Sweet Air

MUSIC IN AMERICAN LIFE

A list of books in the series appears
at the end of this book.

Sweet Air

Modernism, Regionalism, and American Popular Song

EDWARD P. COMENTALE

University of Illinois Press
URBANA, CHICAGO, AND SPRINGFIELD

© 2013 by the Board of Trustees
of the University of Illinois
All rights reserved
Manufactured in the United States of America
1 2 3 4 5 C P 5 4 3 2 1
∞ This book is printed on acid-free paper.

Library of Congress Cataloging-in-Publication Data
Comentale, Edward P.
Sweet air : modernism, regionalism, and American
popular song / Edward P. Comentale.
pages   cm.—(Music in American life)
Includes bibliographical references and index.
ISBN 978-0-252-07892-7 (pbk. : alk. paper)
ISBN 978-0-252-03739-9 (hardback : alk. paper)
1. Popular music—United States—History and criticism.
2. Popular music—Social aspects—United States—History.
I. Title.
ML3477.C66   2013
782.421640973—dc23   2012042309

To Margaret and Fern,
darlings both

Contents

Illustrations

Acknowledgments

Thank you to anyone who has shared music with me in the past and anyone who has, in turn, endured my own musical tastes and passions. *Sweet Air* is only an extension of that intensely gratifying exchange, in the most obsessive terms possible.

Thank you, librarians and archivists encountered along the way, including Harry Rice, sound archivist, at the Hutchins Library, Berea College; John Rumble, senior historian, at the Country Music Hall of Fame; and Tiffany Colannino, archivist, Anna Canoni, publicity director, and Nora Guthrie, president, at the Woody Guthrie Archives.

This project was supported by a generous fellowship from Indiana University's College of Arts and Humanities Institute and a grant from Indiana University's New Frontiers program. Several sections were vetted during talks with the Modernist Studies Colloquium at Penn State University, the Barker Lecture Series at the University of Louisville, and the Americanist Research Colloquium at Indiana University.

I couldn't be more impressed by the hard work and devotion displayed by the staff at University of Illinois Press. Thank you, for your vision and guidance, Laurie Matheson, senior acquisitions editor, and, for your patience and perseverance, Dawn Durante, assistant acquisitions editor. Thank you, too, Jennifer Reichlin, editorial, design, production manager, and Angela Arcese, copyeditor, for your excellent attention to the text in its final stages of production. Thank you, dear readers—for the respect and intelligence with which you approached my manuscript and for helping me shape it into something much more pointed and provocative.

Thank you, friends and colleagues in the Department of English at Indiana University: Judith Brown, Christine Farris, Mary Favret, Paul Gutjahr, Scott Herring, Christoph Irmscher, George Hutchinson, Joshua Kates, Ivan Kreilkamp, Andrew Miller, Jesse Molesworth, Kathy Smith, and Stephen Watt. Your wisdom and kindness mark every page of this book. Thank you, especially, Jonathan Elmer and Jennifer Flessner—your guidance and support have meant the world to me.

Thank you, Barbara Ching, Diane Pecknold, Aaron Jaffe, Marvin Lin, Justus Nieland, and Bill Rasch—for keeping me sane as an academic.

Thank you, Phil and Jeanette Butta, for standing by me from so far away. And thank you, Grandma, for getting in touch.

And thank you, Jack Raglin, Aidan Smith, and Shane Vogel, for your good friendship and good conversation, for knowing exactly what to say when it needs to be said, and for just being decent and cool.

And thank you, most of all, to my sweet and inspiring family—Kimberly, Margaret, and Fern. Thanks for being patient with me, and thanks for providing a warm and loving home where we can play music and dance.

From a Basement on Long Island to a Mansion on the Hill

Taste Biographies and Stylized Gestures

Traditionally, in books of this sort, this is the place where the author establishes his authenticity. This is my chance to display some musical *cred*—my personal intimacy with the blues and country and redneck rock and roll. At the very least, I let you look at my record collection—bootlegs and all—so you know you're dealing with a guy who knows his stuff. But, hell, unlike Robert Palmer, I've never sat in Muddy Waters's kitchen dining on shrimp and champagne. And unlike Guthrie P. Ramsay, I've never sung gospel with a South Side Holiness choir. Unlike Adam Gussow, I've never played blues harmonica with a man who then got himself shot in the chest. And, when it comes to country music, I haven't sung in a North Austin honky-tonk like Bill C. Malone. And I've never been backstage at the Ryman like Richard Peterson. And I'm pretty sure that, unlike Nick Tosches, I've never spent the night in a Cheyenne motel with a transsexual country star. And when it comes to Greil Marcus, American music's most famous scholar-fan, I don't even have the map skills to find Harry Smith's house in Berkeley or Dock Boggs's place in Letcher County.[1]

But I've read the work of each of these writers, and, to be sure, they've all deeply complicated my understanding and appreciation of popular music. As a whole, they've taught me that music matters precisely because its meanings are contingent and its significance—as a form of expression, as a marker of identity or desire—changes with context and time. And yet I find it peculiar that even as these authors challenge the presumed authenticity of musical experience, they all feel some pressure to put their own authenticity on display. Together, they seem to have recreated vernacular music in terms specific to their own generational needs, refashioning its experience according to a series of oppositions that include not just authenticity and inauthenticity, but also expression and exploitation, rebellion and compliance, tradition and modernity. In other words, insofar as their work has preserved any sense of vernacular music in America, that music is now perceived in largely romantic terms, as primitive, passionate, and prelapsarian, or, as Elijah Wald puts it, "a heartfelt, handmade alternative to the plastic products of the pop scene."[2] At best, I think this bias reflects the cultural politics of the Cold War/civil-rights era and, in this, compellingly repackages the desire for social change that informs so much musical expression in America. At worst, though, it sanctions a troublesome sort of fetishism—of race, masculinity, the past—that still marks pop-culture consumption in America. Either way, all of these authors, and many of their fans, seem to believe that music must be *lived* through—and indeed *suffered* through—for it to have any meaning or significance.

No worries about that here—I'll accept not only the inauthenticity of my musical experiences, but also the passive, and at times mindless, inconsistency of my tastes. I came of age on Long Island in the late 1970s and early 1980s, and most of my early musical encounters took place in basement apartments and station wagons. No swamps, no shacks, no barn dances for me—just a lot of linoleum and wood paneling. Most of the songs played to me as a child had little connection to my actual living situation, and they were all piped into our home by artificial means. I remember playing Matchbox cars while my dad blasted Billy Joel's "Movin' Out" on his JVC stereo. I would wait for the sound of the engine revving up in the middle of the song and then race my cars back and forth across the kitchen floor. I remember the day Boy George first sauntered onto MTV singing "Do You Really Want to Hurt Me?" My aunts jumped up from the couch, shrieking in horror, while I sat quietly munching on cereal. I remember when my younger, rowdier brother brought home a cassette version of Guns 'n' Roses' *Appetite for Destruction*. I told him I thought the skulls on the cover looked "retarded," but I secretly played the tape on my Walkman after he went to bed. That's about it, though. If you like to think your author has been down in the flood or racing with the devil, you should know up front that this is all I've got. My early musical experiences were largely conventional, generic, passive even; we listened to whatever the industry offered and accepted it all simply as "music."

But if my "taste biography," to borrow a phrase from Carl Wilson, looks like a series of random or even passive attractions, that doesn't at all diminish its value.[3] My first two 45s were Olivia Newton John's "Let's Get Physical" and Devo's "Whip It"—I loved them both simply because they were musical and they were mine. As I grew older, I moved through a standard suburban catalogue of white-boy idols and influences, and I used them all in typically adolescent ways—to establish poses, to make friends and flirt, to distinguish myself from this group or that. At some point, I picked up a Smiths CD, and that gave me a new way of being a disappointed teen—vaguely queer and slightly British. I found out about David Byrne, who provided a way of being smart, and skinny, and a New Yorker. Later on, in college, I stumbled upon Pavement, and I discovered new possibilities for irony, for tucking in a shirt, for hanging out with other guys. Leonard Cohen introduced me to a certain kinky Canadian Jewishness. Brian Eno showed me how to be blank and empty. Belle and Sebastian gave me a way of feeling sweet. Over time, all this exposure to music expanded my formal repertoire of gestures and attitudes. I slowly built an archive of styles that I could draw upon as the case needed—as son, boyfriend, student, worker, and eventually teacher and writer. Sure, all along, this experience was coded, always already marked by "society and its norms." And I guess, in the end, I've become little more than a white, male, middle-class consumer with indie tastes. But if this process appears mostly passive and largely unconscious, I don't think you can say it was simply reactionary. Indeed, all this was learned through chance and habit, which in itself implies the possibility of other chances and habits.

Sure, psychology plays a role, as we each gravitate toward certain charismatic singers or laid-back bass players or reckless drummers. But I believe our deepest relation to music has less to do with identity and its expressive needs than with a certain feel for aesthetic form. I discovered Bob Dylan, for example, in an introductory poetry course taught by Christopher Ricks. Somewhere toward the end of the course, Ricks lectured on "The Lonesome Death of Hattie Carroll," focusing on meter and enjambment and the poetics of social justice, and then asked us to go home and perform a similar analysis on a song of our choice. I sat in my dorm room, turned on *Another Side of Bob Dylan*, and never heard a thing. In fact, I left the CD in the player for days, living amid its constant folk ramble, but it was the rhythm that got me—the texture—the bare monotonous strumming and the flat twang of the voice. It was the never-ending wall of 1960s folk sound—twelve, fifteen, eighteen verses in a run—all muttering the same thing over and over again, which was really nothing to me, a self-absorbed child of the 1980s. Despite all the social and political values that Dylan is known to express, it was his sheer blankness—the strange inscrutability of his tone—that most appealed to me, precisely because it made no demands on me. Still, today, I don't put on Dylan for political messages or surrealist poetics or even folkish nostalgia. I put on Dylan like someone might carry around a security blanket or suck his thumb—it serves a dumb physical need, filling in the edges of my emotional life with its own sound and rhythm. My life has a momentary shape, a certain affective bearing, and sometimes this song fits my needs, sometimes that one does—sometimes it's *Blonde on Blonde* and sometimes it's *John Wesley Harding*. And while it's hard to say what came first (the song or the need), I know that every time I play some kind of music, I'm expressing both a real demand and its formal ideal.

In fact, I now live in a small midwestern college town where just about everyone seems to love roots music—traditional, primitive, alt, indie, what have you. We can hear fiddle bands and jug bands and rockabilly acts almost every night of the week. A few flatpickers squat on our main street in the evenings and play tunes by Charley Patton, Jimmie Rodgers, and Hank Williams. I recently attended an open-mic night during which three tenth graders performed Carter Family songs in traditional style—they had it down pat: the instruments, the costumes, the blank Carter stare. A few local hipsters hold a hoedown once a month in a real barn; you can catch them walking down the (now defunct) railroad tracks in kitchen aprons and suspenders, carrying pies and big jugs of beer—no joke. It's easy to dismiss all this assumed folkishness as a kind of nostalgic escape or an ironic defense against the present, but it got me thinking about the way musical forms circulate beyond their origins. Most of the people I know in this town are transplants—they all seem to come from elsewhere, and many plan on leaving someday. Students, ex-students, some professors, their spouses and kids—they tend to pack up their lives every four or five years and start over somewhere down the road, finding new jobs, new careers, new homes and friends. So while many of them appreciate the history of the music they like to play, they tend to approach that tradition in ways that are genuinely practical and creative. The sound of fiddles and straws is actively stitched into their daily lives, providing direction and significance, continuity and traction, generating new forms of identity and community. In other words, if my "townsfolk" have found a "fit" in this music, it's not simply because it "expresses" or "represents" authenticity or rootedness, but because it is itself dynamic, migrant, and abstract. They find it useful precisely because it is out of time and space, and they're using it the way it's always been used, as an alternative medium, as a formal means of coping with change in all its stress and pleasure.

In other words, even if music is personally and historically useful, and it reflects the material needs of specific populations, this process seems to take place in a more or less otherworldly space—an "audiotopia," perhaps, to borrow from Josh Kun.[4] My specific past gave me a musical education that was more abstract than sentimental, but it still suggests what is essential to most musical experience in our time. The pop life echoes and doubles over real life, but it remains detached, purposeless, and—thank God—mostly virtual. I might be taking my cues from Byrne and Cohen, or at least the personae in their songs, but there is something irreducibly musical about my relation to them. In fact, we shouldn't even be talking about Byrne or Cohen at all, but rather a "Byrne effect" or a "Cohen effect," in the same way physicists talk about a "Joule effect" or a "Planck effect." I might shape my everyday life according to patterns I find in music, but those patterns spin along quietly in their own ideal space and time without me. We can borrow them, apply them, but they remain available to us (like language itself) only because they are inherently abstract and iterable—airy, empty, ideal. I might have walked into third-period shop class with black mascara like Robert Smith, and a senior in a Skynyrd T-shirt might have, in turn, punched me in the ear. I might have fallen in love with the girl who first played *Slanted and Enchanted* for me, and I might have ended up hating James Taylor because her father's favorite song was "Sweet Baby James." But I can easily see things turning out in other ways. My history is everywhere stitched together and shot through with the thousands of sounds in the air, and this is due to the feelings that may or may not shift back and forth between one space and the other. And so as much as I may be conditioned by my so-called pop life, I am also freed by it—by its inherent *airiness*, its sheer aesthetic purposelessness—to explore other possibilities.

In a way, then, despite the various ways that people have devised to speak about their musical tastes, the best case you can make for any pop song is just four words long—"Hey, check this out." Or, maybe, for a certain emphasis—"Hey, check this shit out." In fact, in the course of writing *Sweet Air*, I've become quite fond of such statements, seeing in their dumb affectivity something like an extension of the musical act itself. *That sucks. That's sweet. That's lame. That's cool*—these outbursts suggest an appeal to an affective body that knows, in its own obvious and unabashed way, which forms fit, which forms move, which give pleasure and which do not. As Robert Musil claimed in his essay "On Stupidity," responses like these are never simply natural or immediate, for they always contain a "kernel of aesthetic analysis." They speak, in their own obtuse way, to what the ancients knew well: sensual experience is founded on an ethical sense of "the good and the just."[5] This doesn't mean that cultural factors don't come into play, or that our responses are ever free of bias and cliché. Nor does it mean that we can't change our judgments over time, suddenly finding ourselves crushing on a new song or style. In fact, while these seemingly gut responses cannot be directly taught, they can be performed, copied, and revised by others. No amount of training, information, or argument can really make someone else feel the value of a song as you feel it, but you can still put your response out there and hope that it sticks. As I try to show in this book, the poses that define fan culture are not only analytical, but pedagogical. In their mutual convulsions and outbursts, fans (and scholars) ultimately enact something like an ad hoc public sphere, putting judgments on display, providing each other with stylish modes of engagement that may or may not prove pleasing or powerful in themselves.

Ultimately, then, I'm not satisfied with the bedroom dimensions of my taste biography, and I want to know what works for other people and how my experiences relate to history at large. If my own feelings are constantly surging into and out of musical forms—decisively *public* forms—I am curious about how these processes work on a larger scale. With *Sweet Air*, I've tried to translate my own experiences as a fan, a scholar, and a displaced Long Islander into a larger, national story. I'm interested in how earlier musical forms generated new attitudes and stances that allowed people to engage and cope with the experiences of being or becoming modern. I'm interested in how popular music created the possibility of a public sphere that was not only expressive, measured by the politics of identity and its representation, but also affective, gestural, and dynamic, measured in terms of its flexibility and vitality. Given my musical experiences, I have a hunch that many of the musicians and audiences that we today associate with gritty authenticity and deep tradition were also invested in performance as an artificial and thus open-ended act of personal re-creation. The best of this music functioned (still functions) as an emphatic gesture, a stylish display, a willful act of self-mediation in a relatively open field of cultural forces and intensities. In this, I believe, the history of American popular music has less to do with "authentic" identities or even representations, some of which find expression and some of which fall into silence. Rather, it's a vast, tumultuous network of overlapping feelings and forms, each three-minute song buzzing alongside thousands of others, each a dynamic node or modality, a tiny emotional circuit, generating relations, attitudes, stances, and poses for the public at large, in a process that is at once contextual, contradictory, unsettling, and perhaps even progressive.

Vernacular Modernism / Pop Modernism

At its most basic level, then, *Sweet Air* seeks to disentangle vernacular music from certain romantic myths of origin and identity and explore its inherent modernism. Each chapter works to uproot a different regional genre, brush off the dirt, and show how it came to address—formally—the new and often overwhelming sensations brought on by modern life. The blues song, we'll find, drew upon the new patterns of rural industry to model alternative forms of personal identity and agency. Country music adapted the detachment and dislocation of the city to advance a more dynamic version of regional life. In response to the Depression and world war, folk music redefined song as a natural resource, akin to coal or oil or labor itself, and thereby as the basis of a new cultural politics. Rock and pop worked through the emotions of the marketplace—the pains and promises of being a consumer and the commercialization of emotion. In all this, though, *Sweet Air* asserts that the value of this music existed not only in what it might have "expressed" or "represented," but in what it enacted, as it formally generated new attitudes and emotions within an otherwise bewildering world. As I show throughout, generic forms like the blues and country reflected modernity back to listeners and fans at the level of gesture and style, each song serving as an emphatic performance of identity and community in affective terms. The relaxed cool of Ma Rainey or Charley Patton, the emotional detachment of Sara Carter, the dark laughter of Woody Guthrie, the tossed-off physicality of Elvis Presley or Wanda Jackson, the geeky aestheticism of Buddy Holly—these all figure here as decisively modernist moves that functioned at the level of everyday sensation and experience. Together, they attest to the power of what Miriam Hansen calls "vernacular modernism": the vast and varied aesthetic experience of modern life that, in its everydayness, sustained a vital forum of exchange and transformation for those otherwise excluded from traditional forms of power and prestige.[6]

Always, though, *Sweet Air* insists on the abstraction of musical space and time. It locates the dynamism of musical culture in what seem to be the most impersonal aspects of musical production—the sensual qualities of sound (timbre, tone, duration), the formal dimensions of song (lyricism, refrain, genre), and the various technological modes of reproduction and transmission (songbook, radio, records, television, etc.). If modernism is defined as an anxious erosion of cultural tradition and authority, it also clears the way for new, more dynamic forms of cultural experience and exchange. Within the abstract space and time of popular song, musicians and fans found new ways of patterning everyday life and grew accustomed to the idea of identity itself as a form of patterning. In fact, as I suggest throughout, in its increased abstraction and dissociation, the music of this era quickly came to mirror the experimental strategies of the modernist avant-garde. As musical production moved further away from traditional sites and contexts, each popular genre came to emphasize certain stylistic features that both reflected and resisted the claims of the modern world—fragmentation in the blues, irony in country music, repetition and refrain in folk music, distortion in rockabilly, abstraction in pop. As I show, new technology only extended this process, as developments in radio and recording estranged traditional music-making practices, driving a wedge between sound and source, and inspired musicians to pursue new creative strategies. In this, you'll find, *Sweet Air* is as much invested in estrangement as it is in identification, anti-regionalism as regionalism. Throughout, music is presented as a moving and thus unstable medium, one in which identity both locates and exceeds its own historical limits. Song is shown not simply to express each performer or place, but also to expand, through its own abstract qualities, local coordinates of space and time, as well as the categories of race, gender, and class embedded within them.

By juxtaposing high art and mass culture in this way, I'm not trying to assert a new hierarchy between them. It is not my intention here to criticize the elitism of the avant-garde or to raise the cultural capital of the popular arts (more on this below). I see value in both ends of what Andreas Huyssen calls the "great divide," and I am just as willing to defend the elite practices of the avant-garde as I am here urging for recognition of vernacular experimentation.[7] Rather, my comparison serves as a way of refocusing standard histories of the era and their possibilities. On the one hand, *Sweet Air* upends traditional accounts of modernism that privilege print, the literary elite, and the bohemian experiences of urban life. On the other, it reverses conventional accounts of vernacular music that look backward in time and ignore the complexities of regional change. Mostly, though, the book suggests that the radicalism of the avant-garde was more widely realized in musical forms that—in their popular appeal and easy transmission—confronted the terms of modern life on a much larger scale. By exposing a modern public sphere that was poor, rural, and musical rather than cosmopolitan and literate, it reframes the geographic and social coordinates of the era and brings alternative forms of cultural production into view. At the same time, *Sweet Air* constructs this alternative history and its possibilities in relation to the marketplace. By considering not just the modernity, but the *modernism—the modernist aesthetics*—of popular music, it navigates the two most persistent myths regarding early twentieth-century culture, both the popular romance of American vernacular music as a form of authentic culture and a closed Frankfurt School–style critique of the culture industry as a form of mass deception. In other words, by exploring the aesthetic gestures of rural and working-class artists, it outlines a more subtle way through the age of high capitalism, one in which techniques such as fragmentation, repetition, shock, and silence are used to negotiate the everyday experiences of industrialization and commodity culture.

More pointedly, I'm interested in the modern period—roughly from 1910 to 1960—insofar as it freed musical culture from the romanticism of the nineteenth century and its emphasis on the lyrical expression of identity. The modern era is most often characterized by its energy and its anxiousness, insofar as it witnessed the shattering of cultural authority as well as the fragmentation of personal and regional identity. Darwin's theories of evolution, for example, dismantled the seemingly natural hierarchy of God, human, and beast. Nietzsche's skeptical philosophy exposed the irony of human progress and laughingly proclaimed that history was over. Freud's psychoanalysis uncovered a deep abyss within the human psyche itself, showing how the self was fractured by irrational desires and perverse commands. But that's nothing compared to the everyday experiences of modernism. Out on the streets and in the factories, modernism was experienced as a widespread and generally anxious release of new feelings and emotions.[8] With trains, automobiles, electrical gridlines, and radio towers, new technology brought about radical shifts in scale and perspective and a complete restructuring of the human senses. Taylorized factories and new consumer markets restructured the rhythms of work and play and upended bodily habits and tastes. Think Chaplin's Little Tramp on the assembly line, jerking to the rhythm of the conveyor belt. Think Dreiser's Sister Carrie in Chicago, her heart exposed to vast displays of wealth and consumption. Think Coney Island, the Chicago Stock Exchange, the trenches of World War I—think the psychoanalyst's couch and all those bourgeois patients rattled by modernity's rush. The shocks and blows of modern life were largely traumatic and often unnamable, and—from farm to factory to urban salon—they upended the sensory limits of the human body and exploded the traditional coordinates of both private and public identity.[9]

At the same time, the modernist period is characterized by its turn to abstraction—the abstraction of reason, the abstraction of labor and property, of machinery, and, of course, art. The sensory overload of modernity was brought about precisely by cold forms, by machines and systems that paid no heed to human limits. Extreme feeling was the unruly byproduct of extreme formalism and so became, at best, a means of negotiating a world of mass-produced forms. In other words, this period is best characterized by its excesses of emotion *and* abstraction, with not much room for anything like an individual, let alone individual expression, in between. Feeling seemed again and again to transgress the boundaries of the individual, flooding both public and private spaces, finding only a momentary coherence in a series of dynamic forms—machines, transportation networks, public buildings, and political discourse, as well as paintings, poems, and songs.[10] Take a look at Picasso's African mask–inspired *Les Demoiselles d'Avignon* or Munch's *The Scream*. Watch Brecht's *Mother Courage* or listen to Stravinsky's *Rite of Spring*. The masterpieces of the modernist era confront their audiences as both creepily abstract and terrifyingly emotional. They are characterized as much by their anti-sentimentalism as by their extreme sensualism, and they use their cold formalism to inspire and manage sensations that are never simply human.[11] Most importantly, all of these works blast through the expressive fantasies of the romantic lyric. Each rejects bourgeois ideals of expression and interiority and instead presents itself as some kind of techno-politico-aesthetic dynamo, adopting the terms of modern life in order to escape them. As Ezra Pound explained, the new art must exceed the merely personal—the bourgeois self—on both ends. It confronts the world inexpressively, but productively, as "an intellectual and emotional complex in an instant of time" and thus as it upends the traditional sureties of identity.[12]

In other words, the modernist intelligentsia was never content with merely recording the changes wrought by modernity. Bucking against an outmoded and more or less stagnant romantic tradition, artists and writers of this period eschewed the essentialism of place and identity and considered how human existence and culture might be shaped (and reshaped) by extrinsic factors. Indeed, once the wedge was placed between reality and its formal mediation, anyone with access to a pen or paintbrush, or a movie camera or recording equipment, could jump into the breach and try to reframe society on some other, presumably more enlightened scheme. Hence the quick succession of avant-garde programs in this period—futurism, cubism, vorticism, expressionism, surrealism, etc.—each touting a revolutionary paradigm in broad-type manifestos. Artists everywhere found new faith in their craft, seeing affective form as the basis of both personal and cultural renewal, using it at once to capture the experience of modernity and renegotiate its basic terms. Pound, for example, juxtaposed classical forms from Greece and China in hopes of restoring a pagan cult of passion and beauty. Virginia Woolf used a stream-of-consciousness narrative technique to dissolve individual egos into a more flexible communal ideal. Other artists—Nathanael West, Djuna Barnes, Bertolt Brecht—turned to the forms of popular culture—the music hall, the circus, dime novels, etc.—seeking to effect cultural change via media already available to the masses. Everywhere, in the realm of poetry, fiction, photography, murals, and music, art crossed over into politics, and vice versa, as the question of form became a question of history—its shape, its meaning, its direction.

But I'm most interested in what popular musicians did with modernism, first because of the everyday and widespread appeal of their performances, and second because they worked through sound and song rather than print and language. With the development of new recording and broadcasting technology, the popular music of this era had a flexibility and range well beyond that of any modernist painting or poem. It quickly reached a significantly different population, one that was often segregated and disenfranchised in terms of race, class, and gender, and whose experiences of modernity differed in both form and intensity. At the same time, the music of this era proved well suited to address the feelings and attitudes that accompanied class-based and racialized experiences of modernity. The decay of home life, the ups and downs of the labor market, the fear and thrill of the roadways, the alluring strangeness of modern technology, the kinky frustration of shopping—these new sensations demanded new forms, and popular music—insofar as it exploited the unique properties of sound—filled this need in different ways. From the city to the farm, via records and radio, listeners found their relation to the modern world newly energized by a cheap and disposable medium that could fade, repeat, and seemingly bend space and time at will. In fact, the lives of musicians and fans were situated between a number of different contexts and networks—work, family, the highway, city, club, studio—each of which provided new structures for musical experience. The jerky rhythms and repetitive refrains of their songs served not simply as metaphors for modernity, but as creative variations on modern living in its sonic aspect. In fact, each song figured as both a stylized expression and an actual product of the new economy, and thus proved an overdetermined site of investment and negotiation, linking listeners physically, technologically, and economically to the new order and thereby mediating their multiple feelings toward it.

Listening to this music in terms of its modernity, though, I detected a certain attitude or tendency that not only distinguishes it from high modernism, but seems to suggest another modernity altogether. I was certainly ready for sadness, nostalgia, and even resentment, but I was surprised by the directness with which many of these artists confront their experiences of destitution and dereliction. Bertha Idaho, Bessie Smith, the Delmores, Woody Guthrie, Ike Turner, etc.—these musicians all seem much more acclimated to experiences of self-negation than the modernist intelligentsia, as if, given their often violent experiences of modern life, they had abandoned liberal-humanist ideologies of the self and self-determination and sought new models of agency in the deathliness of form itself. Here, we need to consider abstraction in a larger sense—as the abstract mediation of the factory, the roadway, the commodity, the consumer marketplace, and, then, of song itself. The blues singer, for example, dives headfirst into the abstract patterns of the industrial network in order to generate new forms of wealth and value. The folk singer projects himself into a series of slogans and phrases, succumbing to public discourse and political rhetoric in order to reshape it from within. The rock star, on the other hand, revels in his own commercial manipulation as a kind of kinky release from the very demands of the marketplace, casually shaping himself again and again according to his own pleasures. Across the boards, these artists were remarkably casual about their own mediation and the processes of mediation, as if they knew that only by engaging the formal dimensions of modernity could they ever hope to survive within it. Many of them saw abstraction—the very deathliness of form—as a creative means of self-negation and self-renewal, and extended it as far is it could go with their music.

Here, *Sweet Air* most clearly suggests how popular music might help us negotiate the larger cultural history of the twentieth century. As most scholars would argue, *modernism* teaches us that our history is always doubled over by its own forms. Everyday life is overlaid or shot through with a virtual archive of forms—cultural, psychological, and industrial patterns—and the one shapes the other via the emotions and desires that pass between them. *Postmodernism* is perhaps only that moment when the scales tip toward the latter and we find ourselves, for better or worse, adrift in a sea of mass-produced forms—caught, affectively, between paranoia and emptiness.[13] But pop music—as feeling and form both, as a *moving* and *motivated* discourse—gives us a unique purchase on this process and its possibilities. Sure, the increasingly abstract nature of musical production in this era amounts to a massive deterritorialization of vernacular tradition; songs begin to drift away from their regional coordinates and acquire a much more generic state—shiny and sleek, short and repetitive. But if by the 1950s, with the consolidation of the music industry, song became less a means of expressing traditional values, it becomes not simply a mode of commercial exploitation, but a source of significant aesthetic investment and exploration in its own right. *Sweet Air* neither denies nor laments this detachment, this pop aestheticism. In fact, taking its cue from countless musicians and fans, it pushes regional tradition toward the pop moment with which it culminates, while also reading pop back onto its earlier forms, seeing it not necessarily as another genre, but as an essential component of modernity itself. Ultimately, the mediation affected via sonic form, and then extended by the commodity form, becomes nothing less than the mediation of modernity itself, the empty noise of the modern world as it finds and loses itself in its own sweet sounding. As I neared the end of this book, I realized that it outlines a much larger trajectory from vernacular culture through "vernacular modernism" to something like "pop modernism." In this, moreover, I began to see how the evolution of musical form corresponds to an evolution in audience and society, culminating in the figure of the fan as the basis of both an alternative economy and an alternative culture—an idea that I take up in chapters four and five.

I am certainly not the first person to note the interconnectedness of modernity and vernacular music. Many others before me have explained the popularity of commercial genres such as blues and country in relation to modern industry and the modernization of rural life (Elijah Wald, Angela Y. Davis, Pamela Fox, Patrick Huber, J. M. Mancini, and many others are cited in this book). No one, however, has compellingly explained how the actual *forms* of popular song address and reshape the experience of modern life. With *Sweet Air*, I'm arguing both for the *modernity* of these songs, as they evolved alongside the wide-scale modernization of rural life, and for their *modernism*, as an increasingly abstract and experimental set of forms designed to manage the novel emotions and sensations brought on by modernization. I'll also note that I'm not the first scholar to explore artists' efforts to cross the "great divide" between high and low culture. However, I've found that previous work on this subject maintains the basic economies and ideologies it claims to critique. Take, for example, Bernard Gendron's excellent study *Between Montmartre and the Mudd Club: Popular*

Music and the Avant-Garde.[14] Beginning with the artistic cabarets of late nineteenth-century Paris, Gendron tracks the avant-garde's efforts to gain notoriety by borrowing from popular musical forms. In turn, he shows, popular music rose within the cultural hierarchy, so that by the 1940s—as bebop, for example—it claimed some degree of aesthetic autonomy and high-art prestige. While Gendron provides a consistent and convincingly illustrated case about these relationships, he concentrates on high art's appropriation of the low and the circulation of cultural capital within an otherwise closed market of artistic value. Thus, while he outlines "a major shift in the cultural-power differential" between high art and mass culture, he leaves the power differential, and all its implicit class biases, intact (7). In the end, this economic model, for all its dynamism, excludes the very possibility of cultural democratization to which it originally alluded: "the art/pop and art/entertainment distinctions are alive and well within the pop music sphere," Gendron concludes, "and as long as there is a struggle for cultural capital and economic capital within the pop field, with winners and losers, there will be an institutionalized hierarchy of 'higher' and 'lower' types of pop musical products" (326).

My work is not so invested in "borrowings" or "accreditations"; rather, it tracks the growth of vernacular modernism on its own terms, as it generated—via music and sound—new forms of investment and exchange within an expansive public sphere and an alternative economy. Consequently, I see it more in line with scholars who begin with decisively popular forms and then construct a larger theory of modernity. Methodologically, I've found the greatest inspiration in studies that explore African American music as an instance of Afro-modernism. Guthrie P. Ramsay's work, for example, characterizes Afro-modernism as, first, a wide-scale confrontation between African Americans and their increasingly modern world and, secondly, a series of cultural forms designed to address and accommodate that process.[15] Ramsay's work focuses on music as both a signifying practice and, better yet, a medium for circulating and negotiating new forms of "social energy." Forms like the blues, jazz, gospel, and R & B, he argues, gave both expression and shape to new publics, providing spaces and times in which modern experience, and its local possibilities, could be negotiated. Ramsay's account is slightly belated, as black musical forms were wrestling with modernity long before the 1940s, and skewed toward northern urban centers, obscuring southern musical cultures that addressed similar challenges. Still, writing from an ethnographic perspective, he recognizes both the historically specific needs of musical cultures and the various ways in which music functions to meet them. "Blackness" thus appears in his work as a "practice," while "race music" becomes one of many dynamic forms through which it operates. A genre like the blues appears as a "modality," a form *and* a presence, a sign *and* an experience, one that, by mingling with other styles, becomes a "durable yet flexible site" of both personal and social identity (46).

Sonic Republic

Beyond Ramsay, though, I believe that the genres tracked in this book sustain not just a set of alternative cultures, but also an alternative economy and an alternative public sphere—a countermodernity within modernity. By defining the possibilities of modern public engagement through song rather than, say, print or even visual images, *Sweet Air* points toward a more dynamic vision of nationhood, one in which the very mechanisms of social production exceed their own economic protocols. First, though, to reach this possible fullness, we must accept a more radical emptiness. While high modernist art and literature have always been perceived as privileged forms of cultural capital and social value, the songs considered in *Sweet Air* are decisively cheap, ad hoc, and disposable; they are lighter than air and just as fluid, and they were embraced insofar as their flexibility and easy transmissibility confounded standard categories of wealth, property, and selfhood. As Woody Guthrie claimed, song generates values and significances "out of nothing," independently of otherwise limited material resources and behind the back of the culture industry. Here, then, for many musicians and their fans, the experiences of loss and exploitation that occasioned the production of popular music also extended the promise of cultural renewal that underlies modernity at large. Song's very airiness—its immateriality, its ephemeral drift—allowed it to fly through the official networks of discourse and exchange and so, in the very act of transmission, generated new possibilities of agency and being. Everywhere, modern history buzzes with these empty, translucent forms, which fracture and distort everyday space and time, cracking open daily life into a number of possible futures. In this, the sonic republic echoes over and against the very conditions of its making in ever-expanding arcs, pushing economic modernity beyond itself in more or less open-ended ways.

As I'd like to show, by looking at the (mostly technologized) production and distribution of popular song, this public sphere figures less as a congeries of competing expressions, established in and through a set of explicit binaries (self and other, center and margins, white and black, etc.) than as an open field of intensities, a modal, immanent, and ceaselessly shifting space of style and gesture. It is not necessarily free of discursive categories—if anything, it sees a proliferation of types and forms—but it sets these forms into dynamic motion, exposing them, through the work of song itself, as singular events and horizons within the "groundless ground" of history at large. While my thinking here is decisively theoretical (recalling a tradition that extends from Spinoza to Deleuze), my most immediate source of inspiration is, once again, recent studies of race music and African American culture. Eric Lott, in his famous account of minstrelsy and working-class subculture, comes closest to laying out the basic terms of what I'm calling the "sonic republic."[16] Lott defines "minstrelsy" as a vernacular form that worked to negotiate, via affect and gesture, the conflicted feelings of a distinctly working-class audience. The figure of the minstrel, in its very inauthenticity (its explicit staginess and stylishness), focused the tensions of race and class feeling, becoming at once an object of fear and fascination, and thus established the terms of a new oppositional public (63–64). As Lott argues, the minstrel was neither a real person venting his confusion and rage, nor a static set of signs through which race, class, and gender were expressed. Rather, the spectacle conjoined form and feeling into a single cultural-political whole, one that exceeded the ideology of expression on both ends. "We might almost call it a precognitive form," he writes, "an encapsulation of the affective order of things in a society that racially ranked human beings. . . . Minstrelsy brought to public form racialized elements of thought and feeling, tone and impulse, residing at the very edge of semantic availability, which Americans only dimly realized they felt, let alone understood" (6).

Insofar as Lott emphasizes modalities and their circulation, he suggests not just the possibility of new social groupings, but also a re-articulation of cultural politics as such. The minstrel show released a set of flexible modes into the cultural ether, a more supple repertoire of race, class, and gender, through which working-class citizens were able to perform their own attitudes and positions within a public setting. At once fake and folksy, the minstrel dislodged social categories from any essentialist logic of identity while nonetheless maintaining their affective charge, and thereby made them available for a range of new engagements and investments: "Where representation once unproblematically seemed to image forth its referent," Lott writes, "we must now think of, say, the blackface mask as . . . a distorted mirror, reflecting displacements and condensations and discontinuities between which and the social field there exists lags, unevennesses, multiple determinations" (8). As Lott further argues, such culture—as an abstraction of culture, one that circulates within its own distinct realm—began to alter the political development of the nation at large. "Cultural *forms*, the various sorts of textuality and subjectivity most closely related to human agency," become inseparable from "social and cultural *formations*, the organizations, processes, and overdetermined conjunctures that bear more significantly on political life" (11). With "minstrelsy," then, the public sphere as a whole finds itself awash in shifting modalities, new and contradictory configurations of thought and feeling, which are never simply expressive of one class interest or another, never simply reactionary or progressive, but by turns resistant, oppositional, and emancipatory, insofar as they are put to various uses in everyday routines, in public spectacles, and, of course, more explicit political confrontations.

With *Sweet Air*, however, I want to track the possibilities of this public sphere as it manifests itself in the modern period proper and through sound and song rather than public theater. In this, I take my cue from Alexander G. Weheliye's excellent book *Phonographies: Grooves in Sonic Afro-Modernity*.[17] Weheliye argues that African American sound culture serves to counter the negative position that African Americans hold within the public regimes of print. According to Weheliye, sonicity speaks to the invisibility of the African American within the mainstream public sphere while providing an alternative form of agency and engagement. The fluidity of sound allows for a more flexible mode of identity, and the constant reiteration of song becomes a means by which both individuals and communities negotiate their relation to modernity. For Weheliye, sound does not figure as some more authentic form or expression of "blackness," but as the medium through which "blackness" is articulated as a contingent set of "materiodiscursive practices" (6). In fact, the modernity of Weheliye's Afro-modernity lies in its connection to the mediations affected by sonic technology. The invention of the phonograph marks the origin of sonic Afro-modernism proper, insofar as it exposes the gap that already exists between identity and its sonic mediation. The phonograph generates an audio-visual break in black culture, not only dissociating "blackness" from the body, but also providing a new forum by which "blackness" may be articulated (7). Modern identity, then, becomes neither its essential expression nor its technological manipulation, but a "chain of singular formations integrally linked" to the modern sphere, a "modernity otherwise" that, in its affectively charged repetitions and displacements, "disrupts and displaces the grand narratives of reason and technological progress by incorporating those who fall outside the mix" (23). In other words, the phonograph radicalizes the kinds of cultural slippage previously enacted on the minstrel stage. It undoes the logic of origin and copy through its own blank machinery, replacing Western ideologies of identity and expression with a ceaseless "repetition of difference," locating new possibilities not *against*, but *through* cultural forms and their circulation. Similarly, as I'll show, recording stars like Bessie Smith, the Delmores, and Buddy Holly did not merely release new identities or desires into the public sphere, but constructed new rhythms and postures that, in their formal repetition, slowly changed the movement and direction of public life. Ultimately, the sonic republic contracts and expands in the circulation of these affectively charged grooves, via overlapping tracks or modalities, ceaseless becomings *within* and *through* an increasingly commercialized and technologized world.

In all this, *Sweet Air* looks back at vernacular tradition to establish not what Greil Marcus calls an "invisible republic," or even a "visible republic," but a *sonic* republic, one attuned to the specific dimensions of modern song as song.[18] In fact, I see this book as a potential antidote to Marcus's incredibly influential work, which, in its celebration of an "old, weird America," has come to shape—and ultimately limit—popular responses to American vernacular music. In a number of famous books—*Mystery Train* and *The Old, Weird America*, most notably—Marcus explores folk music as an expression of the failures of Jeffersonian democracy.[19] He reads the hymns and ballads of the musical past as texts that express the generally tragic struggle for individualism in an otherwise conformist country. No doubt, Marcus's writing is animated by the intense emotions of his largely male, largely southern singer-songwriter canon (Boggs, Presley, Dylan). But, at heart, his claims seem to be grounded in neither folk music nor even the folk movement of the 1960s, but in the paranoia and anxiety of the Cold War. Here, too, emotion informs judgment and thus generates both a new public stance and a substantial body of scholarship, but—as I see it—Marcus's work dissolves both music *and* politics in a romantic and perhaps even imaginary version of American history. In contrast, I hope, in its emphasis on form over identity, song over expression, and modalities over margins, *Sweet Air* shows that vernacular music in America was never simply "old" or "weird," but instead, for many, common, useful, and thrillingly modern. Its "republic" is loud, raucous, and direct—popular, but never totalizing; critical, but rarely hopeless.

Marcus's book *The Old, Weird America* is perhaps his most effective statement on the music considered here. With Harry Smith's *Anthology of American Folk Music* and Bob Dylan's *Basement Tapes* as his models, Marcus claims to be tuning in to an underground tradition of folk expression, a secret and fading language of American promise floating somewhere on the airwaves. Listening to folkies like Clarence Ashley and Dock Boggs, or even troubled rockers like Presley and Dylan, he claims to hear "certain bedrock strains of American cultural language," an "undiscovered country" within the country, a "mystery," hidden away, forced into hiding (xxii; 96). Thus the past plays out as an epic battle between Puritans and pioneers. History figures as the rebel spirit of adventure confronting the slow rot of social conformity. Over time, the "old, free America" has become an "old, weird America," a twisted song of freedom lost. The cry of liberty grows into a perverse hoot, a cuckoo call, signifying nothing but betrayal and shame. As Marcus sees it, then, vernacular culture is upheld by "willful, ornery, displaced, unsatisfied, ambitious individuals"—and their music gives voice to an "occult, Gothic America of terror and deliverance inside the America of anxiety and success" ("American Folk" 122). Again, Marcus offers a potent myth, one that clearly taps the Cold War anxiety of the boomer generation, but it is a skewed version of this music and the history to which it refers. His work at once mythologizes the nation and locks it away; it privileges authenticity and yet displaces it, either in the very distant past or the deepest, most inaccessible regions of the nation or the self. All is conspiracy and paranoia, and song serves mostly to send out secret messages to a scattered remnant of folk-freaks. Everything has been locked away, on a record in the basement, kept secret from those who have succumbed to anything like agency, stability, or community.

More to the point, as I'll explore in chapter four, Marcus's claims are grounded in neither song nor history, but in the figure of the male performer, whether Boggs, Dylan, or Presley, who "beat the black man at his own game" (*Mystery* 142). His work explicitly emphasizes enigmatic "personalities" over material "processes" and thus refigures history itself as a series of heroic gestures, the individual testing of social limits and boundaries, all swaggering twists and thrusts into and against the effete masses (*Mystery* 128). The "question of public life" figures as an issue of charismatic maleness—mysterious, inexplicable, and yet authoritative and transformative, far removed from the messy "distribution of material goods or the governance of moral affairs" (*Mystery* 125). In this, Marcus's work seems to typify the "affirmative culture" first critiqued in 1968 by Herbert Marcuse, a much more radical figure of the postwar counterculture.[20] Marcuse interprets the bourgeois idealization of the human soul—in art, literature, and song—as an abdication of social responsibility. By placing faith in the individual over and against a squalid social reality, he argues, affirmative culture essentially relieves us of the burden of real social change. "This truth has taken on a terrible form," Marcuse writes. "The freedom of the soul was used to excuse the poverty, martyrdom, and bondage of the body. It served the ideological surrender of existence to the economy of capitalism" (80–81). In other words, by locating "the true, the good, and the beautiful" in the mysterious musical soul over and against material existence, Greil Marcus's work not only adopts an outmoded romanticism of the individual, but also affirms the basic principles of bourgeois culture and the competitive marketplace. Its political values are admirable, but its form is suspect. When we listen to pop music, we are meant to marvel at its individualistic agon, and so any potential social energy is poured into the private space of listening, into the pop commodity or body of the pop star as fetish, so it can reflect back a pleasing, but ultimately empty, vision of power and presence.[21]

With *Sweet Air*, I hope to provide a more dynamic theory of popular music and its relation to the modern pubic sphere. At the very least, my study remains attentive to the fullness of cultural life as it plays out beyond the confines of the boomer narrative of conformity and dissent and opens up the discussion to new configurations of public being and belonging. Sure, songs such as Hank Williams's "Mansion on the Hill" and Springsteen's "Mansion on the Hill," or even Elliott Smith's "Memory Lane" ("*where you're dragged against your will / from a basement on the hill*") can be read as texts that address the failures of Jeffersonian America, but they are also at work sounding out entirely new communities. While lyrics are significant, they are only a small part of a much more dynamic knot through which thoughts, emotions, memories, and then real bodies and entire cultures seem to rush. Played in mansions and basements across America, these songs become vital sites around which other spaces and times begin to proliferate, and thus also new opportunities for identity, sociality, and dissent. But this possibility comes through only in a consideration of affective forms instead of ideological codes, musical modes instead of expressive "texts"—as it manifests itself in the structures and patterns of techno-modernity itself. The "sonic republic" expresses nothing and changes everything; it seeps through walls and property, doubles over everyday life in order to effect a massive deterritorialization of its most basic habits and patterns, recreating nationhood itself in its own dynamic sounding and airy openness.

Josh Kun's work on "audiotopias" provides the most compelling alternative to Marcus's theory of the "old, weird America" and comes closest to describing the delicate interplay of form and feeling that I think continues to generate a vital pop musical culture in America. For Kun, too, song marks out a space within space—an ideal "space that we can enter into, encounter, move around in, inhabit, be safe in, learn from" (2). These spaces, in their abstraction, overlap with each other and with everyday life, and thus disrupt mythic unities of both selfhood and nation, such as the kind Marcus seems to celebrate. The sonic sphere, in its fluidity and ceaseless dissociation, suggests an alternative model of citizenship, undecideable, open, and thus serves to oppose homogenization and assimilation. "All music listening," Kun writes, "is a form of confrontation, of encounter, of the meeting of worlds and meanings, when identity is made self-aware and is, therefore, menaced through its own interrogation" (13). Perhaps Kun's study overemphasizes the divisive and estranging effects of popular song. In a way, his model multiplies the rebellious gestures that define Marcus's pop mythology, to the point of obscuring music's galvanizing effects (16–17). But Kun's study is nonetheless valuable for its suggestions about musical form and its social affects, which this book traces back to its modernist origins and pushes forward to its fully aesthetic ends. "Music in American life," Kun writes, "is the story of racial and ethnic difference; it is the story of both nation formation and de-formation, the audible soundtrack to a nation as it continually packs and unpacks itself" (19). Similarly, if my study pays excessive attention to sonic form, and asserts the primacy of form over expression, it is only to understand and preserve this dual process of territorialization and deterritorialization. In fact, more than Kun, I believe that sonic form—in its modern, commercial phase—points beyond human identity and representation as formulated in either nationalist or postnationalist terms. To me, the shimmering, shaling succession of twentieth-century pop audiotopias confounds the experiential horizon by which belonging and citizenship have traditionally been asserted, and thus becomes a necessary object of study in itself.

For me, then, it comes down to an issue of identities versus forms, or, rather, a politics of the marginal versus a politics of the modal. But I believe that the modality of form makes room for the marginal as a contingent gesture or stance within an open field of play. That's why this book ends not with the explicit class politics of Guthrie or even the heated cultural politics of Presley, but with the pop aesthetics of Buddy Holly, a series of seemingly innocuous songs about teenage love that were allowed, in the empty space of the studio, to spin out according to their own formal limits. In this, perhaps, I could be accused of advancing my own generational biases, playing style over substance, putting forth a slacker's vision of cultural exchange and social politics over and against any more direct form of sonic engagement. But I have at my back hordes of musicians and fans who have shown repeatedly that this very airiness—the sheer weightlessness and worthlessness of pop form—carries its own political thrust. The musicians in this book are all abstractionists, using music to create virtual spaces and times, alternative rhythms and bearings, all of which are full of genuine feeling and affect. They pattern the empty air with affective states and stances, and thereby create the possibility of new stances and attitudes, which only then gain circulation as a kind of politics. Their fans, in turn, find themselves caught up in these sonic patterns, inhabiting new configurations of being, some of which prove satisfying and some of which do not. Everywhere, this sonic republic—in its very airiness—remains shot through with gaps and slippages, redundancies and contradictions, and so proves more flexible, more radical, and more whimsical than modernity itself.

Regions, Genres, Chapters

I must confess that I jumped into writing this book like someone might jump into a beat-up car and take to the road. And while I've never been one for driving (or driving metaphors), I was surprised by how often the discussion returned to themes of mobility, transportation, and mapping. Indeed, at times, my research seemed to shift into and out of well-worn grooves, taking me to both established regions of the country and more obscure, less familiar scenes. In the end, I decided to focus each chapter on a specific region and its established regional styles, but only to show how modern experience eroded local ties and opened up the sonic terrain in new ways. In each case, I've tried to pinpoint these processes of deterritorialization by tracking the shifting relations among three rapidly evolving factors—performance, song, and technology—and, in this, my discussion often seems to jump and shift at the speed of modernity itself. That said, some readers might question my decision to organize the discussion around regional boundaries and generic categories at all, as we all know that both musicians and audiences at this time experienced music in more fluid ways. But regional and generic categories remain real focal points for historically consistent sets of concerns and ideals, and it was via these terms that both modernity and its marketplace merged with everyday life and upended its sureties. In the end, my goal is not simply to rehab a traditional genealogy around a modernist foundation, but to revisit the ideas and values that continue to mark popular-music consumption in America and to remap the cultural terrain as we move toward its uncertain future. So, to return to the driving metaphor, let's all make like Chuck Berry and motivate.

Chapter one—"Lord, It Just Won't Stop!: Work and Blues in the Industrial Delta"—begins with the claim that the Mississippi Delta became the heartland of the blues because—of all the regions of the South—it most violently suffered the experience of modernization. Here, the Delta figures as the scene of intense industrial transformation, and its music is depicted as the first flowering of a distinctly modern popular form, one that—in both form and content—provides a startling view of the new kinds of emotions and intimacies brought about by modernity. Drawing on the life and songs of Charley Patton and other popular artists in the region, I try to show that the blues performer—a persistent template for musical identity in America—enters the modern scene only under threat of having his or her individuality destroyed, as emancipation is immediately troubled by both the wild sensorium of modern life (railroads, riverboats, telephones, juke joints) and the more direct threats of Jim Crow (labor, the chain gang, and lynching). But instead of romanticizing the blues musician as hapless victim or romantic drifter, I depict the blues performer as a proto-modernist, an avant-garde performer, whose song adopts and adapts the formal structures of the Delta economy and its evolving landscape, using them to sustain his own career and to provide a new set of stances and attitudes for a working public caught in the grip of industrial change. The final part of the chapter shows how these processes were extended by the production and circulation of "race records." Here, I argue that phonography, as a technology of both sheer reproducibility and sensual excess, undoes the form logic of racial trauma and repetition encoded in the blues. Thus the blues as a recorded form augurs an alternative modernism, one that points beyond itself, ironically enough, by the very technologies of industry and commerce designed to contain it.

If, as the previous chapter showed, blues music provided affective presence to individuals wracked by poverty, racism, and labor, then chapter two, "Thought I Had Your Heart Forever: Death, Detachment, and the Modernity of Early Country Music," shows how country music provided emotional bearing for an entire region gripped by processes of change. Here, I present country song as a dynamic phenomenon of space and time, one that provides an affective link between home and away as well as past and present. In the commercial ballads of the late 1920s and early 1930s, I show, the ground slips away and time moves forward, eaten away by forces larger than singer, song, and the South itself, and the listener is propelled backward and forward on a current of uneasy but thrilling affect that comes to stand in for regional experience itself. This argument is developed through four different moments in the early history of country music. I begin with one of country music's earliest "stars," Fiddlin' John Carson, and consider his popularity in the urban center of Atlanta as it was paradoxically bound to new forces of technology (cinema, phonograph, radio, etc.) and commercial marketing (advertising, publishing, synergy, etc.). In the next section, I turn to the underexplored influence of the Vagabonds and the Delmores, showing that their music appealed to southern listeners precisely because it mixed traditional sentiments with modern, professionalized styles and thereby introduced a new, more progressive attitude into the country scene. Next, in the largest section, I take on the Carter Family, the "First Family of Country Music," arguing that their songs proved important to twentieth-century southerners because they revamped the traditional ballad form to address the anxiety and alienation of a specifically modern life. The Carters' music is here characterized by a fully modern sense of discontinuity and depersonalization, and ultimately, I argue, this detachment—from each other, from home, from the past, and even from their own performances—freed them to construct song as an alternative space and time of southern life. Finally, in the last section, I turn to country radio, which in this period became the primary mode of musical experience for rural listeners and an intense site of debate about the region's future. Here, I consider the popular barn-dance programs of the era, as they seemed both to conjure up images of an idealized rural past and to hook audiences into a new, dynamic network of mass technology and national culture.

Chapter three—"A Rambling Funny Streak: Woody Guthrie, Revolutionary Folk Song, and the Migrant Art of the Refrain"—shifts from issues of personal and regional identity toward explicitly political and popular ones. It provides a bridge from the first half of the book to the second, using Guthrie's songs to track a wider shift from regional song to national culture and, ultimately, pop idealism. My argument begins with Guthrie's own accounts of Oklahoma modernism—the whirlwind cycles of boom and bust that marked life in the Southwest during his early years. As I see it, Guthrie's early experiences, particularly the hungry land grab and migration westward, provided him with a typically modernist sense of cultural drift and discontinuity and attuned him to the growing rift between material reality and its public expression. These sensibilities informed Guthrie's most radical work with the Popular Front; his songwriting of this period, rather than a straightforward expression of folk ideology or class warfare, explores a new economy of sound for an increasingly migrant public. Guthrie's folk songs reflect the aesthetic strategies of other left-leaning writers and artists of the era, such as Walker Evans, James Agee, Ben Shahn, and Diego Rivera; mistrusting the logic of folk authenticity and expression, this group pursued their work as a series of "motivated forms," at once emotive and abstract, and thereby linked art, propaganda, and public activism in a singularly novel appeal to the "people." I show, though, that Guthrie later turned away from the fatalism of the socialist line to explore a certain "comic" mode, one that, in its own sonic rambling, upends the discursive categories of modern public life. Further, in his novel use of the refrain, Guthrie radicalized the ways in which popular song could bind and inspire a community of listeners across time and space. Here, as his anthems of the 1940s came to establish alternative forms of (sonic) nationhood, populism became truly popular—regional song underwent a massive deterritorialization, pointing toward the pop revolution to come.

Approaching the 1950s, though, we are confronted with a moment of apparent betrayal. Here, popular music becomes fully enmeshed in the top-down practices of big business and seems to lose much of its vigor and thrust in its submission to alien media such as photography, television, and film. This chapter, though—"Four Elvises: On the Dada Possibilities of Midcentury Rock and Roll and Modern Fan Culture"—does not lament the business of buying and selling popular music, but works within it to show how the very deadliness of the commodity form—its radical detachment from any traditional context—ultimately extends its affective range and reach. As I argue here, the rock counterculture was founded not against, but through technological manipulation, commercial standardization, and consumer desire, and thus provided fans with new, more thrilling ways of inhabiting a national scene defined by market identities and taste cultures. Somewhere between Marcel Duchamp's arty toss-off and Elvis Presley's tossed-off art, a certain indifference comes to infect popular culture at large; before the blank detachment of the consumer industry, modern art gives in to commercial modernity, and the dada-like iconoclasm of the former becomes a matter of daily life. High and low converge in the cheap, and mostly accidental, production of everyday pleasure, in the casual defacement and deformation of everyday life in the name of aesthetic thrill and stylish revolt. In the end, this chapter is neither a celebration nor a critique of Elvis the charismatic star, or even the music business, but an analysis of the pleasures and pains of modern fan culture. It focuses on the experiences and emergent sites of fandom, arguing that, with each cut, the King presented his body as an affectively charged and fully mediated public body and that, with records, radio, television, and film, his revolt extended—from one savvy fan to the next—across the body politic at large.

Chapter five—(   )—can perhaps best be described as the book's silent track. I am here concerned with the formal silence that pervades pop music in the late modern era, as it both allows for greater experimentation in music and preserves, in the face of complete commercial appropriation, the utopian possibility of some more subtle form of engagement with modernity. This chapter is also this book's most experimental, offering a mash-up of Buddy Holly, John Cage, and Jacques Derrida, all deep purveyors of silence and its critical power. With this grouping, I argue that Holly's music represents the moment when popular music became "pop music," when the ad hoc and mostly local musical traditions in America become a formal institution, free, in its abstraction, to explore its own terms and yet still able to reflect, albeit negatively, upon history at large. To consider this possibility, I begin with the architecture of the recording studio, particularly the sealed reverb chamber, showing how this "silent" space allowed for a more dynamic experience of sonic space and time. As I argue here, both Cage and Holly pursued silence to the point of freeing song (and specifically lyrical song) from the expressive demands of identity and tradition, and in this their work suggests a radical transformation of sonic experience and its place in American culture. The next section takes its cue from Jacques Derrida's *Speech and Phenomena* to show that Holly's vocals work via a process of "indication" rather than "expression" and thus point toward the very world that they fail to name or include. While Holly's lyrics often toy with the forms and themes of lyrical expression, I argue, his actual performances—in their pervasive silence—suggest a radically different kind of speech, one that is ultimately receptive to the contingency of everyday life and the voice of the other. Finally, this chapter returns to history proper, linking Holly's music—and pop music in general—to the Pop Art movement of the late 1950s and early 1960s. Holly's particular brand of pop song, I argue, anticipates Pop Art's own urge to push the emptiness of commercial culture toward something like its aesthetic apotheosis. Like Andy Warhol's "death" series, Holly's melancholic song attenuates decisively modern experiences of incommunicability and alienation to the point of renewed presence within the marketplace itself.

Arguably, all twentieth-century music approaches the condition of pop. With the introduction of technology and commerce, inherited ballads lose their rich textures and become cleaner, repetitive, more mechanical, and more easily consumed. As this last chapter suggests, though, this abstraction allowed pop music to attain its own significant expressiveness. In the slow silencing of region, community, and personality, popular song finds a more thrilling, more open relation to the transience and detachment of late modernity. In the end, Holly's abstract pop exposes popular song as it always anxiously mediates body and identity, as it establishes provisional alliances and exchanges, and so as it lets us experiment with more dynamic ways of being human and being modern.

CHAPTER ONE

Lord, It Just Won't Stop!

Work and Blues in the Industrial Delta

In the opening scene of Richard Wright's 1940 novel *Native Son*, the Thomas family wakes to find that a hungry rat has invaded their dingy one-room apartment. Mother and sister pick up their skirts, screaming, while eldest son Bigger grabs a skillet and takes aim at the beast. The rat is ultimately bested, but the battle leads to a heated dispute about money troubles and Bigger's ability to support his family. The rent's due, jobs are scarce, and the Relief's about to cut them all off. Mother tells her son, "We wouldn't have to live in this garbage dump if you had any manhood in you." Hot and complex feelings trouble the characters long after the argument ends, causing them to retreat to separate corners of their cramped living space. Wright's interest here lies not only in the economic conditions that produce these emotions, but also in the often scanty personal means by which they are addressed. First, he describes Bigger's response, which—in its restless incoherence—drives the entire tragic arc of the novel:

> He hated his family because he knew that they were suffering and that he was powerless to help them. He knew that the moment he allowed himself to feel to its fullness how they lived, the shame and misery of their lives, he would be swept out of himself with fear and despair. So he held toward them an attitude of iron reserve; he lived with them, but behind a wall, and toward himself he was ever more exacting. He knew that the moment he allowed what his life meant to enter fully into his consciousness, he would either kill himself or someone else. So he denied himself and acted tough.

Bigger's response consists of both an excess of emotion and a refusal to acknowledge that emotion. His identity is troubled on both ends: feeling is experienced not as an expression of selfhood, but as a loss of control, while its suppression becomes a deadly pose, fatal to self and others. In contrast, Bigger's mother retreats behind one of the flimsy curtains that partition the apartment and begins to cook breakfast. We can hear her voice, and she is singing:

> Life is like a mountain railroad
> With an engineer that's brave
> We must make the run successful
> From the cradle to the grave[1]

The mother's response is also oddly doubled, caught between the personal and the impersonal. Intense feelings are juxtaposed against the formalism of both chore and song. But, here, emotion finds a certain shape, a comforting groove in the nearly mechanical work of hand and voice. Neither activity seems particularly expressive. The details of the song—a spiritual scrap with a modern locomotive twist—only dimly relate to her immediate context and need. But the act of singing joins the practical and the purposeless, bringing together feeling and form in a single, moving whole, granting her a certain presence and, we'll find, agency. If Bigger shows his emotions too easily, but cannot control them, his mother falls into a satisfying sonic pattern and so regains control of her small world—her blues is the one we want to hear.

As some readers might know, Wright's *Native Son* ultimately indicts not just the blues, but all popular song, as a kind of ruse or cultural opiate. As Bigger heroically maintains, even in the face of arrest and probable death, popular music is nothing more than a form of "surrender, resignation," a sonic palliative for "whipped folks" (254, 356). But even if Wright's leftist commitments led him to reject song as a distraction from more direct political action, we should not ignore its power to accompany, and even transform, the troubled lives of his era. In typically modernist fashion, Bigger can only ironically assert the possibility of community as he heads toward the electric chair. Meanwhile, his mother proves both survivor and provider, and it is precisely the cheap music of the age, rather than its avant-garde fiction, that offered something like a satisfying presence for the black lower classes. As I show throughout this book, the most engaging songs of the day fused everyday feeling and form, and so provided listeners with a viable stance or attitude, a stylish manner, for confronting the world. The blues, though, perhaps more than any other music of the time, dramatizes this process, juxtaposing the hot emotional tumult of the body against a series of cool, abstract forms. As heard from Delta shacks to Chicago tenements to Harlem cabarets, the blues proved—despite its pained origins—a remarkably flexible medium and a new arena for the shaping of identity and community.

In other words, Bigger's mother is an *everyday* modernist, and her songmaking serves to stitch together the fragments of an increasingly incoherent world. Like all those other desperate creations of the age—Pound's *Cantos*, Eliot's *The Waste Land*, Woolf's *To the Lighthouse*—her song strives to produce a certain coherence through aesthetic form. The moderns saw their art as a way of healing the "dissociation of sensibility" brought about by modern life; they turned to the poetic image as a kind of creative restitution, "an intellectual and emotional complex in an instant of time."[2] Similarly, Bigger's mother confronts a world in which words and things no longer match up, a world in which the cunning language of landlord, boss, and the law fails to address her specific circumstances; her song presents itself as a discourse of another sort, and it offers, however briefly, the consolation of form. For Bigger's mother, though, such art is part of her daily routine, and it would be impossible to pinpoint where the daily struggle ends and the poetic act begins. Emotion and art here cannot but fall into each other—in the kitchen, in the factory, on the subway—and no matter how fraught or ironic the result, her song moves apace with the reality of her situation. So, when she finishes her stove-side performance, she calmly returns to the breakfast table with a plan of action: Bigger *is* taking the job, she *will* clean the house—here's the carfare, let's move on. In this, her scrappy song becomes something like a tiny affective motor, providing her with not only a unity of being, but also a certain purpose. In other words, by singing "*We must make the run successful*," Bigger's mother is not simply "expressing" the weary optimism of her race, but creating a space and time in which such optimism becomes a reality—of course, Bigger takes the job.

As I'll show here, though, the blues—as it sounded from the plantations in the South to the factories and tenements in the North, and all the juke joints and tent shows in between—corresponds to a very specific kind of modernity. This music was both embedded in and detached from the sites and routines it addressed, and in this it provided not just criticism, but a rich and poignant negotiation of the various dimensions of its moment: labor relations, the debtor system, transportation, and commodity culture. As is well known, such music was originally and persistently work music. It emerged from the field hollers and work songs of the past, and continued to provide, throughout the twentieth century, sustenance and uplift for a proletarian community. But, also, in the modern era, this music was increasingly individualized, increasingly alienated, particularly from the communal traditions of the African American past. Over time, its forms grew fragmented, more abstract and repetitive, revealing not only a dissociation of identity, but also—I believe—an alternative mode of being. In other words, as I show here, the very abstraction of modern industry and the marketplace became, in the shifting fragments of the blues song, a means of self-invention. The terms of labor and art everywhere overlap and diverge: the blues mobilizes the very excess of modern life—its extreme feelings, its stark formalism—for its own ends, and, in its only very slight abstraction from the habits and routines of everyday life, negotiates another course through history.

This is an agency of another sort. Just as the blues seems to mix categories such as "feeling" and "form," it also resists any simple designation of "worker" or even "self." As I'll show below, the freed slave entered public life only under threat of having his or her promised selfhood (as possession, as right) destroyed. Liberation was immediately overwhelmed by both the vast sensorium of modern life—railroads, riverboats, telephones, juke joints—and the more direct threats of the new southern economy: industrial labor, the chain gang, and lynching. This world seemed much stranger and more complex than anything promised by Emancipation, and the new terms of modern life raised deep ambivalences, proving to be sources of deep pain as well as pleasure. The freed slave was often forced to shift jobs, jump trains, and leave family members and loved ones against his or her will, but—at the same time—this ceaseless dissociation entailed its own forms of release. We should be careful when describing the agency of this figure and his or her music. Not only were blues performers systematically denied the rights of selfhood and self-determination, but their lives and music everywhere suggest suspicion and, at times, outright rejection of these categories. That said, the blues performer was neither a passive victim nor a heroic agent of his or her fate. The blues song suggests neither a simple acceptance nor a flat-out rejection of the modern condition, but a cunning ability to maneuver within its shifting terms, to exploit the new indifference and flexibility of the industrial order for both gain and satisfaction.

I've divided this chapter into three overlapping sections—work, song, and technology. Each tackles this dynamic of self-negation and self-persistence in a different way, as both an everyday experience and an aesthetic strategy, and thereby locates the critical power of the blues as a vernacular modernism. The first section cuts through the swampy romance of the Delta to trace the region's development as a kind a rural factory, as the scene of intense modernization, constant mobility, and hyperproduction. The Delta blues, I argue, emerges out of the unnerving flux of a rural modernity, generating both anxiety and excitement as the plantation system and its workers succumbed to the manic energy and abstract forms of the new economy. By way of example, in the second section, I focus on Charley Patton and the blues ballads that made him famous, particularly as the latter provided a shifting and ultimately open template for both personal and regional identity. Here, I will explore how singer and song inhabit the various contexts of Delta life—the countryside, the highway, the lover's shack, the railroad station; the blues voice, specifically, proves as dislocated and dissociated as the modernity it seeks to address, at times restless and fretful, but also thrilling in its mobility and plasticity. The third section shifts from the technology of blues production to the technology of blues consumption, focusing on the blues as a *recorded* form. In general, the blues, with its repetitive stanza form, its recycled lyricism, and its obsessive re-creation of past violence, suggests an endless effort to master some prior wound or loss—a pain at once racial, sexual, and economic. Here, though, the recorded form of the blues—rather than merely replaying such traumas—points toward a more progressive theory of repetition and mimicry, one that, even as it conjures up seemingly primitive forms of African American magic, opens up history for both musicians and audiences. The reproductive power of the phonograph links the "primitive" and "progressive" dimensions of the blues and forces us to reconsider not just the modernity of African American culture, but the cultural possibilities of techno-modernity at large.

One—The Rural Factory and the Modern Blues

How do you picture the Mississippi Delta? What images come to mind? A muddy river? A dusty highway? The dark outline of a man in natty suit and hat, guitar case in hand, waiting for a ride? This mythic iconography works to establish—on record covers and book jackets, in movies and documentaries and television shows—the rootsiness, the rawness, the gritty authenticity of both the region and its song. Think dirt, think poverty, think loneliness—the somber outlines of the region seem to confirm the truth of its music—its "real" pain, its "real" joy—as if a troubled life could only be experienced directly, earnestly, objectively. Yet, at the same time, these popular images only ever present the music, for all its presumed immediacy, in hazy, mystical terms—the region at once appears and vanishes; the singer's identity is both asserted and denied. Such iconography—insofar as it derives from the work of the early blues archivists and the blues revivalists of the 1960s—raises a mist of romance and thereby obscures the material dimensions of the blues. We are led to believe that the blues is unfathomable and its origins obscure, buried deeply in the individual soul, or, further back, in the alluvial plane of the Delta or, even further, the tribal mysteries of Africa.

Take Martin Scorsese's celebrated blues documentary *Feel Like Going Home*.[3] Largely a work of heavy editing, the film consists of a series of down-home blues tracks played over stark archival imagery of lone plowmen, yellow floods, beaten shacks, and angry dogs. The flow of blues voices seems ghostly, disembodied, as if their owners only ever existed in some muddy limbo, ceaselessly haunting their own lives, while the visuals are all perfectly grainy, perfectly beaten, making the entire region seem like its own lost home movie. "Hell Hound on My Trail" drifts onto the soundtrack, and then the ghostly image of Robert Johnson's head fills the screen, superimposed over a tracking shot of a dusty Delta highway. The camera follows the white lines in the road, then cuts to a spinning disc on a phonograph player, and finally closes in on Johnson's death certificate. Over these cagey markers of authenticity, Scorsese whispers, "A high haunting voice, pitched on the razor's edge between joy and pain. Dead at twenty-seven, twenty-nine songs, and just two known photographs. We'll never have more than just a few scattered memories and details about the life of Robert Johnson." *What joy? What pain? What happened in those twenty-nine years? Why mention the death, the photographs—at all—if not to shroud them both in some shady mystery?*

Something solid must exist between this region and its song, something that shapes one to the other and explains their joint meaning. But it is *work* and mostly *work*, the one thing resistant to all blues mythologizing. Not *slavery*, mind you, but the crappy, anti-romantic work typical of modern life—pained, repetitive, meaningless, uncertain. Of course, work and workers appear throughout accounts such as *Feel Like Going Home*. Men and women are seen toiling away on the land—digging, cutting, plowing—but only in isolation, only as individuals, as if their one restriction, their one adversary, was nature itself: stubborn trees, fitful rivers, pesky insects. Work appears here as a basic human liability, a God-given chore, and, even, at times, part of an agrarian ideal. Its terms and conditions are obscured by the rural setting in which it occurs; the specificity of the plantation system is replaced by a near-biblical language of size and scale.

In this, we lose sight of the one reality that makes sense of the blues as a historical form: the capitalist network of investments and rewards, and all the complex technologies, architectures, and routines that constituted the modern plantation system. Ultimately, this swamp needs to be dredged of its romantic ooze. We need to think clearly about how the region, and its racial hierarchies, evolved through the process of industrialization. By situating the blues fully within the context of the Delta as a "rural factory," we can better understand not just certain blues lyrics, but also the blues itself as a product of that factory, as a thoroughly modern art that helped worker and community relate to industrial modernity at large.

The Delta was, of course, one tough swamp to clear—miles and miles of mud, roots, disease, bugs, alligators, bears, and rats. The earliest settlers found it nothing less than a "seething lush hell"—no paths in or out, no ready sustenance, and no reliable weather. But if the region became the heartland of the blues, it was because, of all the regions of the South, it most violently and extensively suffered the processes of *modernization*—the brutal feat of draining the swamps, the struggle to attain soil consistency, the construction of a transportation network, and, most importantly, the development of a stable workforce. In all this, it was a place fit for devils, but devils of a particularly modern cast—one thinks of Joseph Conrad's Kurtz or William Faulkner's Sutpen—white, naked, beast-like, with a whip in one hand and a spreadsheet in the other. The region would make brutes of us all, but only because its development demanded a fully modern juxtaposition of savage violence and rational technique. As James C. Cobb explains, the Delta's transformation can only be understood in terms of the "determination, rapacity and cruelty" that humanity can display, "if the proper incentives are in place." It commenced once the weakness of Reconstruction gave way to the oppressive measures of Redemption and a "cadre of white leaders sought to create through an ironic combination of economic modernization and racial resubjugation a prosperous and politically insulated cotton kingdom."[4] In this, the black worker was exposed to all the hostility of the market without any of the (meager) protection that may have been granted as property under the plantation system. His or her very identity, poor as it already was, was liquidated, made fungible, reduced to its productive minimum and then channeled through the abstract forms of the economy.

Seeking not just larger yields, but also lower costs, Delta owners rationalized all aspects of the plantation system. From planting, storage, and shipping to milking the cow and feeding the worker, success demanded the implementation of new structures and managerial techniques. Over time, the paternalistic order of the Old South gave way to the impersonal reign of the "rural factory," highly efficient and micromanaged in all respects. "A central office," Harold Woodman explains, "made all major management decisions, determining hours of work, the amount and kind of fertilizer and seed used, the maintenance and improvements required, the tools, equipment and mules to be used, the boll weevil poisoning to be applied. Supervisors or overseers directed the work and saw to it that the workers followed the routine set by the manager."[5] Indeed, by the early twentieth century, the region was gaining international attention not for its picturesque landscape or its tortured music, but for its modern business techniques. In 1937, *Fortune* magazine published an article on an English corporation that owned the Delta & Pine Land Company of Scott, Mississippi—38,000 acres, 3,300 working hands, and 1,000 "blacks." As the company president explained, the plantation's success was due to "expert management." The whole operation was neatly organized into twelve units, each with its own supervisor; it maintained its own gin, a company store, and all equipment and animals; it even ran an "experimental farm" where "an expert breeder succeeded in producing seed that matured early (to lessen boll weevil damage), had a long staple, and had a high ration of lint per acre."[6]

For early black migrants, those who flocked to the Delta in the 1870s and 1880s, this new system seemed to represent independence and advancement. Planters lured workers with promises of better wages and more autonomy, benefits not seen anywhere else in the South. Some leaders even courted the possibility of suffrage and outwardly adopted a policy of political "fusion," touting racial cooperation as the basis of economic stability.[7] Rather than dismantle the hierarchy of the plantation system, however, the Delta gave it a decisively modern twist. The familiar domestic values of the old order, conditioned by an ambivalent paternalism, were trampled under the sheer rationalism of the new one, so that racism continued under the guise of efficiency itself, embedding itself deeply in the faceless economy. As one worker explained, "You know when a man owned you he had to be careful not to kill you or even bruise you, but the poor white overseer didn't own nothing and didn't have anything to loose [sic]" (Cobb 23). With *this* Emancipation, blacks in the South confronted, in more or less direct ways, the limits of the free market and the work ethic through which it was promoted. They had been freed into a modernity that—economically, morally, physically—betrayed its own foundations of privacy, property, and self-determination.[8] Having given up the past, the ex-slave was now confronted with a world that was both brutal *and* inhuman, his existence caught, in a way, "between two deaths," between the loss of organic tradition and the cold abstraction of the economy.[9] As Alan Lomax put it, "Feelings of anomie and alienation, of orphaning and restlessness—the sense of being a commodity rather than a person; the loss of love and of family and of place—this modern syndrome was the norm for the cotton farmers and the transient laborers of the Deep South."[10]

But we need to look closer at these feelings, particularly as they inspired complex responses and—in the collusion of feeling and form—new models of agency for both male and female workers in the region. First, this modernity moved at a breakneck speed, churning up everything in its wake, and, in its sheer physicality, assaulted the body at the level of both sense and feeling. Not only was there work to be done all year long on the plantation—clearing, reaping, ditching, building, plowing, picking, hacking, baling—but, again, the work itself had been divided and distributed so that each task became its own constant activity over and over again.[11] The recently emancipated worker often seemed to exist as little more than the motion of labor itself. He or she seemed free only to lift more, dig more, chop more, cook more, to work more hours, to owe more money, and to be replaced by someone else. As Marx might claim, all that was solid in the South melted into air, and so the black body was caught up in the perpetual motion of the economic machine. Or, as the men in the labor gangs hollered:

> We had to move.
> > Look out, Shot,
> > Here I come,
> > And you standin up there,
> > With your big shotgun.
> But we gotta keep moving.
> > We got a man,
> > He done fell dead,
> > But alls I heard
> > Was what he said,
> Keep on moving. (Lomax 68)

These are conditions only a futurist would love. The machine must move without restraint and labor extracted at all costs, by threat of rope or shotgun. In fact, there's no room for "men" in this factory. The individual is a swamp of sentiment, blocking the way of complete mobilization; the body is a resource that must be consumed over and over again, sacrificed slowly for the sake of progress and economic gain. Thus, one worker described Delta life as a *perpetuum mobile* of machine and metal:

> When they first started building levees all the work was done with wheel-barrows. I rolled many a wheel-barrow up there. Went from wheel-barrow to slip—a big shovel with two mules attached to it. There'd be one man to load, one man to drive it, and one man to stay on the dump and dump it. It would never stop, just come right around. Then they went to wheelers. A wheeler was like a slip, only it was bigger with wheels. It would carry three or four times as much as a slip. You hitched two mules to it. From wheelers they went to wagons and carts hitched to four mules. Then they used a turning plow and a belt. Then they come to the present time with these trucks, dippers and tractors. (37)

As the worker slips out of this passage, so his identity slips out of history. By the time we get to the "present time" in this passage, with its trucks and tractors, he has been reduced to a bare minimum, nothing more than a series of affective positions, forced to conform to a world of large machines.

Secondly, then, this modernity was defined by cold abstraction, a massive denaturalization of identity and culture according to an entirely new set of sizes and scales—the deathliness of form itself. First, work in the Delta exceeded any natural order. It did not rise and fall with the seasonal cycle, but continued all year round as a series of simple, unchanging tasks. It did not end with the individual plot of land or even the larger boundary of the plantation, but extended infinitely with the planter's ability to increase his holdings. At the same time, its rationalization trampled over the connections of home and family. The law of supply and demand had no patience for domesticity, breaking apart intimate ties of kith and kin, replacing them with cold contracts and debtor slips. Indeed, even at the level of the individual body, motion was abstracted, reduced to series of repetitive forms—the repetitive rhythms used by groups of loggers to cut down trees, the mangled postures and awkward gaits of the heavy-lifting stevedores, or the ceaseless folding and ironing done by domestic servants. Generally, the worker's entire life—where, when, and how he or she worked—was determined according to the "rational" needs of the economic order. Work songs, in turn, explored the limitlessness of this system, its dissociation from anything like human value and perspective, and the radical dissociation of effort and return:

> Done worked all summer
> Done worked all the fall

And here come Christmas
And I ain't got nothing at all
I'm just a po' cold nigger[12]

At the end of the day, the worker seemed to have cultivated nothing but bewilderment and fear. Nothing he touched belonged to him, and all he made could be taken away at a moment's notice. Over time, everywhere in his life, he experienced the irrationality of his newly rationalized world. His experience revealed a widening gap between reality and its abstract manipulation, between his emotional investments and the machinery of labor and economy to which they were forced to conform.

Of course, when it comes to this work, blues singers were often openly hostile about its terms and conditions. They all knew the fate of John Henry, the steel-driving man, who went down with his hammer beside him on the road. But this was only one of many songs that lamented the demeaning nature of labor, the threat of industrial machinery, the hostility of the overseer, and the ever-present fear of replacement and unemployment. Sometimes their criticism was quite direct: singers peppered their songs with the names of cruel overseers and warned listeners to stay away from specific plantations. Other times, as in Sampson Pittman's "Cotton Farmer Blues," it was deeply structural: in a few quick verses, Pittman outlines the whole insidious network of debt, exploitation, and legal restriction.[13] Similarly, Bessie Smith, in "House Rent Blues," gave voice to the unprotected life of the single woman, hounded by creditors, and Ida Cox, in "Pink Slip Blues," lamented the fickleness of relief efforts.[14] Regarding the free agency of the marketplace, it was a luxury no worker or domestic servant could sing about with any confidence. Working or quitting, saving or spending, having a name or not, such distinctions were meaningless in the Delta, where, as Son House lamented in "Country Farm Blues," any white captain could take your identity away and replace it with his own perverse will.[15] Oddly, then, while many commentators emphasize the individualism of blues *performance*, few see that most blues *songs* reveal a deep failure or even a refusal to assert anything like a traditional "self." As the communal vibe of the spirituals and work songs faded into the cultural background, the blues emerged as an expression of not simply pride, but also of isolation and alienation, failure and submission. The music's celebrated freedom—its "element of pure self," as Lawrence Levine famously claimed—never existed in a pure form, for it was always complicated by the forms of the economy and troubled by extreme feelings of loneliness, anxiety, and apathy.[16]

Still, for many blacks in the region, the feelings generated by the plantation economy—of quick and sudden motion, extreme emotional violence,
personal dislocation and detachment—suggested new kinds of pleasure and
horizons of expectation. Often, blacks in the region, dissatisfied with the
modicum of privacy granted by sharecropping, exploited the inconsistency
and uncanny indifference of the marketplace, cherishing displacement and
divestment as potential freedoms and new sources of dignity.[17] Switch jobs,
take a line of credit, jump a train, ride the flood out of town—with a little
pluck you could make a break and start all over again somewhere down
the line. Such maneuvers are best described not as "rambling" (there's too
much romance in the word), but as a kind of "slipping," a term that better
captures the cagey uncertainty and chancy violence of this motion. The
Delta worker was constantly "slipping" through the gaps in the system, riding its currents, skimming off the top, and beginning again at the next farm,
the next station, the next town, the next crop. In "Revenue Man Blues,"
for example, Charley Patton sings—in his own loud, risky way—of both
endless debt and the thrill of evading it. He takes only three short verses
to attain the desired bottle, grab his girl, and slip through the cracks. As in
many blues songs, the singer's sheer velocity allows him to elude the law,
while his anonymity becomes a decent disguise. He successfully adapts
the conditions of his own dereliction, situating himself both within and
against a generally treacherous economy.[18] The most popular blues songs
in the region, such as Ida Cox's "Wild Women Don't Get the Blues" and
Clara Smith's "Every Woman's Blues," explored these same possibilities for
women. Smith's song first outlines the ways in which society devises to trap
women, only to declare, with a sneaky half rhyme, her own sly escape:

> You can read your hymnbook, read your Bible, read your history,
>   and spell on down,
> You can read my letters, but you sho' can't read my mind.
> When you think I'm crazy about you, I'm leaving you all the time.[19]

As we'll find in the next section, the shaky uncertainty of the blues form
serves a positive function in this regard. As singers like Patton and Smith
slip from verse to verse, from voice to voice, they quickly adopt and adapt
one stance after another—"hand to hand," as Bessie Smith described it—
reveling in their ability to move between stances and attitudes.

In this, Delta blues culture seems to reflect a much larger process in
which the region's chaotic lushness was overlaid with a series of abstract
patterns—not just labor and commerce, but transportation networks,

communication systems, and power grids—each providing new means of mobility and investment. Paradoxically, as the renovated plantation economy expanded to control the various flows of Delta life, it also provided new possibilities for slipping away, opening pathways both within and beyond the region.[20] Over time, a certain doubleness came to mark all the networks of daily life, so that the road to work also functioned as the road away from work, the railroad became a site for trading goods as well as guitar licks, and the worker himself slowly became, in a way, a savvy performer of his own fate. Many of these networks overlapped, multiplying the possibilities for deterritorialization. Railroads, for example, carried not only hundreds of thousands of blacks into and out of the region, but also copies of the *Chicago Defender* and pressings from Paramount Records. The automobile, too, became a means of transportation, a mode of sociability, and, with the addition of radio, a technology of cultural diffusion. In these ways, the region became a "staging area" for a Great Migration—or, rather, a *Great Slipping*—that was at once demographic, economic, and cultural. In fact, the Delta soon came to be known as a great cosmopolitan hub, a rural city of sorts, "part of one of the great mainstreams of national commerce," famous, in accounts of the time, for its "cosmopolitanism."[21] In other words, the region quickly came to dissolve its own regional determinants as they encoded both economic and racial identities, setting the terms for both blues culture and, as we'll see in the next section, the blues form.

Take the celebrated blues experience of the road, a key site for "slipping" away. If the bluesman had "ramblin' on his mind," the harried nature of his flight was experienced as both thrill and terror. On the one hand, movement in the region was compulsory. It painfully defined the activity of the worker, on both the newly Taylorized farms and on the roadways, in the desperate motion from one work site to another. As Robert Johnson famously sang, with the hell hound hot on his trail, "I got to keep movin' / I've got to keep movin' / Blues fallin' down like hail."[22] On the other hand, life on the road implied a certain autonomy and even pleasure. Movement—from one town or job or lover to another—provided some control over one's fate and became, at times, a freedom in itself. As Jeff Todd Titon explains, the frequent, surreptitious flights of Delta workers figured as a kind of "protest." In a society defined by the collusion of legal and illegal restriction, motion was undertaken in defiance, as a quiet but effective revolt against repressive structures.[23] For some, though, this movement was simply exhilarating; the new landscape, crisscrossed with roads and tracks, appeared excitingly open, beckoning anyone who sought a more immediate release. For both men and women, travel became a thrilling end in itself, a sensual experience in excess of any goal, economic or otherwise, and thus a genuine source of personal identity. As Johnson sang, staring down the Devil himself: "You may bury my body down by the highway side / So my old spirit can catch a Greyhound bus and ride." Similarly, the narrator of Patton's "34 Blues" has been run off of Dockery Farms. Broke and lonely, he looks around him at the landscape and sees nothing but fear and failure. Then, however, he spies a "big six Chevrolet car"—"My God!" he exclaims, as if immediately rejuvenated, "what solid power!"[24] The blues queens outraced their male counterparts, both literally and figuratively. In songs like Anita Hill's "Sports Model Blues," Cleo Gibson's "I've Got a Ford Engine Movement in My Hips," and Virginia Liston's "Rolls Royce Papa," female singers claimed the privileges of techno-modernity and celebrated the open life of the road. Gibson comes across like a kinky cyborg in her double-entendre-laden song of the open road: "I got Ford engine movements in my hips," she sings with raunchy glee, "Ten thousand miles guarantee."[25]

If car and road signified the alluring openness of the territory, the Delta shack suggested the uncanny persistence of stability and form. As a form of regional architecture, the shack was inherently porous, leaky, exposed. You could literally stand in the front door and look right out through the back. As a dwelling, little separated interior and exterior, and the cruel world was felt pushing on all sides through the split pine shingles and rusted tin roof. Here, property came to function at the barest minimum, a grim reminder of home in a world determined to deny all comfort and shelter.[26] As with the car, though, we need to understand the emotional doubleness of the shack. On the one hand, the shack appears in the blues as a site of fear and anxiety. Many songs begin with the "blues at my door" and end with the terrifying image of the "blues all around my bed." As Bessie Smith sings in "In the House Blues":

> Oh, the blues has got me on the go.
> Oh, they've got me on the go.
> They runs around my house, in and out of my front door.[27]

On the other hand, the open shack also often implies personal freedom, a release from domestic routine and the closed family circuit. The blues singer often appears waiting at the door or the gate, beckoning his or her lover inside or ready to leave in search of another. In many women's blues, especially, the singer exploits the new flexibility of the economic order and takes control of the domestic space, granting access to whomever she pleases. In Smith's "Sam Jones Blues," for example, poor Sam returns home to find a newly liberated (and newly named) Mrs. Wilson blocking the doorway—she knows her rights and now she's queen of the shack.[28] In a way, then, the Delta shack encouraged an alternative kind of sociability, a more fluid engagement with the outside world that seemed to contradict bourgeois boundaries of private and public life. In fact, as some have argued, the dissolution of property in the modern South signaled a return to more traditional forms of African American community, restoring a sense of public intimacy and exchange for otherwise anxious and alienated individuals. For all its faults, the shack, with its open architecture and easy accessibility, became a key site of new/old black sociability, an odd but persistent space of cultural difference spawned from within the plantation system itself.[29]

These processes, insofar as they entailed a massive deterritorialization of regional life, also determined the popularity of certain kinds of blues in the region. As Elijah Wald explains, the most popular blues songs in the Delta expressed a thoroughly modern worldview, and the most popular blues performers were celebrated for their urban style and professionalism. Indeed, despite the preference for primitive hollers established by early folklorists and latter-day revivalists, Delta audiences demanded music that was cosmopolitan and slick, as it connected them to the novel forms and sensations of modern life. Hymns and hollers were old news, ragtime was a dying fad, but the blues—as it was purveyed in big cities like Chicago and New York—represented a "a hot new pop style," a modernity just in reach (9). Here, of course, we cannot underestimate the popularity of the blues queens in the region. Stars like Ma Rainey, Ida Cox, Bessie Smith, Victoria Spivey, and Clara Smith dazzled audiences not just with their peppy songs of city life, but also with their dazzling gowns and elaborate stage shows. As the original "blues" stars, they represented the first wave of modern African Americans who had "slipped away" from the confines of regional life to establish a certain independence elsewhere, either in the big city or in the very transit of their professional lives. In their performances, these early stars juxtaposed traces of racial and regional identity with new markers of success and wealth. This combination of old and new, doubled everywhere by peppy jazz arrangements, created a sharp affective charge for black audiences in the South, as, for example, in the case of Ma Rainey's stage show. As Daphne Duval Harrison explains, Rainey's blues lyrics tended to focus on black rural life, and her earthy, powerful contralto established a regional intimacy with her southern audience, but the setting and style of her act everywhere asserted the singer's iconoclastic modernity. The highlight of Rainey's act occurred when she emerged dripping with jewels from a stage set designed to look like a Paramount talking machine; as the *Chicago Defender* exclaimed, "Oh Boy! What a flash Ma does make in her gorgeous gowns backed up by her Georgia Jazz Band."[30] Similarly, ads for Rainey and her peers contained images of stereotyped black mammies alongside up-to-date photos of the singers with modern hairstyles and fancy gowns. On all levels—sound, image, even in the technology and commerce of popular music consumption—blues audiences were confronted with the processes of change occurring around them.[31]

As Wald suggests, the music of the blues queens "came to Delta dwellers as the sound of hope and promise, of faraway cities with good jobs and a more liberal racial climate," and thus inspired the next wave of male blues performers in the region (97). As significantly, I believe, it provided listeners with a chance to explore and evaluate the possibilities of modernization. Simply put, living on the fringes of the community, as both black women and professionals, the blues queens represented the avant-garde of regional deterritorialization and, in content alone (I'll discuss form in the next section), their songs acclimated listeners to the pleasures of a more completely modern life. As Clara Smith put it in "Mama's Gone, Goodbye": "Fare the well, I've been excused, now there's brand new rules and I ain't no fool."[32] Even when such songs expressed ambivalence about modern life, they maintained a keen sense of independence and offered new models of agency for listeners.[33] The blues queens certainly liked to boast about their experiences in the city, and a quick glance at the charts of the day shows that audiences simply couldn't get enough of songs about Chicago, Baltimore, Pittsburgh, Houston, and Kansas City. While many of these songs outlined the dangers of city life—poverty, disease, unemployment, prostitution, and alcoholism—they just as often flirted with the surreal freedoms of the city. In "Kansas City Man Blues," for example, Clara Smith boasts of her lush life in the city clubs with a new, high-stepping man; similarly, Bertha "Chippie" Hill, in "Pratt City Blues," outlines the good things to be had "nice and neat" on Baltimore's streets, far away from the dreary farms and dusty fields of Sandusky.[34] What intrigues me most is the pleasure these songs seem to take in the very dissociation of experience and identity brought on by modern life. They are most notable for their attention to the city as a place of abstraction—the openness of the urban economy, in which anything could be bought and sold, and the self-stylization made possible by urban anonymity. In "All Around

Mama," for example, Mary Dixon describes herself as a woman with an open mind, one cultivated no doubt by her experiences with (paid) men in the city. Bertha Idaho's hit "Down on Pennsylvania Avenue" presents the city as a space of radical transformation, outlining a night full of chance encounters, cheap thrills, and cunning shape-shifters: "Let's take a trip down to that cabaret," goes one verse, "Where they turn night into day / Some freakish sights you will surely see / You can't tell a he from a she / You'll find them every night on Pennsylvania Avenue."[35]

Again, blues music is often defined as the raw expression of the fears and hopes of the emancipated African American. With its intimate lyricism, bruised melodic lines, and individualized performances, the music seems to arise out of the pained private spaces of southern black life and reveals the tormented existence and vague pride of black individuals as they confront the conflicted terms of their existence.[36] But the condition of Emancipation was specifically one of extreme feeling and form, of overwhelming sensation and abstract, impersonal structure. The deep emotions of the freed slave were brought about precisely through extrinsic processes of dissociation via work, technology, and law, and thus were deeply embedded in the modern features of the landscape. As I hope to show in the next section, then, the significance of the blues is not just that it gives voice to individual identity—in fact, it is a quite *in*expressive art—but that it performs, in its very abstraction, an ultimately open-ended process of self-creation and self-revision. In a world without props or property, without the very property of the self, the blues is only always a temporary claim or contract, a provisional statement or stance of allegiance and investment, but one that nonetheless generates a sense of value for its holder. In this, the music is more actively engaged with the landscape it addresses, sounding somewhere between the road and the shack, between country and city, mobility and abstraction, generating provisional, but no doubt genuine and productive, stances in a constantly changing world.

Two—The Cunning Mobility of the Blues Singer and the Blues Form

So let's take another listen to Charley Patton, the "Masked Marvel"—the Delta's first *homegrown* professional bluesman, if not the country's first rock-and-roll star. Patton was a boozer, a scrapper, and a repeat offender who led a restless life, slipping up and down the South and Midwest, playing when he could as loud as he could. To other blues performers, he seemed both a wild musical genius and a cheap showman: he could easily whip up a gut-wrenching blues, but he was mostly famous for twirling his guitar, spinning it behind his back, and playing it on his head.[37] Today, Patton's biographers suggest that his life was as confused and crossed as the Delta itself. The oldest son of a mixed-race sharecropping family, he seemed fated for a bluesy life, endlessly roaming the region in search of an impossible satisfaction. His career, no doubt, proves a crossroads in more ways than one, a constant transit between the tenant shack and the railroad, the back porch and the recording studio, tradition and modernity. His songs, too, seem caught—on a series of Paramount records—between rural idealism (lazy rivers, bird nests, and stone ponies) and the complex signs of modernity (Buicks, telephones, and revenue men). As we'll find, though, this restless movement and dislocation—between houses, classes, races, and styles—proved for Patton a solution in itself, the basis of both a genuine career and a true aesthetic. Simply put, as "the Masked Marvel," Patton was able to slip along the currents of the new economy, exploit its flexibility and constant dislocation, and thus expand his world and its possibilities. He entered the tumultuous flow of modernity in order to re-map it on his own terms, giving up conventional notions of identity—racial or otherwise—to establish both a new aesthetic and a more flexible, more satisfying form of existence for himself and his listeners.

Patton's pathbreaking career as a blues singer makes most sense within the context of the upwardly mobile mixed-race family in which he was raised. If, as is often claimed, he was the guitar-toting "missing link" between older forms of African American music and the modern blues, his career marks a transition from passive endurance under Jim Crow to a more cunning negotiation of the modern marketplace. Patton's grandfather was a white man from Vicksburg. He owned real estate and worked as an overseer on a Bolton-area plantation. Soon after the Civil War, he left his wife and married a "black Indian" woman, with whom he had three children. Patton's father, in turn, had started off as a cropper, renting space from Will Dockery for one-fourth his yield. He eventually earned enough to own his own land, a company store, and a profitable hauling company. With his wife Annie, also of partial Indian descent, he enjoyed a prosperous life; his status as "bossman" raised the Pattons well above the standard sharecropping lot, linking them to some of the most powerful families in the region. Through both work and migration, then, the Patton family resisted racial categorization in a way previously impossible for blacks in the South. They neither denied nor succumbed to their mixed ancestry, but used the features of the new economy to maneuver upward within it; dissatisfied with the limits of the color line, they found—through renting, ownership, mobility, and, eventually, music—a life of greater freedom and opportunity. In this, of course, the industrial Delta provided an ideal base of operations. Bolton had long been known as a haven for upwardly mobile blacks, and it provided an ideal setting for mixed families after the war. According to David Evans, Dockery Farms was run by a "paternalistic planter who by all accounts treated his tenants very fairly and frequently gained their loyalty and residency for stretches of many years"; like the plantations described above, it was "a modern operation, at once efficiently managed and technologically advanced, and it provided many middle-level positions and ownership opportunities for eager blacks" (132).

Charley Patton benefited from this environment in more ways than one. His family's status provided him with an advanced education, a decent home life, a steady stream of adequate employment, and, later on, as a musician, a built-in network of fans and gigs. But we need to distinguish how Patton himself negotiated his position in this *milieu*. While it might be true that—given his ambiguous racial/economic status—he never truly found his niche, he was also able, like his father and grandfather before him, to capitalize on the increased fluidity of the region. As Evans explains, "His 'niche' in the system consisted of placing himself outside the system and actually avoiding a niche, never permanently accommodating, never letting himself be pinned down" (133). As I'd like to add, though, Patton's songs suggest that this "choice" only became available within a fully modernized Delta. Patton's blues career exploits not only the unique sites and routines of the region, but also its technology—the commissary, the roadway, the train station, the juke joint, the radio, the phonograph. He established himself by slipping into the machinery of this system, making a name for himself alongside its sanctioned modes of operation, riding its smooth economic flows and skimming off what he could (sometimes as much as $75 a night). For Patton, in fact, music making was itself a kind of abstract labor defined *within*, but also increasingly *against*, other kinds of work. With guitar in hand, he was able to live more prosperously than his father and establish for himself a greater deal of freedom and dignity than those within even the upper echelons of the sharecropping system. Beyond the frustration of rent and debt and contracts, beyond even the complacent life of the propertied classes, the musician maintained a lifestyle that was neither simply proletarian nor entrepreneurial, neither simply black nor white, but always indeed modern.

In other words, there's more to the commercial image of the "the Masked Marvel" than we might think (see image 1). Paramount released Patton's first two records—"Mississippi Bo Weavil Blues" and "Screamin' and

IMAGE 1 Paramount "race" record advertisement featuring the Masked Marvel. *Chicago Defender*, September 1929.

Hollerin' the Blues"—under this seductive moniker in 1929, promising listeners a free record if they could guess the artist's identity. More than just a promotional device, or even a form of commercial passing, the name reflects, as we'll see in a moment, the kind of creative ambiguity and anonymous mobility that marks all of Patton's blues. It speaks not just to the ambivalence of his life and career, but also to the novel form of expressiveness—even the cunning *in*-expressiveness—of his cultivated art. We should recall here that Patton's success as a recording star came after the initial breakthrough of the blues queens. While he was always a local favorite, he represents a second wave of blues performers who gained commercial attention in the later 1920s, when record executives realized the marketability of regional forms. In this, his fame and reputation were situated not just between races and classes, but also between regions, landscapes, and economies. Tellingly, then, while Paramount's advertisements announced each new song as a "Race" record, as a presumably authentic expression of rural feeling, they depicted Patton as an urbane man in a dapper tux and bowtie, with well-oiled hair and a witty smirk on his lips. One ad, in fact, for "Spoonful Blues," set Patton in the middle of a swanky uptown café; surrounded by high fashion and quality service, he bears the expression of a thoroughly modern ennui.[38] In general, these ads positioned the "Marvel" within a complex iconography of primitivism and progress and, much like the music itself, presented the Delta as a site of both deep emotion and worldly sophistication. They suggested that identity in the Delta was not only displaced and disaffected, but always in motion, a mercurial and thoroughly modern stance, one that could be, in its very abstraction, a source of pleasure and gain. Again and again, we'll find, the Masked Marvel disappears only to find himself again, slips away to reemerge somewhere else, carrying off some new trick or thrill, some new position or form that, for the time being, gets the job done.

In Patton's music, then, the blues takes many forms and ultimately comes to signal both the mutability and provisionality of all form. It is variously a feeling, a mood, a nameless threat, a person, a lover, a boss-man, a mob, and, of course, the Devil himself. It is often experienced as both cause and effect, action and reaction, and it can be used as both hex and counterhex, poison and antidote, pain and relief. Most importantly, the blues is both the cause of song and song itself, both an active emotion and its formal expression, and, in this, it blurs the boundary between inside and out, depth and surface, form and feeling. In fact, Patton's blues always begin with some real danger, some specific threat of attack or annihilation. But whether it's a flood, a strike, a murder, or a lover's betrayal, each disaster turns out to be curiously pervasive, implacable, infectious. The blues floods the region and—like the economy described above—dissolves all in its path, seeping through towns, homes, beds, and hearts, destroying every surety, every stability of self and property. In Patton's "Mean Black Moan," for example, the blues spreads from a workers' strike in Chicago to the singer's front door and, ultimately, all around his bed.[39] The hungry men he describes are both tormented and tormentors, persistent figures of a persistent and contagious dread; they appear on all horizons, and indeed destroy all horizons, collapsing world and perspective into one dark blur. "Lord, it just won't stop," the singer cries in despair, after seven pained verses. Thus his fall figures not as a physical death (although such deaths are common in the blues), but as a kind of personal dispersal; identity gives way to psychological malaise, plot gives way to desperate gesture, and ballad form melts into shapeless moan. And yet, as I'd like to show, Patton's blues, like the modernity to which they respond, always somehow signal renewed presence and persistence. The emotional flooding of identity clears the way for new mobility, while the ceaseless mutation of form signals the possibility of new habituations. In other words, the performer develops a new kind of song out of this very tumult, a song that is affectively open and startlingly creative, harnessing the strange currents of the moment to his own obscure ends. Indeed, even the protagonist of "Mean Black Moan" ultimately regains his footing, using sound itself to cut through the murk, asserting that, when this evil ends, he'll be "all right" again.

In a way, the very fact of blues performance—the persistence of voice alone—suggests survival, but some of Patton's performances, charged with high emotion and multiple positions/perspectives, establishes an altogether more flexible and creative form of identity. Take, for example, "High Water Everywhere." Here, Patton's performance, recorded in two long, rollicking parts, more clearly displays a startling energy and bravura.[40] As the flood seeps across the region, dissolving everything in its path, the bluesman slips from site to site, hollerin' all the way with reckless glee. The singer's frantic search for higher ground, accompanied by an anxious percussive beat, barely exceeds the movement of the flood, and yet it proves surprisingly productive, matching its own shifting persistence against the overwhelming threat of drowning. With each verse, the singer becomes more and more like some protean deity, a swampy shape-shifter, appearing in a number of different voices and guises, adding one response after another. Patton, in fact, a master of commercial manipulation, recorded a second version of the song for his Arkansas listeners, which includes a comparable list of places from across the state line and a slew of new characters—a family man, a praying man, a working man, etc. This second version generates a whole new set of emotions and stances (despair, fear, shame, and sadness), the piece charged by an increasingly manic energy, so that its concluding moment of despair also sounds like a moment of personal triumph, as if the singer had repopulated the entire forsaken region with his own song.

In this, Patton's recorded repertoire suggests the idea of a man freed by the very forces that oppress him. Taken together, his songs present him as a vast host of attitudes and personae—farmer, factory worker, prostitute, mother, moonshiner, striker, striker's lover, striker's child—a whole range of public poses in response to the strange phenomena of his day. And yet the colorful details of these changes should not distract us from the more subtle play of feelings and forms that underlie them. In fact, when Patton focuses on more personal crises, we begin to see that the startling dynamism of his performances corresponds to a much deeper reformulation of identity in relation to its given environment. "Screamin' and Hollerin' the Blues," for example, carefully dissects Patton's conflicted relation toward a single lover and her dilapidated shack.[41] Following the singer's rapid emotional shifts, the song is pushed this way and that through a series of charged, but open-ended, states. The singer frets between road and bedroom, city and country, past and present, and so each verse functions as a provisional site of habitation and comfort. In this, self-presence and stability are always deferred, displaced, elsewhere; existence becomes a perennial leave-taking, a perpetual motion both toward and away from somewhere or someone else. But even as the singer's own feeling seems to get in the way of his stability, this tension becomes a source of energy and pleasure in itself. In fact, failing to come to any coherent stance or resolution, the singer decides to take the entire dilemma, and even his lover, onto the road. In the end, his own affective motion—no matter how fraught—generates something like personal presence and the constant possibility of its revision:

> Oh, I'm going away, baby, don't you want to go?
> I'm goin' away, sweet mama, don't you want to go?
> Take God to tell when I'll be back here anymore.

As Angela Davis points out, romantic relations in the blues often serve as "tangible expressions of freedom." To pick one's own lover, to travel miles in order to find him or her, to abandon or establish a home or job—such choices were the everyday expression of the new mobility of life after emancipation (8). For Patton, though, the course or tour of his feelings, as they push him both toward and away from any stable scene, from one form or another, becomes itself a compelling source of freedom and power, so that, in the end, his song appears as determined and dynamic as the landscape in which it sounds.

In this, we can begin to appreciate the specifically sonic qualities of Patton's performances and the blues at large, which are never simply expressive, but enactive and provisional. Sound, here, precisely that which gives the singer's declarations both presence and weight, also serves to expose each one as only momentary. "Screamin' and Hollerin' the Blues" is a perfect case in point. Here, Patton uses his voice to establish a new stance or attitude for each verse: sometimes, with a bellow, he presents his position as willed, determined; elsewhere, with a carefully placed crack or sigh, he conveys uncertainty, weariness, strain; and, then, in other places, he declares his intentions with a chuckle, as if he knows he's just fooling himself. But almost every line ends in uncertainty, with a shaky fall down the scale. Each verse peters out with mumbling resignation or smug indifference, an excess of meaningless sound, and thus prepares the way for the next, for some new vocalization that proves just as powerful. Similarly, Patton's guitar bucks and bolts from one figure to the next. Sometimes it builds toward a thumping groove suggestive of forceful progress; sometimes it rushes forward in harried flight, with a series of tonal leaps; at times, even, it falls into a syncopated strut, suggesting cocksure strides. But most figures screech to a halt with piercing sets of triplets, as if both speed and direction were all wrong, and the player must start all over again. In a way, the restlessness of the guitar conveys more than lyrics or even voice. The emotional compulsion to move is precisely what cannot be named here, only felt, and the accompaniment, with its shifting rhythm, demonstrates an uncertainty that is itself both powerful and exhilarating.

But it would be a mistake to distinguish between lyrics and accompaniment in this way. Patton, like all the best blues players, worked voice and guitar deftly in relation to each other. Some lyrics are answered by an expressive riff; some are doubled, some counterpointed by a plucked melody; others are simply cut short by a squall of notes. Throughout, meaningful language gives way to fluid sound, while fluid sound is shown to be always already structured, and the process as a whole restores something like the underlying openness of discourse. In fact, Patton's songs, as songs, approach the entire Delta landscape in this way, through the flexible medium of sound, and thus work through the everyday forms and forces of the region. Sound becomes a means of both claiming and dissolving the restrictions of his environment, a fluid material that simultaneously upholds and upends predetermined structures. Take, for example, "Green River Blues," which provides a typical mix of responses to the train as a form of modern technology.[42] Throughout, the train proves a remarkably fluid technology, making new emotional connections and dissolving old ones, but it is at every step exceeded by the startling fluidity of voice and guitar. In a typical move, Patton first compares the sound of the whistle to his lover's cry, and so gives voice to intense loneliness. But, in the second verse, the engine is just as quickly eroticized, proving—more than just a metaphor—an actual conduit for erotic encounter. In the next, the lyrics slip from the moaning lover to the man she rides, who is now contemplating departure on another route. And so on and so on, in a jaunty metamorphosis that is deeply sensual yet duly formal, bound to the schedules and shapes of the railroad itself, and yet everywhere veering off on new affective tracks. The song could have just as well been called "Thirteen Ways of Looking at a Railroad," if it didn't so enjoyably replace the stillness of looking with sonic motion. The guitar here, too, functions like a sonic rail switch, changing track from verse to verse, generating unnameable, yet undeniably thrilling, sensations along the way. While each verse name-checks a different station on the actual Delta rail system, the accompaniment jumps from one rhythmic pattern to the next, shifting the energy and feel of the piece each time. In this, Patton's song reveals itself to be as much a product and manifestation of the modern world as a comment upon it. Like some sonic engineer, the bluesman jumps tracks, rides the clichéd lyrics and standardized riffs of the blues repertoire like he uses the train itself, as empty cars waiting to be filled with his own affective freight.

Again, Patton's songs actively slip from one state to the next, from one form to another, always exceeding their own demand for stability; they work within and against the landscape in which they resound, taking energy from the various structures along the way in order to move through and beyond them. In other words, they move by way of feeling *and* form, always one in excess of the other, in what often seem to be charged, yet often abstract, configurations of sound. Given this motion, we'd be fools to turn to the blues for traditional notions of identity or expressive consistency; rather, these songs test possibilities of being and experience by way of sound itself, and so attain—along the way—a much more flexible form of identity and exchange. In fact, any given blues song, with its unique coordination of guitar and voice, makes it impossible to assert the primacy of either feeling or form, or even distinguish between them. At first glance, feeling seems primary, as if the song were nothing more than a raw and intense energy seeking out and then overcharging the otherwise lifeless clichés of the lyric tradition. However, at times, feeling often seems only to arise off of the very surface of the blues as a discursive form, after the fact, as some subtle effect of each song's particular lyrics, format, context, and history.[43] To borrow the language of Brian Massumi, we can only really say that every blues event is received on two levels, the "discursive" and the "affective." On the one hand, the lyric fixes the meaning of the song; it restricts responses in terms of culturally established patterns or norms. On the other, feeling is experienced as strength and duration; it registers the brute force of an experience, its sensual impact before or beyond any simple act of naming. For Massumi, as for Patton, cognition entails a subtle negotiation between these two registers, the "amplification" or "dampening" of one by the other. Some songs are more discursive, more logical than others, and some are more moving, more gripping than others. Most, though, slip back and forth between these two extremes, from one register to the other, and their pleasure exists in how they careen, in sonic space and time, between different states and stances.[44] Or, as Simon Frith puts it, "The meaning of a piece of music is embodied 'within' it, formally, structurally, and syntactically"; on both sides of musical experience, for performer and audience, there is a constant *slippage* of categories, for "interpreting, feeling, and evaluating thus constitute a single process."[45]

Of all genres, the blues, with its stark juxtaposition of voice and guitar, gives us a unique and, indeed, more immediate access to these processes. On the one hand, lyrics are constantly disrupted or distorted by sensual phenomena that are not so much understood or interpreted, but felt. Moaning, groaning, hooting, and howling, the blues singer exceeds any simple notion of expression and yet still manages to refer to his everyday experiences. These vocal effects seem both more and less expressive than our established language; they point toward and away from some more solid or stable meaning. At the same time, this sensual experience is extended beyond the voice to the wordless counterpart of the guitar. A lyric is finished by a lick, a bass riff leads into a fluid moan, the rhythm of the mouth is syncopated by slaps on wood. In fact, for a bluesman like Patton, success depended precisely on his ability to make a guitar "talk"—to moan, to murmur, to sing, and even, as in "Prayer of Death," beg for salvation.[46] And yet we cannot ignore the other side of this mix. For while blues music makes bold use of sound's physical qualities— its "grain," to borrow from Roland Barthes—it is equally dependent on ready-made forms.[47] Its lyricism is mostly standardized and repetitive, and the best singers are not necessarily inventors, but interpreters of long-familiar lines, from the generically banal (*Good morning, blues, how do you do?*) to the local and idiosyncratic (*Going where the Southern cross the Dog*). Ultimately, if unbounded emotion fuels blues production, the blues song itself figures as a kind of linguistic shaping, a technical manipulation of ready-made forms. Meaning is generated in or perhaps between the repetition and juxtaposition of various prefabricated lines, in a near-alchemical process of symbolism and suggestion. Thus David Evans defines the blues as a compositional "process" and distances it from Western ideals of aesthetic "completion." As he explains, the blues does not provide "coherence" of theme or expression, for each song is composed "at a deeper level," in terms of "emotional continuity." Formal features such as repetition, juxtaposition, and metaphor "serve to create contrasts, tensions and release of tension, and a sense of ambiguity and uncertainty . . . within an extremely compact form."[48]

And so the slippages of an increasingly industrialized world become the slippages of blues song and blues identity. But if Patton strikes a number of compelling, if contradictory, poses in his songs, we should also define the overarching attitude that makes them all possible. Sure, the singer appears in his music by turns cocksure and contrite, bold and frightened; he often asserts a traditional form of masculinity, but also a more humble, if not humiliated, sense of duty and remorse. He confronts his world with humor, with anger, and even at times with love; he knows his possibilities are limited, yet he continually finds pleasure and wonder in both the natural landscape and its expanding economic other. But, overall, his music reveals a consistent sense of ease, a willingness to take it all in stride and a casual refusal to give in, to burn out, or give up or go down in the flood. Indeed, the image of man presented in these songs is a crafty, provisional one, ceaselessly mediating himself and his future, cutting new paths and figures across the terrain, never quite satisfied, but always thinking up some greater satisfaction down the line. Perhaps, then, of all the emotions presented in Patton's blues, his *cool* is the most persistent and the most productive. Patton's cool is both stable and dynamic—it entails both an indifference to change and a refusal to accept anything as final or static, and so reveals at once the pained legacy of modernism and its eventual overturning. "I'm goin' away to a world unknown," Patton sings in "Down the Dirt Road Blues"—"I'm worried now, but I won't be worried long."[49] Simply put, beyond any single stance or attitude, beyond any recognizable narrative of change or betterment, this coolness, born of dereliction itself, reveals and sustains the possibility of a better life.

Of course, this derelict cool becomes the allure of pop music as such, as it was purveyed not just by the next generation of blues stars (House, Johnson, Waters, etc.), but also by white country and folk singers (Rodgers, Guthrie, for example) and the rock and pop stars of the 1950s. Here, though, it is important to note how the coolness of the blues, in the very *singing* of the blues, provides a worldly alternative to an older sense of sin and salvation in African American music. As has often been noted, the Christian hope of transcendence makes itself felt in the blues as a desire for worldly "satisfaction." For the blues singer, the promised land is no longer a romantic Africa or a spiritual Heaven, but a new plot of land, a lover's bed, a bottle of whiskey. The bluesman wanders through an essentially godless terrain, wearied and uncertain, and his imagined pleasures are all completely mundane: Patton yearns for a stone pony, a five-pound ax, a jelly roll; Johnson loves his phonograph, his Terraplane, and a 32–20; Son House sings about finding "womens and whiskey" in Heaven. But there is a more formal distinction to make between these two traditions. In spirituals, the primary response to "sinning" is "moaning," a sound that both acknowledges the worldly impoverishment of the self and calls for some extraworldly grace. The moan—as wordless voice—seems both embodied and abstract, mired and transcendent: even as it arises from a world it can neither name nor control, it reaches for an impossible otherness, for some airy space beyond language itself. In the blues, though, this moan—in its dynamic doubleness—proves a mundane, but no less deep, source of satisfaction in itself; pleasure is found in the very movement of the song, in sound itself, in its own cool flow from one sonic form to another.

In other words, with the blues, the hierarchy of the spiritual is set into dynamic motion, laid out flat, coolly, across the modern face of the earth, making of that impossible journey something like a thrilling joyride. Patton's "Bird Nest Bound" best conveys—in both theme and sound—the dynamic I am trying to describe, as it loosely slips from one highly charged form to another and ultimately comes to celebrate that slippage itself.[50] The disturbing core of the song appears in the third verse. The blues here pervades the scene, seeps through doors and walls and floors, spreading fear and despair, threatening all selfhood. The singer asks, perhaps of himself as much as his lover, "What is going to become of you?" The troubled house is at once source and symbol of this anxiety, its inhabitants beset by conflicting desires and doubts—"Sometime I think I'll quit you, then again I won't." At this moment, the song can only point elsewhere, and the singer, looking back in time, confronts the ceaseless motion of his life; if the present situation occasions weariness and perplexity, just like the past, he turns to movement itself—of identity, of voice, of language, too—as a source of presence and comfort. Thus, in a fascinating slip, the house is replaced with a bird's nest, an aerie free of all mortal restraints. This new image brings together motion and stability both, signals flight as well as comfort. It suggests the persistence and pleasure of mobility, of constant bounding and, thus, boundlessness. But, then, in the next verse, the image slips again. The nest now becomes a "shiny star." Here, home, sweet home—the scene of habit, stability, usualness—appears utterly elsewhere, impossible, alluring, and strange. The spoken aside hints at an ironic shift in attitude. The singer declares that he's "just stayin' there," and, in this, "stayin'" becomes a state of cool indifference—"*just* stayin'"—and so turns into its very opposite, just moving. In one final lyrical slip, Patton brings us back down to earth again and reveals the utter modernity of his condition. The shining star becomes a shining car, and the song ends—or never ends—in praise of transit and dislocation. In this last moment, with the entrance of this automotive *deus ex machina*, movement—both sonic and automotive—is embraced as a kind of cool, giddy grace.

Three—Race Trauma, Race Records, and the Compulsion to (Press) Repeat

But let's skip forward forty years. Watching the 1969 television video of Son House performing "Death Letter Blues," I'm frightened not only by the sheer brutality of the performance, but also by its utter formalism.[51] Son House appears alone onstage in a minimalist mock-up of the Old South. He sits on a wooden stool in a sharp circle of light, with only some undulating wisps of color to mark out the hills and clouds of a bygone world. Next to him, we see a fat wooden barrel and a tall, skinny microphone stand, two simple icons of the blues' otherwise long, complicated history. Suddenly, the performer's arm swings into motion, cutting out an angular space around the guitar. His weathered hand beats against the steel, over and over again, the same monotonous pattern, punctuated at the end of each line by a loud ring off the metal slide. The movement spreads to his entire body, which heaves and jerks in forceful counterpoint, until his face finally crumples in pain—eyes closed, teeth clenched—as if wincing against the very sound of his song. Once set in full motion, with all parts flailing, the bluesman seems stuck in a violent groove, at once frenzied and fearful. He becomes a manic sound-making machine, so many parts moving together—bone, muscle, pick, slide, microphone, camera, wires—all linked up, hooked up, and pulsing together to make, for our viewing pleasure, an endless black pain.

Here, the term "revival" takes a completely different meaning. As the legend goes, eager white blues fans rediscovered Son House in 1964 and retaught him to play the music he had long since given up. Seeking some downhome blues to cure their own suburban blues, they set him up on a national touring circuit and eventually landed him a gig at Carnegie Hall. In this, alone, Son House's return seems less like a personal triumph than a brutal reenactment, a whitewashed conjure act of the racial violence the singer had long since left behind. But we need to confront the performer's own willingness to re-create, over forty years later, the musical forms of his past. For all its immediacy, this is a decisively compulsive spectacle; House seems to have fallen into a well-worn pattern that satisfies in its very violence, in its intense re-creation of fear and rage. He appears onstage like a chronic ghost, emerging out of his own timeless limbo, woken to repeat the crimes of the past. In this, for sure, the song most associated with House's revival, "Death Letter Blues," seems less like a famous calling card than a fateful series of violent attitudes and poses. The titular letter arrives only to set the singer off on a circuitous route that he has clearly taken many times before, forcing him, in verse after verse, to "do the things you don't want to do":

> I got a letter this mornin', how you reckon it read?
> It said, "Hurry, hurry, the gal you love is dead."
> I got a letter this mornin', yeah, how you reckon it read?
> It said, "Hurry, hurry, because the gal you love is dead."

In a way, the mysterious missive tells us everything and nothing. As it announces the lover's death, it inspires the same nameless dread we heard in Patton's songs. Racing off to see his lover's corpse, the singer moves through all the common blues emotions—grief, remorse, loneliness, fear, and, of course, anger, hostility, meanness—until, in most versions, he simply exhausts himself, transformed into the very ghost that has been haunting him. The song, in fact, contains up to at least seventeen verses (although House never recorded them all at once), and each one fails to address, let alone resolve, the singer's dilemma. We can guess that he is torn up by the death, and we might even venture, upon hearing about the woman's "low-down ways," that he himself caused her death. But nothing points clearly toward a knowable past or a usable future. The singer seems caught between two moments of forgetting, or perhaps two kinds of in-existence, "between two deaths." His life is suspended, held up, between the letter that announces his lover's demise and the corpse that awaits his return, or, worse, between the pain he has suffered and the pain he will suffer again. And so his performance seems outside of time altogether, the stage his limbo, an artificial platform where he must enact this bluesy ritual night after night. Ultimately, the letter becomes his own, a script that he must, in guilt and fear, perform in all its blind fury, from beginning to end, for all of eternity.

As suggested above, the blues exists somewhere between a traumatic event and its discursive manipulation, between an excess of unnameable emotion and the comforts of form. But when structure itself seems simply or grossly repetitive—a tendency of the AAA/AAB stanza form, perhaps, or the recycling of standardized lyrics and licks—it seems to leave both singer and song suspended in time, endlessly circling or fretting around a wound that can never be fully named or grasped. Such repetition, moreover, seems to take a specifically vicious form on records and recordings, which tend to lock both singer and song in an ahistorical groove, insisting over and over again upon a violence that may otherwise no longer exist. Indeed, many of the popular blues records of the 1920s—by Bessie Smith, Ma Rainey, Blind Lemon Jefferson, Blind Willie McTell, Charley Patton—can be characterized by a near-pathological reenactment of delinquency and violence. Here, in precise three-minute form, in increasingly slick crooning and standardized progressions, the violent cycles of racial trauma spin out over and over again. Cutting, shooting, rape and murder, violent sex and cold rejection, humiliations public and private—everything the blues performer presumably seeks to leave behind—is carried forth, portable, replayable, and decisively public, recast as pervasive and ethereal sound, spinning abstractly in space. Over time, Patton, "the Masked Marvel," in all his thrilling plasticity, gives way to Son House, the "chronic ghost," locked forever in recorded form, congealed in wax, doomed to repeat a past he never quite experienced. Here, though, I'd like to give the ghost his due and, rather than take a dubious aesthetic pleasure in his pain, tend to his malady. I'd like to defend him as not simply a traumatized and repetitive subject, but as a specifically phonographic and mimetic artist, one that, by way of recording technology itself, feels his way toward some other future. Here, then, I'd like to advance claims originally made by Adam Gussow regarding blues violence and its persistence, pushing them in the direction of recorded form.[52] The following discussion straddles two lines of thought, one that is psychological in its account of trauma and the "compulsion to repeat," and another that moves by way of recorded sound toward a more open kind of repetition. Insofar as Freudian therapy figures as a "talking cure," I want to argue, we can look to the "talking machine" as a means of personal and cultural transference, a modern device capable, in its technological fusion of feeling and form, of "repeating, remembering, and working through" the frightening experiences of modernity and thereby sustaining the original dynamism of the blues.[53]

Of course, violence marked the blues tradition long before the invention of records, and it surely underlies its persistent appeal. It appears in the blues in strange sadomasochistic configurations, not just as a personal power to be wielded, but also as a recursive and ultimately self-defeating structure. Blues*men*, specifically, often turn to violence as a cocky assertion of gendered power. In Skip James's "22–20 Blues," the singer shoots at a man, a woman, and then the law itself, each imagined killing leading to the next, in a bluesy Oresteia of retributive violence.[54] Robert Johnson upgrades the tune and the weaponry in "32–20 Blues," shooting and singing with a reckless glee, trying to kill, mutilate, and erase all trace of his intended victim.[55] Both of these songs, though, end in dissatisfaction and defeat. Each singer's pleasure ultimately proves fleeting, inconclusive, their assertions in need of constant augmentation and desperate repetition. James is left wandering along the dusty road, measuring his gun against his own arm. Johnson is pumped up with nowhere to go, erect with unspent energy—"Lord, I just can't take my rest," he wearily declares. Later, with amplification, bluesmen began to revel in the violence of sound itself, and thereby exposed its formal dimensions. Johnny Lee Hooker, for example, used amplified voice and electric guitar to shoot down lovers and listeners in a single sonic blow:

> Boom boom boom boom
> I'm gonna shoot you right down
> Right offa your feet
> Boom boom boom boom . . . a-haw haw haw haw . . . [56]

With Hooker's turn to wordless scat, he transfers all power to sound itself. The song becomes a sonic assault, the listener placed in the position of feminized other, experiencing the thrill of power through his or her own annihilation. With this formal turn, though, blues violence seems to exceed the simple logic of personal or retributive violence. In a way, as the humiliations of race and gender are replayed as formal, sonic satisfactions, violence itself turns abstract, immaterial, eternal, making, for better or worse, endless victims of performer and audience both.

This dynamic is complicated by its frequent appearance in women's blues. As Angela Davis and Hazel Carby have both argued, women's blues do not shy away from vengeful violence.[57] In "Send Me to the 'Lectric Chair," for example, Bessie Smith depicts herself in a murderous rage, slashing and cutting at her unfaithful lover with a Barlow knife and then laughing over his dying body. In another strain, however, female blues singers seem to indulge in their own pain and mistreatment suffered at the hand of a male lover. Whether as the playful "stinging" of Memphis Minnie's "Bumble Bee" or the more intense violence of Ma Rainey's "Sweet Rough Man," this tradition is notable for depicting the intense pleasure of pain with only a very small irony.[58] So, for instance, while a real sense of despair pervades Bessie Smith's "Hard Driving Papa," she's clearly having a hoot in "Empty Bed Blues, Part 2":

He came home one evening with his spirit way up high.
What he had to give me made me wring my hands and cry.
He give me a lesson that I had never had before.
When he got through teaching me from my elbows down were sore.[59]

As in Hooker's song, the pleasure of this pain is decisively formal. Smith reserves her most playful vocal tricks for the song's most brutal lines. At the end of the first verse, for example, she offers up the word "had" on a long, sexy blue note and then brightens her tone for the word "cry." She sings the first line of the second verse—which already contains a hokey educational metaphor—with a dirty syncopated bounce and then curves the word "sore" with a smile. In this, the song seems less like a "celebration of masochism," as one clueless writer put it, than an oddly satisfying performance of it, one in which the pleasure of pain is bound to the pleasure of form itself.[60] Of course, we might be disturbed by the regressive nature of this strategy; such art can just as likely extend as well as curb the cruelty it addresses. But the ability to sing pain—to repeat it and thus shape it into sonic form—seems to imply a certain presence as well as mastery, pleasures otherwise denied African American women. As Davis suggests, in songs such as these, blueswomen drew upon an ancient African tradition in which naming figures as a form of power and control: "The blues preserve and transform the West African philosophical centrality of the naming process. In the Dogon, Yoruba, and other West African cultural traditions, the process of nommo—naming things, forces, or modes—is a means of establishing magical (or, in the case of the blues, aesthetic) control over the object of the naming process" (33).

We might here recall Ralph Ellison's famous claim: "The blues is an impulse to keep the painful details and episodes of a brutal experience alive in one's aching consciousness, to finger its jagged grain, and then transcend it, not by the consolation of philosophy but by squeezing from it a near-tragic, near-comic lyricism."[61] Think "cutting" (dermatillomania)—the blues singer cuts him- or herself open in order to master some prior cutting, to turn an otherwise vague pain into a recognizable and thus containable form. Similarly, the pleasure of song lies in its doubleness, in the fact that it is experienced as both a sensual and a formal phenomenon, both a passively endured hurt and a creative act. As Adam Gussow argues, blues culture at heart is defined by violence—by racial subjugation and the ever-present threat of lynching; the singer's aggression, in turn, serves to copy and wield this violence against its perpetrators, as if the very form of subjugation could establish a certain presence and agency.

Gussow, in fact, distinguishes between three kinds of blues violence—the disciplinary violence of the white regime, the retributive violence of the black victim, and the intimate violence between blacks ("the gun-and-blade-borne damage black folk inflict on each other") (4). We can certainly appreciate the retributive satisfactions of the "bad man" tradition; Stack-O-Lee swallows all the violence of the white regime and spews it back out without any regard of race or class—*watch your Stetson hat!* But as Gussow explains, even the intimate violence of black-on-black relationships can "be sexy, enlivening, a crucial prop in the struggle to make one's mark within a black social milieu" (5). In these songs, too, the loss of self, as a form of destitution or dereliction, leads to its reconstitution in other ways. The ability to stab, slash, or shoot another black person, or be stabbed, slashed, or shot at in return, works to establish presence and agency in a world that systematically denies both. Such violence—in the juke, in the bedroom, on the work gang—figures as part of a significant personal and social ritual. Each cut recalls—and reenacts—a primal lynching scene, serving to dismember or dissolve the slave, worker, lover, so that he or she can miraculously rise again. In the vitality and intensity of repeated violence—in the very marks scrawled across the battered body, as in the lyrics used to describe them—both singer and listener attain a new kind of presence and self-satisfaction, both a genuine sense of being and a momentary sense of control.

In this, we can begin to re-hear the violence in women's blues as specifically mimetic and re-creative. In "Sweet Rough Man," for example, Ma Rainey beats Elizabeth Browning at her own sweet game, counting and thereby claiming all the ways of sexual violence. Her song opens up on her own bruised body, presenting it—in the form of split lips and blackened eyes—as a testament to the work of true love. She wakes from bed with a headache, moaning, "My man beat me last night with five feet of copper coil," but the listener quickly detects a note of pride—in both the defiant delivery of her song and in the specific tonal qualities of her voice. Slowly, urged on by the building vamp of the rhythm section and the increasingly complicated riffs of the lead guitar, the singer regains her strength and begins to piece together a common, if forceful, justification of her relationship. As in other songs of this genre, Rainey first balances the pain of abuse against the pleasure of sex, citing in her defense the satisfying strength and stamina of her otherwise abusive lover. By verse four, the distinction collapses, so that the sex itself proves the greatest source of pain, a passionate act that at once destroys and restores her sense of being. "But when he starts to lovin," Rainey sings, "I wring and twist and scream." At this moment, the listener is made intensely aware that the singer's own presence exists in and through the process of re-enactment. Rainey's voice, skimming energy off the surface of her own re-created past, reveals a new directness and an increase of sensual force. By repeating the violence of the bedroom, wielding its intensity in her voice, in sonic form, she becomes an active agent within it—her body is marked out once more and the self grows clearer, proudly declaring that "it ain't no maybe." Potency has been transferred from abuser to victim, whose delivery, as redelivery, spins into the future as another possible future. Her song, like the traces of pain on her body, affirms her place in the world and her community along with it.

Freud, of course, tried to mobilize the "compulsion to repeat" in similar ways; he defined therapy as a process of "remembering, repeating, and working through," and he saw his couch as a site where the patient could safely and more effectively relate feeling and form, replaying the pain of the past in order to master it. Similarly, we might say, the blues functions as a kind of sonic therapy, repetition as a form of difference and mastery; it functions as a second illness—hair-of-the-dog homeopathy—a willed trauma endured to correct past trauma, as if the pain of the past could be reshaped in the mouth. This is, in fact, precisely how W. C. Handy described his own interest in the blues form: finding the triple repetition of the traditional blues verse "too monotonous," he "adopted the style of making a statement, repeating the statement in the second line, and then retelling in the third line why the statement was made."[62] But here, I want to consider repetitive blues violence in the form by which it was most commonly experienced and dispersed—the record. What happens when formal repetition becomes mechanical repetition? Do records imply repetition *with* or *without* difference? Is listening to records bad therapy, a failing to work through the traumatic event? Does the recorded artifact, a compulsive form in shellac, ever accomplish anything new? Playback only guarantees the insertion of the past into the present, the undue preservation or transposition of time into space (or, really, into non-space), such as the one in which Son House endlessly frets. In a way, phono-graphy, as a form of sound-writing, only freezes the dynamic interplay by which personal and communal values are created, capturing in sonic form, in an engraved form, an exchange that might otherwise open up upon time and space both.

Many early accounts of phonography and the recording industry ex-pressed similar worries, often presenting the record as a fetish object, a frozen, and ultimately false, emblem of human presence. As Theodor

Adorno argued—with characteristic disdain for all pop culture—popular forms such as jazz and blues, with their cheap and easy play of improvisation and structure, work to trap the ego of an otherwise abused listener. The record as commodity-fetish provides with one hand what the marketplace has already stolen with the other; the disembodied voice on the disc at once fills the listener with power and takes it away, demanding, as it fades, another spin.[63] Accounts like this suggest a deep connection between the traumatic formalism of the blues and the traumatic form of the record. In either case, an initial wounding or breach in psychic identity leads to manic repetition, a compulsive fretting around a single image or object that represents power and restitution. Indeed, in the blues world, fetishes are both obvious and multiple—guns, knives, fast cars, a new suit, a pair of shoes, a letter, a hambone, a jellyroll, a mojo hand, etc. Some songs, though, such as Robert Johnson's "Phonograph Blues," offer up, not without irony, a fetishism of the phonograph itself.[64] In Johnson's anxious ode to record playing, sound technology promises to restore presence but always gives way to its opposite—fears of inadequacy, dysfunction, and replaceability:

> Beatrice, I love my phonograph, but you have broke my
> 	windin' chain.
> Beatrice, I love my phonograph-ooo, but you have broke my
> 	windin' chain.
> And you've taken my lovin' and give it to your other man.

On one level, Johnson's song simply celebrates the joys of making love with the record player on. The machine is depicted, in its industrial strength and power, as a kind of prosthetic manhood, an object designed to extend and enlarge an otherwise lost potency. Yet it is precisely this dependency that saps the singer's strength and brings about his ultimate replacement. The phallic needle quickly becomes a detachable dildo, and thus a form of castration, tracing a very different kind of cut. In turn, the machine reveals itself as feminine, a fickle lover who holds all the power in her ability to grant or withhold satisfaction. This is Beatrice's phonograph, after all, and she refuses to let it moan, playing what she wants when she wants. Lying behind the singer's fear is perhaps a more general fear of modern commerce as a new outlet for feminine desire. Beatrice represents a new female prestige on the open market; she can easily take her good lovin' and spend it on another man or another record.[65] Thus, if the commodity-fetish is alienated labor power (according to Marx, rather than Freud), the singer faces the loss of his manhood in the form of economic abstraction and indifference. In the end, the amplification he sought in recorded sound, the potent immortality of a disembodied voice—what Adorno calls its "mirror-function"—begins to fade.[66]

But this is not the only, or even the most common, way that records were perceived or experienced by the audiences for which they were intended. As mentioned, the formal category of the blues was established through the professional, northward-leaning careers of figures such as W. C. Handy, Ma Rainey, and Bessie Smith. These musicians translated the rough, unnamed musical traditions of the black South into marketable forms that immediately signaled their modernity—on the vaudeville stage, on sheet music, and, most importantly, on records. In fact, the now celebrated group of Delta blues musicians, which includes Charley Patton, Son House, and, later, Robert Johnson and Muddy Waters, represents a second wave of specifically regional performers who played for record companies seeking to bring new life into a struggling format. As Wald's study deftly shows, by the time these musicians began to record their own blues in the late 1920s and 1930s, the phonograph had already infiltrated the region, and records had transformed compositional styles, leading to a greater emphasis on production and the thematic unity of each song. Indeed, the very records on which these songs were stamped seemed to signal modernity broadly. Discs arrived from faraway cities such as Chicago and New York and, for both musicians and fans, implied some nearly possible elsewhere to the local round of toil and grief. Thus flying in the face of record companies' efforts to sell "regional" music back to black audiences, most consumers were drawn to new music, new gadgets, fashionable designs, big-name stars, and dance crazes. They sought records as records, as fascinating objects in their own right—sleek new things to fondle, collect, display—to crowd out the familiar spaces and objects of a more ordinary life.[67]

But I'd like to assert here that phonography itself, the very logic of recording and distributing sound, worked against both the fatalism of the racist past and the presumed closure of the marketplace. Simply put, the record format suggests repetition of another sort, one that, in a largely technological process of self-negation and restoration, extends the sensual power of the blues and the critical capacity of Afro-modernity at large. Here, Zora Neale Hurston provides a lead by beginning her famous essay "Characteristics of Negro Expression" with the bold claim that "The Negro's universal mimicry is not so much a thing in itself as an evidence of something that permeates his entire self."[68] Hurston's essay explores what she believes is the African American's deep tendency to copy. With mimicry, she argues, the African American demonstrates an alternative mode of being and exchange, one that—in contrast to Western forms of reason and power—has both a more direct and a more supple relation to the everyday world. For proof, Hurston offers a bit of comparative linguistics: "The primitive man exchanges descriptive words," she writes; "His terms are all close fitting." This alternative language contains signs that are physical and vital in themselves: "So we can say the white man thinks in a written language and the Negro thinks in hieroglyphics" (49–50). For Hurston, such mimicry is both natural and cultured, sensual and significant, and thus a more vital, more ethical form of language and communication. The African American uses this innate art to negotiate rather than master the oppressive forms of his environment; he works through rather then against "outward signs," at once yielding to their shapes as he manipulates them from within. Thus the seemingly primitive repetitions that define African American culture prove creative and original. They are always repetitions with a difference: "What we really mean by originality is the modification of ideas. . . . So if we look at it squarely, the Negro is a very original being. While he lives and moves in the midst of a white civilization, everything that he touches is re-interpreted for his own use. He has modified the language, mode of food preparation, practice of medicine, and most certainly the religion of his new country" (58).

Ultimately, such mimesis represents a different kind of naming or "nommo." We might even say that it represents a unique kind of magic, one that underlies many "primitive" rituals that seemed, to many, to be reemerging in the early twentieth century. Freud's 1913 study *Totem and Taboo*, for example, opens up with the rather startling claim that "sympathetic magic" is making a comeback in the modern world.[69] According to Freud, the neurotic patient, much like the primitive magician, tries to influence the world by means of its reproduction. Rattled by modern life, he or she intentionally "mistakes" imaginary forms for real ones, producing copies of that which otherwise seems beyond any personal control. Mentally repeating the traumas of, say, family life or war or work is tantamount to performing a crop cycle or making a voodoo doll; in such cases, the sufferer not only expresses certain psychological needs, but also seeks to alter the shape of the world in his or her favor (101–6). For Freud, in fact, all such magic—as "black magic"—figures as an alternative process of signification, one that combines naming as well as influence, copy and contact. Re-presenting the environment is tantamount to reorganizing it, and thereby makes room for new position and power within it. In this, blues repetition appears less as a form of cultural pathology than as an alternative model of agency designed for present life. Regarding the magic of the "mojo hand," for example, Paul Oliver writes,

> Such "mojo hands" . . . were made with great care from personal fragments and from natural objects. Hair from the armpits or pubic region, finger-nail parings, pieces of skin were considered especially effective in love charms, as were fragments of underclothing, of a menstrual cloth, and other closely personal effects. Combined with parts of night creatures, bats or toads, and with ashes and feathers from sources selected for a symbolic significance relative to the purpose for which they had been prepared, they were tied into small "conjure-bags" or put into an innocuous-looking receptacle and either carried to exert their power upon the victim when contact was made with him, or buried beneath his doorstep, hidden in his bed or hearth. (126)

In Muddy Waters's "Louisiana Blues," for example, the singer seeks the "hand" not just as a symbol of virility, but as part of a larger redistribution of power, one that will "show all you good women how to treat your man."[70] Similarly, in "Lucky Rock Blues," Ma Rainey seeks out a totemic stone to ward off bad luck; in "Louisiana Hoodoo Blues," she consults a hoodoo hand, a black-cat bone, and some goofer dust in order to keep away the sexual competition.[71] In each case, mimesis generates actual power and presence for the performer. In each case, the copy is never just a copy, but also a form of gritty contact and vital exchange.[72] The blues performer re-arranges as he or she re-presents the environment. The copied fetish, rather than sapping power, as in Johnson's "Phonograph Blues," makes power available, serving as a source of energy and a point of access to an otherwise hostile world.

This same magic no doubt characterizes much African and African American music, particularly in contrast to traditional Western canons of originality and expression. As Joel Dinerstein explains, "West African–derived sociomusical practice involves *re-presenting* the soundscape in rhythmic phrases, not in correctly playing a written score through notes." As heir to this tradition, the blues performer was no mere copyist, but "a musician creating a dialogue among culture, music, and technology"; his art extends a "sociocultural imperative to recreate the world in sound. Every detail in the landscape must be repeated, revised, represented, and stylized in public rituals to recognize and rechannel its power."[73] Thus W. C. Handy opens his autobiography with an account of his youthful efforts to imitate the sounds of the Alabama countryside, specifically the "great outdoor choir" of robins, bobolinks, crows, crickets, bullfrogs,

moo-cows and whippoorwills (14–15). As he later explains, his most successful compositions—*Memphis Blues* and *St. Louis Blues*—mimic the
cacophony of industrialized life, the rumble of boxcars and riverboats, the
hum of chitterling joints and train stations, the noise of Beale Street and
the docks of St. Louis (118ff). Similarly, Patton's records show that he was
able to imitate the various rhythms of the steam train, and it is frequently
claimed that, as part of his show, he could perfectly duplicate—by request—
all the different whistles heard along the Delta rails. In "Terraplane Blues,"
Robert Johnson shows off his slide and hammering tricks to mimic the
sound of a man working under the hood of a car. Ma Rainey's "Black Cat
Hoot Owl Blues" begins with a trumpeted rendition of an angry cat's howl,
and Bessie Smith's "Sam Jones Blues" opens with an ominous knock on
the door.[74] With similar examples in mind, Jeff Titon rejects expressivist
theories of the music and instead defines it as an active "imitation of life."
Blues performances are decisively imitative, he argues, but not static; rather,
they recreate experiences in sonic form as a way of shaping new responses
toward them. Here, as in Hurston's account, mimicry becomes progressive, a means of explanation as well as influence, an attempt to "adjust and
adapt" responses to modern life in its various forms (192–93).

In the Delta, records took this process to a whole new level, at once
formalizing and multiplying the possibilities of mimicry. As mentioned,
Delta blues musicians honed their craft through records, and the average
farmhouse was crammed full of spinning black discs, giving listeners a
chance to try out the new attitudes and styles engraved upon them. As
many field researchers noted, the phonograph was central to a dual process
of assimilation and dissimilation, and became, over time, a critical device
for both defining and transforming black identity in the region. According
to John Work, writing in the early 1940s, "Folk instrumental performances
are practically all improvisation upon the idioms and patterns . . . developed by countless players for a particular instrument. . . . Rarely are they
'copied' exactly. They constantly are being modified and altered by the
temperament of the players, and the incoming of new idioms and style
of performance via visitors, radio, and juke-box."[75] Similarly, listeners in
the South were by no means passive when it came to buying and playing
records. Some were quite vocal about their tastes and choices, asking re-
tailers to carry certain performers and songs and writing to record scouts
and distributors with specific requests.[76] Moreover, no song ever made it
into the local culture without alteration. Listeners quickly spun off their
own repetitions, changing words and phrases, altering tones and modes,
copying commercial songs in order to control their meanings and affects.

As Hurston elsewhere notes, "The song on the phonograph record soon becomes the music of the work-crew, but with this interesting change: the original words and music are changed to satisfy the taste of the community's own singers."[77] This statement reverses the entire history of blues music, placing records at its origins and work songs at its end. But, really, with such mimicry in mind, there is no beginning or end, just copies of copies and their contextual usages; musical exchange slips its historical coordinates and starts to develop as an alternative region of engagement and exchange.

To return to the issue of the record as a commodity, then, we might now also begin to see how it affects an ultimately open-ended exchange of feeling and identity. As suggested above, the recorded voice often functions as a fetish or magical totem, generating—for beaten and weary listeners—fantasies of restored identity and power. But perhaps even more than the reproduced image (with its flat surface and passive submission to the gaze), the recorded voice plays with the possibilities of copying as a form of contact. This voice is always both a real voice and a copy of voice, and thus implies directness as well as detachment, immediacy and mediation. In fact, the recorded event is always still an event, the complete sound of that event, but freed from—*abstracted from*—the other determining dimensions of that event. In this abstraction, the record, as with any fetish-commodity (defined by both Marx and Freud as an abstraction of human power), opens the possibility for sensual investment, renews the potential for sensual exchange, for a kind of purposeless yielding and exploration (as in Hurston's account of mimicry). In other words, in its reproduction, sound is detached (however slightly) from its origin and becomes both inherently empty and overbearingly present, exploding both the "aural unconscious" and the history it encodes.[78] Indeed, in dozens of memoirs and works of fiction about the blues, such as Ralph Ellison's *Invisible Man* and Richard Wright's "Long Black Song," it is specifically this sensual encounter with a recorded voice that inspires new forms of personal and public identity. At the moment of trauma's repetition in sound, racial history is emptied of its force, and its actors are made aware of its sheer lightness and potential transformation.

As Alexander G. Weheliye suggests, phonography presents a serious challenge not just to everyday racial discourse in America, but to the very notions of identity and history upon which it is based.[79] According to Weheliye, modern black identity exists in and through its mediation via technologies of print and sound. While print defines the black subject in his or her absence, making him or her legible through illegibility (or invisibility), sound provides a suppler, more critical model of engagement. In the audio-visual break that defines phonographic culture—the gash between source and sound—the black subject is at once de-materialized and re-materialized and thereby finds a new, more flexible mode of being. Sonic invisibility entails neither simple negation nor subjection, but becomes the precondition for another kind of presence altogether—"a positive condition of possibility"; the body folded into sound remakes selfhood as a series of contingent opacities or intensities—"slippages," perhaps—at once open and defined, immanent and singular (32, 54). As we saw in Patton's music, the appeal of this kind of selfhood cannot be underestimated, and perhaps in itself explains the allure of phonography for an otherwise traumatized community. As Weheliye writes, in phonography, "the original/copy distinction vanishes and only the singular and sui generis becomings of the source remain in the clearing. . . . the source is always (re)produced as (anti)origin while also appearing as a differently produced occasion in each of its singular formations" (32). Thus phonographic culture at large, born out of this audio-visual disjuncture, surpasses the limited and often damning logic of origin and copy, of authenticity and expression, and becomes, instead, a series of "potent, yet fragile singularities as modes of becoming-in-the-world" (68).

So with phonographic magic in mind, we can begin to re-hear the blues as both "primitive" and "progressive," a cultural phenomenon that, by pointing backward, pushes history forward—or, by copying, even on records, becomes original. In other words, by presenting sonic mimicry in this way, we can rethink its primitivist associations as decisively modern, and indeed potentially progressive. For Weheliye, in fact, phonography transforms history itself into a series of tracks or grooves, varying rhythms and virtual forms that sound with and against each other in a more or less dynamic mix. Such grooves—insofar as they imply both a kind of formal writing (graphism) and an affective mo(o)vement—suggest a mode of temporal change that is both multivalent and nonlinear; mimetic culture as such entails a proliferation of emotionally charged spaces and temporalities, all cross-fading into and out of each other, creating ruptures, displacements, and syncopations within history proper. For Weheliye, borrowing from Édouard Glissant: "Nodes, monads, opacities, and folds all offer hypotheses of time not encased by the constraints of linearity and unimpeded progress . . . . They conjure a different form of temporal materiality, in which the material is interrupted and in constant flux rather than held in the abyss of universal time" (80).

Ultimately, then, on circulating records, the collusion of feeling and form that defined everyday life in the industrial Delta, and then found creative form in Patton's popular blues songs, becomes the basis of an alternative history, at once virtual and affective. The blues star, still dragging a painful history up on the stage for all the world to see, laying it on records for all time to come, bears witness to both the sheer emptiness and possible redemption of racialized modernity. His or her very abstraction and technologized manipulation—enforced by labor, extended into song, marketed through records—at once upholds and retains the openness of space and time. The very commodification of this once vital art—congealed forever in cheap wax, spinning endlessly in space—yet maintains the promise of reconciliation, some future moment of release, when the train actually stops, the paycheck arrives, the lover finally returns. At the very least, it opens up the space and time of public life and thus the possibility of an alternative public sphere, one that, as we'll see throughout this book, proved both alluring and productive for countless fans and musicians both within and beyond the Delta as a staging ground for rural modernity.

CHAPTER TWO

Thought I Had
Your Heart Forever

Death, Detachment,
and the Modernity of
Early Country Music

So I walked down to the local store and picked up all seven volumes of Fiddlin' John Carson's *Complete Recorded Works* (1923–34). And, yes, I listened—with my earbuds in—to 156 ballads, minstrel songs, reels, agrarian anthems, and rustic hymns. And like many others, I quickly learned that listening to the oft-proclaimed "Father of Country Music" can be a painful experience. His fiddle scratches back and forth across the strings like some rusty lathe blade, moving in seemingly random, often brutal motion. His voice is at once reedy, mealy, and sharp; most lines are choked and garbled, but then some warble off into strange, unsettling highs and others fall away into a listless hum. As a whole, his *oeuvre* is nothing less than exhausting; almost every note grates, each melody wanders, all harmony off, and still the music seems utterly monotonous. As Bob Coltman once wrote, "I hesitate to suggest this, but was he slightly deaf? I don't mean that as a criticism; he was so good he shouldn't sound any other way. But his treatments have the same ranting, wayward stubbornness you notice in musicians with slight hearing loss, and he's not always in tune, so that his music has a sprained, disorienting quality."[1]

And yet—like Coltman and many others—I couldn't stop listening. Granted, styles and tastes change over time, and what may grate on contemporary ears may have soothed listeners from another era. However, at least part of the allure of Carson's music is the same today as it was back in the day: its very "disorientation"—its thrilling ability to seem both far and near, archaic and immediate, respectful and rebellious. Perhaps this racket derived from years of playing outdoors, in the heat and without amplification, where Carson would have had to raise a very loud hell in order to capture the attention of an audience. But it is hard not to imagine that there wasn't something peculiar to the musician himself, some inner turmoil that pitted bow and fiddle against the very music they couldn't stop playing. Or maybe something about his time and place, some regional panic that at once enflamed and twisted its own song. As the *first* country star with the *first* country hit, Carson's fame rose in Atlanta, Georgia, where his trick fiddling drew newly displaced farmers working the mills and factories. Between gigs as a planter, railroad man, and moonshiner, he cultivated an act that was part nostalgia trip, part musical marvel, and part hillbilly comedy routine. For his earliest fans, it seems, this restless music conjured up both rural authenticity and its impossible other—big-city flash—and so revealed something of their own struggles.

Because, really, you can't go back, and this chapter begins with the premise that country music nostalgia signals its own modernity. If Carson is the "Father of Country Music"—and, when it comes to country music, we're all family—he was the first of many performers at the threshold of southern modernity, part of that rural vanguard that transformed local disaster into commercial success. Carson, Rodgers, Williams, Haggard, Lynn, and beyond—so many country singers tend to romanticize and ruin, betray as they mourn the already fallen homestead; they sing sadly, defiantly, gleefully of their beloved corner of the country as it fades from view. The power and allure of such music, however, rests not just in the opposition it establishes between rural life and modernity, but rather in its ability to accommodate one to the other. Indeed, if blues music provided a sense of presence and agency for the *individual* wracked by poverty, racism, and labor, country song explores similar possibilities for an entire *region* gripped by change. Country song translates the anxiety of its moment into sonic form and thus creates an alternative presence and consistency for listeners confronting their own implacable modernity. The following discussion links the experiences of dislocation and disorientation that, for many, defined modern rural life with the sonic detachment that frames some of the most significant performances of early country song. This detachment, this very anxious and painful uprooting, I'll show, might have led some musicians and fans to a reactionary immersion in song itself, but it also proved the formal precondition for other, more dynamic feelings and attitudes toward the region.

Country's complex relation to modernity has long-been established, but commentators seem to dwell on a rather shallow struggle between authenticity and artifice. For example, Richard Peterson's excellent book *Creating Country Music: Fabricating Authenticity* explores the development of country music in relation to the commercial market and its various technologies.[2] Peterson's work cuts through many of the myths concerning country music's roots and shows how its fabled authenticity was fabricated to sustain a growing industry. Between 1923 and 1953, he explains, "authenticity had become commodified, and thousands of men and women learned how to make a living from the music not only as performers and singers, but also as songwriters, comics, instrument makers, costumers, disk jockeys, managers, promoters, producers, publishers, photographers, video makers, and the like" (3). While I appreciate Peterson's modern-leaning approach, his account focuses more on the country music industry than the songs it produced. While he notes that the significance of country music is negotiated by performers and fans, his discussion is framed from a "production perspective," focusing on the "institution" of country music as a "machine that was capable of making and merchandising new records and new artists on a predictable basis using the evolving concept of authenticity" (9). This chapter also tracks the processes of institutionalization, but primarily as it generated new *forms* of country music that appealed to a transitional country audience. Moreover, it shows how institutionalization signaled new possibilities of rural identity and how inauthenticity itself became a source of significant emotional investment for rural musicians and fans.

In this, I prefer Aaron Fox's notion that country music authenticity is always already "contaminated and compromised" by commercialism.[3] For Fox, country music is less an authentic expression of the folk than a self-conscious style that sets conventional categories—such as authenticity and inauthenticity, private and public, past and present—into "complex, indeterminate motion." Fox focuses on mid- to late-century performers (from Hank Williams to Randy Travis) who were forced to reckon with a consolidated industry. Looking back from this moment, I want to show that earlier country music—of the 1920s and 1930s—responds to a much more quotidian, more pervasive experience of becoming modern. The songs discussed in this chapter depict characters and states of mind that seem to flit anxiously between home and away, presence and absence, past and present. The best music of the period worked through and beyond these everyday fragments; at once intimate and alienated, engorged with sentiment and flat in tone, it helped adequate listeners to personal and regional change. For me, then, this music was not yet, as Fox argues, an ironic and playful form of postmodern culture, but an emotionally deracinated form of modernist culture, consisting of charged but free-floating bits of both past and present life. In the music of Carson, the Delmores, the Carters, and many others, the markers of rural and modern life—the family, the farm, the fiddle, the grave, the city, the train, the radio, the automobile—appear loosed, detached, spinning abstractly in sonic space, available for both old evasions and new investments.

Certainly, there is sadness to this music, a yearning for home, for mother, the old dog by the fire, and even the old slave. Every country song, in its airy abstraction and fleeting temporality, extends the experience of loss; all are copies of copies, fading into the past, measuring again and again their distance from home. But something new inevitably arises out of this gap, as an affective charge or surge, and—even if only within its own musical context—proves productive, generative, forward-looking. Following Kathleen Stewart, then, we'll find that country music nostalgia structures the present as well as the past; it positions the listener in relation to a dynamic world, in a complex narrative of development and change. It signals not just persistence, but mobility—and here the mobility of song doubles the mobility of history—a movement out of the past and into the future. Here, then, I am interested in not just the creative interplay of feeling and form that we saw in the blues, but the sonic creation of alternative temporalities and spaces.[4] As I hope to show, the *time of decay* and the *space of ruin* is carried over into country song itself, into its very structure, which produces the new and affirms the possibility of change. Sadness, grief, loss—the circle is indeed broken, but the emotions it once contained carry the listener toward some thrilling elsewhere. Each performance spins out in ever-widening circles, breaking open again and again, tracing new arcs in the southern dust, toward and away from home.

To define this music and its potential, I will correlate several aspects of this emerging culture, tracking in turn a career, a trend, a repertoire, and then a new technology. First, I'll provide an overview of John Carson's career as it reveals the social and economic forces that country music needed in order to establish its wide acclaim. Then, with an analysis of two early country hits that reworked sentimental themes in a "cool" modern style, I'll outline the formal qualities of the professional country song and explain how they acclimated listeners to the possibilities of regional change. In the third section, I will consider the ballads of the Carter family as they translate modern experiences of anxiety and alienation into sonic form, and specifically as they reveal the productive potential of sonic detachment. The last section presents country radio as a technological manifestation of regional death and dispersion. It shows how radio broadcasters, specifically John Lair, used sound and voice to dis-embody and re-embody southern culture on a mythic scale. If my examples seem to reflect a grossly sentimental strain of early country music, I hope it will become clear that I am less interested in self-conscious engagements with modernity than with the "disorientation" and "defamiliarization" of traditional musical forms. Many other country stars worked with risqué themes and styles that could be termed modern (Jimmie Rodgers, Cliff Carlisle, Buddy Jones, for example), and some performed songs that offered a decisively modern form of escapism (Gene Autry, Patsy Montana, and Bob Wills), but the music discussed here, in its very sentimentalism, more clearly offsets its formal innovations. In the end, I hope to show that the nostalgic gap opened by Carson's fiddling proved the precondition for a mode of rural engagement that was utterly modern and truly critical in its awareness and vision.

The First and Last "Real" Country Star

The arc of Carson's career, while brief and fortuitous, provides us with a comprehensive sketch of the emerging country music industry. In the early decades of the century, his ballads and reels carried him from ad hoc "pass the hat" venues on Carroll and Decatur Streets to the organized fiddlers' contests of the 1910s and then to early country radio programs and eventually the booming market for records. A true musical mercenary, Carson shamelessly borrowed from folk dances, minstrel shows, vaudeville, churches, and even broadsides written up by big-city composers. He was, in a word, a fiddler for hire, and he fiddled all the old songs—at carnivals, store openings, and political rallies—for anyone looking to draw a crowd, a buck, a vote. Unlike Patton, though, whose career somewhat fortuitously followed the channels of the Delta's industrial economy, Carson self-consciously tapped into a growing series of technological and professional networks, including those of the budding music industry, and worked the spatial/temporal paradoxes of his career in novel aesthetic ways. While this history has been the subject of much commentary, in the work of Richard Peterson, Patrick Huber, and others, its formal innovation has been overlooked and underappreciated. Carson's hillbilly music was also big-city business, but, in its dependence on the new economy, it spoke to the newly displaced and disaffected in complex and often ironic ways. It appealed to a newly formed class of rural refugees, but rather than striking a nostalgic chord for those dreaming of a home they had left behind, it forced its audience to confront and explore their own changing history in often startling ways.

This dynamic was on display as early as the 1913 Atlanta fiddlers' contests. From the very first day of the very first contest, promoters and press agents mocked and exploited the event's hillbilly cred. Contestants were depicted as dim virtuosos of a dead but difficult art. The typical fiddler didn't read music, loved a drop of 'shine, and frequently fought over straws. When convinced to take the stage, he appeared in torn trousers, bare feet, and "two feet of white whiskers," often trailed by a sorry-looking hound. But when the old coot finally pulled his fiddle (homemade) out of a sack (burlap), he'd play nothing but heavenly music from the hills.[5] As Gene Wiggins notes, newspapers falsely reported that Fiddlin' John hailed from "Blue Ridge," because it sounded mountainy. Articles exaggerated his mealy accent, tattered clothing, and poor personal hygiene, but these traits were used to offset and affirm the authentic beauty of his playing.[6] In all, this epic buffoonery worked over an audience that needed both to romanticize and reject its own past. Here was a bit of rural life made available for both commemoration and mockery, just the thing for those who thought they had left behind the past for good. The press, of course, never let you forget the transcultural twist. As a reporter for the *Atlanta Journal* wrote, the songs played were "old favorites . . . your granddaddies used to dance to in the country cabins before they moved to Atlanta and got rich in real estate and turned to grand opera lovers" (Daniel 19).

After the war, Carson's career set the mold to which most country performers would later conform, drawing upon its professional paradoxes to attract listeners. Despite the relative smallness of his circuit, he became a typical touring artist. With a few banjo buddies, he would hit the road and play, looking for crowds, passing the hat, and slowly learning the values of advertising. By the early 1920s, he had the routine down pat, arranging shows in advance, finding sponsors, and selling songsheets. Throughout, the old-time feel kept the operation running—Carson's rustic repertoire and bumpkin ease linked together an increasingly vast network of technological media and commercial know-how. In 1922, he took a chance and shuffled into the brand-new WSB studio on the fifth floor of the *Atlanta Journal* building. He stammered his way through an introduction and almost instantly found himself on air singing his crowd-pleaser "The Little

Old Log Cabin in the Lane." The landmark broadcast embodied the central paradox of Carson's entire career, namely, that this very old music found its greatest significance in a decisively modern setting. As one of the station managers explained, "He played and sang until, shall we say, exhaustion set in. But not before he had scored a signal triumph and the phones were jumping up and down with requests from listeners who liked this return to the old-time mountain music" (Wiggins 70). Here, as throughout the history of commercial country music, dissociation becomes a precondition for cultural integrity, alienation precedes any kind of wholeness. Carson himself often joked about this paradox of his career: "Radio made me. . . . Until I began to play over WSB, more than two years ago, just a few people in and around Atlanta knew me, but now my wife thinks she's a widow most of the time because I stay away from home so much playing around over this part of the country."[7]

The speed of this transition was matched only by Carson's jump to records in 1923, another "first" that completed the commercial nexus of touring–recording–broadcasting. The well-known story begins with Polk Brockman, a furniture salesman who worked as the Southeast distributor for OKeh Records. Brockman likely knew Carson from his Atlanta fame, but the idea of recording the performer first struck him when he was seated in a Times Square theater watching a newsreel of a fiddler contest. Back home, he convinced Ralph Peer, a production assistant for OKeh, to give Carson a chance, and 500 copies of "Little Old Log Cabin in the Lane" were made for distribution in the local area. While Peer had little faith in the recording ("Pluperfect awful!" he supposedly exclaimed), the group had an "accidental hit" on their hands. The first sales rush occurred at a fiddlers' contest arranged by Brockman for the release. Carson played the record—not the song, but the actual record— onstage, sold copies during the performance, and then took to the road in a new Model T with "OKeh Recording Artist" painted on the side.[8] Here, too, the presumed directness and authenticity of the event overlaps with its stunning dislocation and staginess. No doubt, the presence of records onstage lent a certain esteem to the rustic performance, just as the authenticity of the performance validated its recording. Either way, Carson went down the highway feeling all right, and the industry moved on to bigger things, using better microphones, brighter promotions, and the intricacies of copyright law to translate tradition into solid gold. As a story of American pluck, this one hardly seems original, but as an instant of emergent rural modernity, it can't be beat: traveling the hard road back to the origin of country music, we find a furniture store, a record company, a movie theater, and a Model T.

The growth of this industry was surely matched by changes in southern demographics and attitudes. As Patrick Huber explains, Carson's audience consisted of recent migrants, men and women who, like Carson himself, had been driven off their farms in the hills and forced to work in Atlanta's textile factories. Confronted with the harsh regime of the mill and crowded into small, impoverished tenements, these rural refugees turned to fiddlin' in order "to cope with the challenges of an uncertain and sometimes bewildering modern life. . . . [to] acclimate themselves to their new working-class lives and to assuage those anxieties spawned by social dislocation, industrial expansion, and shifting social attitudes and morals." At the same time, many of these workers were exposed to consumer culture for the first time, and their newly found leisure and disposable income (however meager it might have been) gave them access to country song, as it maintained a "strong sense of community and regional identity" (xvi). But while Huber nicely depicts the development of this vibrant culture, and the variety of its musical tastes, he tends to simplify the appeal of Carson's music. He acknowledges that Carson was no "old-fashioned, untutored folk musician," for his song bag contained a range of modern themes and styles, and his career was, as we've seen, deeply bound up in modern technologies (50). Yet, at the same time, Huber's analysis doesn't move far beyond the claims made by early journalists themselves, namely, that early country music "conjured up nostalgic longings for a lost agrarian world" (65). In contrast, I'd like to explore the very form of this hillbilly shtick, its complex relation to tradition, and the various and often conflicted emotions it generated, as they signaled the possibilities of the present as well as the distant past.

Even the most casual look at the genealogy of country song shows what a strange mongrel it can be. Think Jimmie Rodgers's yodel, the Carters' railroad blues, Hank's Hawaiian numbers. As Bill C. Malone originally argued, rural music has always been responsive to larger forces of commercial and technological change, and its forms have evolved in relation to a diverse American tradition that includes gospel, blues, Tin Pan Alley, and Spanish and Hawaiian guitar.[9] Carson's varied repertoire is typical insofar as it immediately dispels any simple romance of rural "authenticity" or even "rootsiness." His songs derive from a range of periods, cultures, and traditions, and they are each performed with a freewheeling disregard of historical precedent as well as formal consistency. Indeed, the repertoire reveals an almost iconoclastic disrespect for origins, a willingness to revamp any traditional song, often in mid-song, as the occasion demanded. He often played recent tunes in ancient styles (as with his stripped-down revival of the 1906 hit "The Orphan Child") and ancient tunes in modern styles (listen to his beautifully expressive version of "All Alone by the Sea").[10] Also, he remixed melodies and lyrics, fusing together different musical genres to create songs that sounded both familiar and strange. He sings the popular verses of "The Baggage Coach Ahead," but the accompaniment is pure mountain folk; his drunken rendition of "Old Aunt Peggy, Won't You Set 'Em Up Again" is sung to "Glory, Glory Hallelujah." At the same time, Carson constantly revised traditional music for more contemporary purposes and venues. He used a "Hesitation Blues" for plugging Tom Watson's governor bid, and then he used it again for hawking True Blue beer at a country fair. On courthouse steps, playing for enraged Leo Frank haters, he followed the inflammatory "Little Mary Phagan" with "Give Me that Old Time Religion" and "The Little Old Log Cabin by the Lane."[11]

Carson, no doubt, sang often about the modern world. Songs such as "The Farmer Is the Man Who Feeds Them All" and "Dixie Boll Weevil" address, in their own rambling way, insurance and farming support, credit and taxation, social respect, and class bias. But Carson's more traditional and overtly sentimental songs reveal a more startling confrontation with modernity. Certainly, his hits all tend to focus on the past, but they depict a region already in decline, and they are sung with an odd mixture of pathos, pride, humor, and relief. From first to last, these performances cut against the very sentiments they supposedly express; traditional melodies and lyrics comes across as material to be used, to be manipulated in the present for the present, rather than expressions of a sanctified past. In fact, each of the fourteen sides first recorded by Carson deals with some form of death, dissipation, and failure, but hardly any of these performances can be described as specifically nostalgic or even sad. First, any sense of homecoming is vexed by calamity—death, crime, train crash, pestilence, storm. Nostalgic reverie is clouded by either a sense of impossibility or active refusal; even if there were a way back home, the singer hardly seems interested in returning. Moreover, as these songs depict a fading rural ideal, they rise and fall and then rise again with affective energy. As Patton sings of death and decay, his fiddle screeching endlessly, the ground seems to slip away and time moves forward on a thrilling current of feeling. Each performance is driven by an active, forward-moving set of southern emotions—pride, guff, grit—carrying both singer and song out of the past and into the present. Indeed, in Carson's best performances—"The Little Old Log Cabin in the Lane," "When You and I Were Young, Maggie," "You Will Never Miss Your Mother Until She's Gone," and "Be Kind to a

Man When He Is Down"—he seems nothing less than proud and vital, even flirty and adventurous. Sure, here and there, one detects a certain wistfulness, but each song rises again in defiant glee, as if even naming the past as past represents a triumph of the present.

For example, Carson's signature tune, "The Little Old Log Cabin in the Lane," was commercially written and produced as far back as 1871.[12] It had appeared in countless minstrel shows and songbooks through-out the decades, so that by Carson's time, it would no doubt have come across as an older, if fondly remembered, tune. Lyrically, both sentiment (wistfulness, longing, loss) and setting (run-down cabin, weedy plot, old dog) belonged to an earlier, mustier tradition of rural nostalgia. Indeed, given that the song's lyrics already depict a fading rural ideal, it must have seemed doubly, even triply, anachronistic on the Atlanta stage:[13]

> The chimney's falling down, and the roof's all caved in,
> Lets in the sunshine and the rain.
> But the angel's watching over me
> When I lay down to sleep
> In my little old log cabin in the lane.

But, despite setting and theme, Carson's rendition bears no trace of de-cline. Almost immediately, his delivery distracts from the song's weary lyricism, redirecting attention to the singer himself and his clearly undi-minished vitality. As Mark Wilson says, "Carson does not croon the song. He practically shouts it, and in his performance the song seems almost a celebration of life amidst the decay it chronicles" (Wiggins 221). From first to last, Carson's handling of the maudlin lyrics is slyly ironic. He delivers the song's title line with a knowing smirk, while he resists the excessive pathos of the verses with sets of knowingly drawn vowels and a mocking flourish at the end of each line. Throughout, he overshoots the minstrel shtick as he hams up his own modern shtick, working the gravel in his voice to humorous effect and emphasizing slips in grammar with extra volume and duration. Sure, he's a creaky old coot, but he knows how to laugh at his image; in fact, he seems to be laughing at the entire tragic economy of southern nostalgia. In the end, his performance offers up a very different kind of feeling than the one implied by the original com-position: the presumed authenticity of the past is reapplied to the singer himself, who acknowledges death and decay and yet, by dint of strength and irony, continues to push forward in the present.

Carson frequently camped it up on the Atlanta stage, exaggerating his source material and its rural underpinnings. In a way, though, his largely comical act—with its trick fiddling and hokey jokes—provided audiences with a serious forum to explore feelings of fear and fascination in relation to their own past. As mentioned, Carson's hit was a cover of an old minstrel tune—a whiteface version of a blackface lament for an imaginary South that never existed in the first place. The complexities of time here everywhere overlap with the complexities of race, making themselves felt in the very performance of the song. As Huber points out, Carson was an active member of the revived Ku Klux Klan in Atlanta, having joined after the race riots in 1906. He often played at Klan functions in the Atlanta area, including Klan-sponsored fiddler contests, and he worked as a campaign fiddler for gubernatorial candidate and Klansman Clifford Walker in the 1922 state elections (61, 92). Yet Huber also notes that Carson's neighborhood in Atlanta ("Cabbagetown") bordered on a black neighborhood ("Niggertown"), from which he picked up new musical styles. Carson often played his repertoire—which included both minstrel songs and many black-penned tunes—to mixed-race audiences on Decatur Street, and he once, strangely enough, played a racially integrated benefit for an African American communist organizer (53, 84, 94). With these contradictions in mind, Carson's rendition of "The Little Old Log Cabin in the Lane" seems shaped by the psychological dynamics of minstrelsy in a much more complex way. As Eric Lott might argue, the performance works through a series of established cultural forms, here settled in published song, in order to manage ambivalent feelings of racial and regional repulsion. Most apparently, the clearly undiminished vitality and urban success of the performer, in all his whitewashed loudness, stands in direct opposition to the images of rural life depicted in lines such as,

> Now I'm getting old and feeble, and I cannot work no more
> That rusty bladed hoe I've laid to rest
> And old Massus and old Missus they are sleepin' side by side
> Their spirits now are roaming with the blest.

What seems most remarkable here is that Carson's minstrelsy cut both ways, turning around on his own southern whiteness as much as directing it toward established notions of blackness. In fact, his stage performance of "The Little Old Log Cabin in the Lane" explicitly avoids the racist cast of previous renditions; he sings the song in a decisively "white" hillbilly manner, at once establishing a respectful connection with its protagonist and exceeding it with his own sly irony. In this, Carson's minstrelsy is also decisively temporal. If it caricatures ethnic or racial difference, it does so within the context of regional change. He frames his counterfeit portrayal

of race—white or black—within a larger narrative of southern transformation, and so exposes, for better or worse, the motion of history itself.

In *Natural Acts: Gender, Race, and Rusticity in Country Music*, Pamela
Fox argues similarly that country music works through minstrel-like
representations of rural and non-rural identities.[14] The country music
stage, she argues, is crowded with fabricated types—the poor rube, the
shrill cowgirl, the oversexed negro, the honky-tonk angel, the modern
entrepreneur—and these "masks" work to generate complicated processes
of identification and disidentification. As she explains, "Rural poor or
working-class whites who performed as rubes, like *blacks* performing in
burnt cork, may have then achieved a 'type of shame management through
hyperbolic self-representation' . . . Like their black counterparts, they may
have resorted to 'theatrical grotesques as ways of marking distance between themselves and their horror,' in order to 'mark' themselves in turn
as modern civilized subjects" (32). Although Fox doesn't consider Carson's
early act (her work focuses on radio barn dances), we may note here that,
in its campy humor and hyperbolic imagery, it similarly allowed audiences
to think through the various dimensions of their own history. Here was
not only a black man and a white man, but a hayseed and a professional, a
worker and a performer, and, beyond that, both the past and the present,
the city and the country at once, a dizzying set of overlapping relays that
must have set Atlanta audiences on ecstatic edge. Indeed, the performance
itself—as the repeat performance of an even older song, a sound seeming
both near and far—flickered between two worlds; as temporal minstrelsy,
it functions as neither nostalgic escape nor insidious mockery, but as a
confrontation with history as such.

As a whole, I think, Carson's performance maintains this deep but productive relation to the past, one that will inform all I have to say in the
following sections. While his act was framed for a recently urbanized
crowd, it drew upon a set of temporal relays, momentous encounters with
the olden days that proved in excess of mere nostalgia. The floppy felt hat,
the fiddle, the old hound, the old slave himself—these objects had been
lifted out of their original contexts and displayed onstage as emotionally
charged fragments of present time. The formal quality of song only in-
tensified this process, not just because of its liveliness and immediacy, but
because its very immateriality, its very detachment, provided an unsettling
link between past and present. Technically, it was the same song heard
long ago, and yet it was there, present, bearing a strange but powerful
doubleness in its own repetition. At times, the press would hit upon this
temporal dissonance and struggle to convey the emotional currents that

it seemed to generate. One writer claimed that the best fiddler recreates "the thrill of forest throats, and mountain wind" and "the whisperings of April voices in the leaves or raindrops dripping from the eaves of some lone cabin on the hill." Another urges, "Shut your eyes and you forget you are in Atlanta's big auditorium. . . . You can see the rafters of the old barn and smell the hay up in the mow and 'most hear the lowing of the cattle and the rustle of the hen who complains about her disturbed nest" (Daniel 23). If such statements attest to the transmissibility of sonic form, they also suggest that its function can change across time and space. As we'll find, country song is intimately bound to regional history, but it accomplishes its cultural work through a set of immaterial sounds and related images. Its power is founded on its detachment, on the very dematerialization of regional space and time, and with this, its unreal lightness, it can be used to advance either creative or reactionary forms of regional identity.

The Delmores, the Vagabonds, and the Formal Turn

So with modernity and modernization in mind, let's hack away at some of the myths concerning country music. The most common strain assigns an organic rootsiness to the music itself, as if it rose directly from southern soil, like some delicate wildwood flower, in a sorrowful yet glorious process of regional expression. Here, a certain sluggishness of musical evolution comes across as authenticity and commitment, and in turn supports a self-pleasing narrative of southern resistance to modern life as cultural degeneration. Of course, given the historical factors that accompanied the growing popularity of country music—tenantry and sharecropping, the spread of industrialized labor, inflation, Depression, the Dust Bowl, and two great migrations to the North—one expects it to have a bit more political bite. Many critics, though, argue that country music responds to modernity in a purely negative fashion; it unashamedly presents itself as an imaginary respite, projecting all manner of ideal abodes—log cabins, moonlit stills, and angelic palaces—to which the weary modern listener may retreat and rest his weary head.[15] But while country music often does serve this function, a careful consideration of its form shows a more complex relationship to historical change. Indeed, while other critics have gotten around the reactionary nature of this music by considering its contextual uses and increasing institutionalization, I'd like to add an analysis of form to the conversation.[16] Cultural trauma is encoded not only in country's lyrical content, in its self-conscious myths of loss and restoration, but also in its internal relations of structure and style. As we'll find, when these songs are taken as songs, as the sonic patterning of the region's emotional life, they confound spatial configurations of home and away as well as temporal narratives of rise and fall, and thus cut new paths through the region.

According to Richard Peterson, the early development of country music—from, say, the Bristol Sessions of 1927 to the start of World War II—vacillated, in its search for authenticity, between "soft" and "hard" forms, between the sentimental songs of the parlor and the rougher fiddle breakdowns of the barn. But Peterson smartly notes that both of these styles harken back to earlier, largely commercialized forms, and, in this, the evolution of the form doesn't seem to follow any obvious linear progression (138–39). Nonetheless, I'd like to show that, by the early 1930s, *form* itself became a distinctive feature of country song and a genuine aesthetic value for both musicians and fans. In other words, the most successful country music of this period juxtaposes warm feeling with cool style, and in this came to signal its own modernity. While lyrics remained transfixed on the broken past, endlessly repeating moments of loss or rejection, performance styles—driven by the commercial marketplace and new recording technology—grew increasingly formal, detached, and even distracted by their own virtuosity. No way but through, it seems—the slick new music of this era does not abandon the past, but recasts it in dynamic tension with the present. Cool country adopts the abstraction of the age as an aesthetic strategy, using it both to attract the modern-day listener and to foreground the dissociation of regional space and time. This formal irony, if we may call it such, reflects the aesthetic peak of modernism as represented by, say, T. S. Eliot's *The Waste Land* or William Faulkner's *The Sound and the Fury*, texts in which the very alienation and critical negativity of modernity always also implies the possibility of cultural restitution. Similarly, early country music grips the listener with its own formal coldness, frustrating his or her sentimental demands: these songs pass away before our very ears, at once raising and resisting the possibility of some better time and place, suggesting only within their own cruel formalism a way through the modern impasse.

Let's turn to two acts from the 1930s noted for their "professionalism" and formal "sophistication." First, the Vagabonds—a slick pop group that found success on Chicago radio before they were lured by WSM as part of an effort to update the station's image. Up north, the group was known for its experiments with new technologies and new programming formats, but down south they were celebrated for their ability to update old-time

tunes for modern audiences. When they turned to the beloved "Heart and
Home" songs of the region, they kept all the rustic iconography and melancholic lore but gave it a pop shine, adding their own "patented, smooth
three-part harmony" as well as "slick, snappy arrangements."[17] Take their
1933 hit "When It's Lamp Lighting Time in the Valley."[18] As Charles K.
Wolfe points out, the song's lyrics anxiously juxtapose a modern world of
passion, crime, and the city against a lost bucolic past (*Riot* 184). But the
song registers a much more complex doubleness through the psychology
of its narrator and its own ambiguous arrangement. "I've sinned against
my home . . . and now I must ever more roam," the narrator explains with
an unsettling matter-of-factness, and so begins to outline the cold, hard
facts of his otherwise tragic life. With no luck in the city and no way back
home, he seems caught not only between spaces and times, but also between forms and feelings—between the hard-boiled toughness of the city
and the sentimental weight of the country. The same tension riddles the
song's performance. At first, sweet harmonics and gentle stringwork offer
to ease the pain of this otherwise unbearable tale. The song presents itself
as a traditional ballad with a nice melodic resolution, and thus seems ready
to provide a purely sonic comfort. But the singer recounts the tale with a
sort of blank efficiency, and the sound of the whole seems to emerge from
an empty, featureless space—a studio. Both voice and instrumentation are
remarkably grainless, too polished, too precise for the emotional messiness
of their own tale. In fact, the musical accompaniment is so obsessively
neat, so pure and thin, that its very perfection distracts us from the tragic
plot, overshadowing its pathos and perhaps even its moral. Thus, if the
song presents itself as a respite, an imaginary dwelling, it remains both
warm and distant, soothing and abstract, only always potential. Sonic
relief is both offered and denied, and the listener is left, anxiously, with
only a distant, fading, receding promise of homecoming, stuck between
two impossible realms.

The Delmores were similarly embraced as innovators, mixing a range
of popular styles in arrangements that were slick, intricate, and utterly
catchy. Their subtle vocal harmonies and quick guitar work were well
suited to the new technologies of records and radio. Their arrangements
would have been impossible without recent innovations in microphone
technology, which had transformed country music at large from a raucous public exchange into an evocative experience of psychology and
mood.[19] But the Delmores' version of "The Frozen Girl" (1933) uses these
very features to undercut its own sentimental import.[20] Take the song's
opening, with its plaintive iambs—"no home, no home." The cry of the

orphan child is provided here by two professional voices in delicate harmony; the phrase is fully aestheticized, detached from its own emotional content, and thus reaches the ear of the listener as a source of primarily sonic pleasure. Indeed, each line of the song seems committed to the brothers' own stunning harmonic maneuvers. Intimacy itself appears as a formal, or even technical, feature of the song itself. Paradoxically, the very technology used to bring the human voice straight to the heart creates an abstract space for the play of vocality, one that is undeniably thrilling but perhaps uncommunicative and not a little bit uncanny (see chapter five). Lyrically, too, the Delmores distance themselves from the sentimental scene. The song's narrator appears aloof, providing, through a series of flat quotations, a seemingly objective but oddly indifferent stance toward the tale. By the end, the song's stylish presentation seems to reflect, with only a very slight irony, the rich man's rejection of the orphan:

> The snow fell fast as she shrank on the steps
> And strove to wrap her feet,
> In a tattered dress all covered with snow
> Yes, covered with snow and sleet.

The performance—at once impersonal and detached—puts a new spin on the sentimental scene. What began as a tender gesture of comfort turns out to be a cold refusal, and the ghostly murmuring of voice and string serve to wrap, perhaps mute, both girl and earth in a blank "winding sheet." In this, the song occupies a ghostly space, between two uninhabitable realms of feeling and two impossible styles. The listener, too, remains orphaned at the doorstep at the South, so close and so far from the comforts and intimacies of home and family.

No doubt, though, for rural listeners, this affective tension proved a significant pleasure in itself and pointed toward the future rather than the past. Looking at the production, promotion, and reception of these more "professional" country acts, it becomes clear that their uncanny modernity was a real source of curiosity and investment. First and foremost, the experience of country music in the 1930s was carefully mediated by the urbane rhetoric of the industry's promotional material. While performers were encouraged to exaggerate rustic accents and mannerisms, the shtick was always offered up in reference to its own commercialization, framed by the thrilling logistics of big technology, big business, and big living. In other words, the musical event was never simply experienced as a form of regional comfort or even as regional shame (to borrow Pamela Fox's terms). Rather, in its clash of styles and conflicting terms, it came across as an inquiry into the process of being or becoming modern. Fan journals devoted lengthy columns to readers' queries about studio techniques and professional routines. They answered questions about stars' birthdays, heights, weights, eyes, and hair, as well as job experiences, work routines, and growing salaries. Distinctions were frequently made between the stage persona and the "real" performer: photos presented stars with and without costume, while articles described difficult work schedules and busy travel plans. *Rural Radio*, in its October 1938 feature article on Mountain Pete and his Mountaineers, candidly outlined the difference between the performers' public image and their actual backgrounds: "The strange thing is that they hail from all parts of the globe," and, given the group's professional training, "It's hard to believe that they would know anything about American folk music."[21] Even George Hay, a master of hillbilly gimcrackery, knew his Opry audience wanted more than corncob pipes and apple pies. In his promotional biography of the Opry, he comes clean on Harry Stone's work schedule, Roy Acuff's growing income, and Little Jimmie's record-breaking personal appearances. He never once doubts that fans appreciate these more or less rough equation of heart and wallet: "Asher Sizemore is a shrewd showman," he writes; "their programme pulls the heart strings, which in our language means a sure-fire hit."[22]

Given such instances of casual disclosure, one can safely assume that fans in the 1920s and 1930s sought more than tradition in their country music. They were equally invested in modern professional life, and they were curious about the alternative careers and trajectories made possible by new technology and commodity culture. In fact, the most successful musicians of the late 1920s and early 1930s were those who managed to perform their own modernization, their acts seamlessly blending the old and new, tradition and progress, earnestness and success into a single pleasing image charged with the weight of history itself. Take Hay's brief biography of the Vagabonds, which focuses on the way the band cleaned up the markers of rural authenticity: "They could hardly be called 'country boys,'" he explains, "but they loved folk music and handled it with a background of formal musical training, which smoothed it as against the usual renditions handled in a strictly rural fashion" (28–29). Similarly, the preface to the Vagabonds' *Collection of Mountain Ballads, Old-Time Songs, and Hymns* stresses their early travels along the circuit-rider ring, "when they played in the hills and valleys, and learned to live from the people of the sod, who are very near to their hearts." But, lest we forget, the report asserts that "[t]heir Vagabondage is not one as described as being of very low caste or the common bum. Far from that, they quickly tell you that their kind of Vagabond is one who travels through the country, visiting cities and calling via radio upon millions of people."[23] Such documents negotiate a range of competing emotions and investments; moreover, they affirm rural identities that are mobile, productive, and future-oriented. The lives of the Vagabonds are as fluid and open as the economy through which they travel; their happiness is the happiness of mobility, of a newly flexible community of consumer/fans. Indeed, the end of the songbook provides the real scoop; here, fans are privy to the professional routines and complex moral virtues of the Vagabonds behind the Vagabonds:

> It may be interesting to you, who read this little book and sing the songs contained therein, to know that The VAGABONDS—Herald, Dean, and Curt—are constantly employed in their chosen profession, and at all times are busily seeking new ways of entertaining the millions who have become their regular fans.
>
> They start their day very early, usually doing their first broadcast as early as 6:30 A.M. or 7:00 A.M. Then their next job is to get together in their office quarters and go carefully over the mail received the preceding day. Each letter must have careful attention, and where an answer is needed they take time to attend to it at once.
>
> Usually following this morning meeting they take time to eat their second breakfast. They are well known for their Table Power. Eat! When that word is spoken they all smile and start following their noses to where the coffee odor is strongest.
>
> Back to the studio for rehearsal. This morning rehearsal lasts from two to three hours. If you think singing and rehearsing for three hours is fun, and no work, try singing for three hours and see then if you can speak.
>
> One day each week is set aside for recreation. Hunting is the greatest hobby. Then comes golf, fishing, and other outdoor sports of interest.
>
> The Vagabonds find that even in the Great Outdoors much radio material is to be discovered. They use many illustrations in each program which have been taken from some actual experience of one or the other, Herald, Dean, or Curt. (30)

Again, like the songs described above, this promotional material refracts country values through a modern lens. Deep emotions and professional values—that's how they do it in the new South. Big business and busy schedules, hard work, hearty appetites, and scheduled relaxation—country values bring modern success, while modern success leads right back to the country, and so, on the level of musical production and consumption, the region at large is set into dynamic motion.

Again, the slick songs and promotional materials of this era suggest that early country music culture served to negotiate affective tensions brought on by modernization. Rural fans were drawn to this music and its performers as they signaled a possible reconciliation between older ways of life and new, more dynamic modes of being. In a way, all popular musical experience draws upon an uneven relay of emotions and forms. It moves from everyday life to song and back again, at once redirecting and reshaping the affective terrain in more or less novel ways. In this, I'd like to show, country music should be defined less as a symbolic formation, less as an expression of southern ideology, than as an alternative space and time of emotional engagement. Specifically, the *space of country song* floats above the soil, in its own abstract orbit, removed from other country spaces, and yet undeniably tangible, affective, and inclusive; it is a projection and a province, an impossible elsewhere and a physical feeling of home. Relatedly, the *time of country song* liberates the listener from everyday time, from the brute fatalism of historical time, but still initiates an affective change—an open event—by which we can evaluate our movement through everyday time. Call it an "imagined community," call it an "invisible republic"—country song is that strange southern space at once real and imagined, everywhere and nowhere, in which tenant farmers, rail-yard workers, truckers, curators, and even scholars can pursue their emotional responses to modernity.[24] In this, we might begin to detect a more positive feeling, a more productive use, for detachment and dissociation. As we'll find with the Carters, the very gap between experience and abstraction, while occasioned by historical tragedy, becomes the thrilling precondition for some more satisfying present, perhaps even a radical future.

The Carters, the Corpse, and the Lament

In most accounts, the Carters seem to sprout literally from the soil of Scott County, Virginia, their shoes clogged with dirt, their hair entwined with lilies. They are great Appalachian gods of yore who tapped the woods and streams of their Clinch Mountain home for a buzz far greater than wine or weed. They are preservers of the old ways, guardians of the folk, celebrants of hearth, home, and the country store—and they're singing our songs. "All the songs had deep-gutted meaning," offers a Carter family niece. "They were always about a feeling somebody had *had*." Even today, scholars find themselves gushing, placing the music somewhere between religious reliquary, magical elixir, and fairy balm. From Mark Zwonitzer's biography:

"Carter Family music was a song of what [the weary traveler] left behind. The lonesomest, neediest, most cut-off listeners could lean forward toward their radio sets, hear those songs, and think, *That's just how it was—they understand.*"[25] Call me city-jaded, but regarding the Carter family—the so-called First Family of Country Music—two simple biographical facts tend to trouble this account. One: while the trio was promoted as a family act (a common practice at the time) and celebrated for their commitment to the virtues of domestic life, A. P. and Sara were divorced at the height of the group's career and remained estranged during some of their most successful recording sessions. Two: while the group was largely responsible for preserving and popularizing Appalachian folk culture and their songs have become synonymous with American musical tradition, their national fame coincided with a series of commercial radio shows broadcasted from a barely legitimate station over the Mexico border.

The Carters' lives were nothing if not cynically modern, and their repertoire represents one of the most radical revolutions in the history of popular music. Although the group is associated with the shacks and streams of Scott Valley, Virginia, and their music grew out of the airs and ballads of the Old World, their compositional method and performance style signaled drastic changes in the experience of popular music. If their songs proved essential to American lives, it was because they confronted the pain and alienation of a specifically modern life and turned contemporary feelings of loss and detachment into a virtue of form. As the sober-minded Bill Malone notes, "The Carter Family sang of an America that was gradually disappearing. . . . fading since even before the Carters were children" (*Country* 67–68). Similarly, Curtis W. Ellison claims that of the many different strands that compose country music tradition, the Carters offered "a pervasive evocation of transience, of present things fading away, of personal tragedy and death" (26). I'd like to push these descriptions a step further, arguing that not simply "transience" or even "death," but a fully modern, fully aesthetic sense of detachment, the deathliness of form itself, shaped the Carters' relation to the South as well as the widespread success of their music. It was not their rootedness, but their detachment—from each other, from their home, from the past, and from their own performances—that shaped their best music and guided it toward a series of anxious but compelling resolutions.

The persistent romance that surrounds the Carters is startling, given what is already known about their path-making career as musicians— the initial Bristol sessions, the transition to recorded sound, the royalty system that yoked them to Ralph Peer, and, of course, their employment

under Consolidated Royal Chemical on XERA radio. Also, this romance
flies in the face of all that has been said of the formal dimensions of their
music—A. P.'s updated lyricism, Sara's expressive voice, and, of course,
Maybelle's barn-thumpin' guitar scratch. By building songs off of set chord
patterns and a rhythmic guitar, the group tamed the modal excesses of
the rural musical past, offering standardized and simplified structures for
an otherwise distracted modern audience.[26] Together, the group worked
together like a set of country Imagists, shortening, simplifying, polishing
their tunes, smoothing over all the rough edges so that they would appeal
to a world beyond that of the overalled mountain men and apple-cheeked
grannies who supplied them. Indeed, no matter what we hear today (as
it might be refracted through our own postmodern nostalgia), the music
was known then as smooth and up-to-date, and its popularity signified
a general trend away from the old-timey feel of Carson and the fiddling
contests. As Bob Coltman explains, their sound was "just plain futuristic
compared to the older, less developed styles prevalent in 1927." It was not
their traditionalism, but "the way they'd 'changed' or 'modernised' (some
even say 'spoiled') the old songs" that gave them success and a place in
American culture.[27]

But to appreciate the Carters' aesthetic *modernism* (in addition to their
historical *modernity*), we specifically need to consider their approach to
the ballad form. By the time the Carters began recording, folk scholars
had already begun to discern a decisive shift in ballad form and performance. On American soil, they noted, early European models faced a
certain adulteration. Songs shed their intricate narratives and became
shorter, fragmented, more emotional, more expressive. Lyrically, American performers tended to focus on the affective core of each piece, cutting
extraneous narrative details (particularly of the mythic or supernatural
kind) and emphasizing the intense but common emotions of the dramatic
situation.[28] The Carters pushed these tendencies to their breaking point.
Having access to a wealth of material, they were drawn to ballads that
explored traumatic states of loss and alienation. They mostly avoided
traditional melodramatic topics—murder, class strife, natural disaster,
etc.—in favor of more decisively modern states of ennui, anxiety, and
melancholia. Moreover, whereas the sentimental ballads of the nineteenth
century tried to assuage the listener's sadness and alienation, with either
peaceful imagery or melodic resolutions, the Carters' songs seemed to
dwell, obsessively, morbidly, on their own anxiety and despair.[29] With these
shifts, the Carters' songs not only paved the way for the pop revolution to
come, but typified the modernist dictum to "Make it new!"—translating the

foreign world of the British ballad into a provocative idiom for their own regional audience. The storm-tossed sea became the economy-wracked South, while snooty barons, cursed sailors, and starving street urchins reappeared in contemporary forms, as broken farming families, workers looking for jobs, or lovers parted by war.[30]

But we cannot underestimate the significance of *form* here. On the one hand, the Carters' ballads proved distinctly modern in their lyrical promiscuity, moving freely in terms of plot, character, and even point of view. Voices rarely occupy any coherent space or time, and the details of both biography and experience remain murky; rather, each voice seems to emerge out of an empty, nihilistic space, appearing only to trace out stark, nearly impersonal configurations of pain and hope, recalling the fragmented subjectivities found in "The Love Song of J. Alfred Prufrock" and Gertrude Stein's *Three Lives*. At the same time, the Carters' songs avoided any overt display of moral judgment or sentimental investment. Rather, they find coherence in a certain coolness of delivery, by restricting rather than extending lyrical expression. Far more than the Delmores or Vagabonds, the Carters excelled at stylish detachment and indifference. They worked against the excesses of traditional balladry by presenting the emotional core of each song in the sonic equivalent of blank-face; even when singing of murdered lovers or hunted criminals, their performances maintain an emotional coldness that draws more attention to each song's formal features than its contents. Relatedly, each Carter song appears as a remarkably consistent structure, standardized in terms of verse and chorus, and severely restricted in tone, tempo, and range. These songs mean business—and industry; driven by Maybelle's unvarying strum, they surge forward with the force of heavy machinery, a series of inter-locking rhythms and tonal levers designed not so much to express, but to produce new emotion. Again, "Make it new!"—but here the Carters estrange listeners from the intimacies of music itself, recalling Eliot's own call for depersonalization in poetics, specifically his claim that "The progress of an artist is a continual self-sacrifice, a continual extinction of personality."[31]

So while the group might have inherited the reserved, unadorned style of Appalachian singing, their sense of abstraction and cool, restricted delivery, not to mention their speed, cut against the entire tradition.[32] One might argue that they had no choice but to shorten their songs, standardize their repertoire, and create an easily recognizable sound; these changes were forced upon the group by the record format itself, with its limitations of range and duration, and by changing consumer tastes in a competitive pop-culture market.[33] But, still, the Carters' disjointed formalism served specific aesthetic purposes. First, it reflected the lived fragmentation of the region; as we'll see, it proved a fitting correlative to the abstract shifts in space and time that increasingly came to mark modern rural life. Secondly, it allowed for a stable vantage point from which to explore new emotions. In their detachment and indifference, these songs gave listeners a way of recognizing the changeability of modern southern life and even, at times, protecting themselves against its seeming dangers. Thirdly, the Carters' detachment worked, consistently, willfully, against their own inheritance, their own mythic past, and provided listeners with a new attitude and a new means of adequation. As Katie Doman explains, the music's driving rhythm and "strong, sure" tones tamed "the sentimentality of the material" and instead offered listeners a "powerful exigency," a new emotional stance in relation to a changed world (76–77).

At least some of this energy and innovation can be traced back to A. P., the group's principal song gatherer/updater. For sure, A. P. was a strange dude—"wifty," the neighbors called him—shaking all the time, and distracted at home or away, even in the midst of his chosen work. He was, it seems, born to a typical but recently disturbed corner of the South. The foot of Clinch Mountain had always been too small for the ambitious, but too poor for them to do anything about it. By the early 1920s, the sleepy valley had caught a glimpse of the emerging modern world, and it wracked the nerves of anyone with a greater sense of purpose. There was Neal's up the road, which served as railroad depot, post office, and consumer outlet; the electric lights and growing commercial district of Bristol nearby; the brother's new phonograph and his small, but expanding record collection; and the newly paved roads, luring small, shaky boys away from home. No doubt, A. P. was charged up—he was literally struck by lightning in his mother's womb—but his energy was largely unfocused, whipping about his frame like a loose telegraph wire, making him shake and stammer. His condition, however, only seemed to worsen as the region around him seemed to expand. The neighbors watched him fretting up and down the railroad tracks, or pacing across the front porch. They knew he was "a-searchin'," but he just seemed a crazy fool, his brains scrambled by that electricity.[34]

Nevertheless, while A. P. had the drive to get out, he always found himself returning, beaten and dissatisfied and poor once more. His first major venture led him to Richmond, Indiana, where he worked briefly on the railroad. As would become his habit, he hurried back quickly, raging with homesickness and fever, but he returned with a song, "My

Clinch Mountain Home," and from that point on, it seemed, wandering and song gathering went hand in hand.[35] Not surprisingly, like many of A. P.'s compositions, this first song is preoccupied with anxious partings and arrivals, a dual process of dislocation and desperate return:

> Far away on the hill to a sunny mountain side,
> Many years ago we parted, my little Ruth and I
> From the sunny mountainside.
>
> She clung to me and trembled when I told her we must part.
> She said don't go my darling; it almost breaks my heart.
> To think of you so far apart.

Maybe A. P. shook so much because he was trying to be in two places at once. Even his song is torn—between spaces, between times, between ways of life. It moves anxiously across vast affective regions, offering a cartography of heart and nation both. The lyrics are remarkable as much for their vertiginous shifts in scope and scale as for their emotional resonances. First the singer provides an intimate view of himself at his lover's breast; then he finds himself way out west with all of rural America separating him from home; next he holds a photograph in his hand, and the scene bends inside and out, giving us memory and photograph, past and present both. The penultimate verse is particularly fraught with uncertainty—the singer is both home and away, holding a picture of the place in which he stands, thinking of a lover who appears to be right next to him. In this lyrical space, all is in flux: here is there, memory becomes presence, but presence seems to fade without warning. While the traveler expects some return, his life has become, as in Carson's music or the Vagabonds', a series of mediated images and a continual parting. In the end, the wifty fragments all but cancel each other out, and he seems everywhere and nowhere at once, at once going and staying, flickering in and out of time, his lovely tremolo providing a haunting double of itself.

But if there is nostalgia here, it exists in relation to the future. The singer actively straddles two moments, looking back as he continues to move forward, holding the picture not so much as a memory or reminder, but as a hope or protective device, or even a ticket, to some other place or time. In this, A. P.'s tremolo becomes the trembling of the future, a second incarnation of himself, in the grip of change. His voice is the voice of self-differentiation, measuring the flickering of identity on its way to some other home. Indeed, A. P.'s best compositions are almost always doubled, tripled, quadrupled in this way, registering abrupt shifts in space and time, shaking at the transition from country to city, from home to highway, from poverty to fame and back again. Often, as in the Vagabonds' song above, the act of parting is repeated over and over, compulsively, cosmically. While no one knows exactly the passions that drive the likes of John Hardy, Georgie the engineer, or that aggravatin' beauty Lulu Walls, we nonetheless feel its effects: one simple dissent opens up an entire world of dissatisfaction and difference, and so drives the rural soul across the face of the earth. The act of parting, no matter how painful, proves remarkably productive, extends well into the past as well as the future, and thus seems infinite, endless, and dynamic. In one continuous cycle, the desire for wholeness entails the recognition of failure, while that failure in turn restores the desire for some future wholeness. Indeed, this is an extremely active nostalgia. At best, it contains the promise of a better life; at worst, as maddening flight, it is still a critical activity—with each letdown, with each betrayal, something like dissatisfaction spreads through the region like wildfire.

But if A. P.'s songs reflect the anxiety and upheaval of modern life, Sara's performances seem to represent its cool detachment and stylish excess. No doubt, Sara saw her fair share of regional tragedy, and, when it comes to country music history, she will forever be cast in a maternal role. But her best performances are notable for their outright rejection of traditional southern womanhood and their explicitly anti-sentimental presentation of "female" emotion. Indeed, biographically, Sara comes across as a thoroughly modern woman forced to contend with the limited rituals and traditions of country life. From a very early age, when she was essentially orphaned by the death of her mother, she confronted the tragedies of life with a stoic reserve. Her childhood nickname was "Jake," reflecting perhaps her nearly masculine bearing and her aggressive work ethic; as a teen, she sold greeting cards to raise money for instruments and then started her own girl group. Later in life, she would be seen hunting, fishing, cutting trees, working the mill, and wearing pants. To courters, she came across just like "Lulu Walls," "pretty as a queen" but "aggravatin'" to the end, refusing to play her part in the dating rites of the day.[36] After marriage, in fact, she shocked A. P. by cutting her hair short, and then, later, she had an affair with a thoroughly modern young man, Coy Bays. Moreover, Sara had taste. To the extent possible in the region, she stylized her life according to her own sensibility. "She had a taste just like she had an ear for a song," claims her son; whether cooking a meal, decorating the house, cutting her hair, or singing a ballad, the final product had to be "perfect every time." In all this, Zwonitzer explains, Sara was known in the region as "liberated before there was such a thing," and this "liberation wasn't an idea Sara and her friends got from women's magazines. It came right out of life" (60–61).

Still, Zwonitzer, like many commentators, casts Sara in the classic role of southern mother and hears her music in traditionally gendered ways. Her music, he claims, served to embrace regional tragedy—every death, accident, and orphaning in the valley—and bestow it with greater, spiritual meaning; each song gave voice to rural helplessness and abandonment and then covered it over with the "romantic cloak of martyrdom" (102, 43). Clearly, though, Sara's performances captivated audiences as much for their modernism as for the traditionalism. Onstage, she appeared fiercely unsentimental, even when singing the most gut-wrenching ballads, while, on records, her isolated voice seems not so much to express, but to contain or even bury, the pain of the lyrics. Take, for example, the two songs she chose to sing on the second day of recording in Bristol. The first, "Single Girl, Married Girl," takes only three short verses to unpick the entire romance of southern womanhood, casting it in opposition to the very freedoms of modernity:

> Single girl, single girl, she's going where she please.
> Oh, she's going where she please.
> Married girl, married girl, baby on her knees.
> Oh, baby on her knees.[37]

Lyrics aside, the stylized performance everywhere cuts against its own emotionality. Sara severely restricts the song's melodic range, choking down most of the song's sentiment at the back of her throat. At the same time, she breaks up the romantic flow of the melody, so that quick clusters of sound are juxtaposed against astounding moments of release. Most notably, she begins and ends each line with an oddly extended note, a high, flat tone that floats slightly out of tune and well past its allotted measure. At such moments, the voice seems to outstrip the word of its meaning, drawing attention to its own texture and the obscure agency of the singer herself. The sound it makes comes across as both a rural wail, part of a larger tradition of lament, as well as an abstract bit of noise—empty, meaningless, open. Either way, with these notes, the voice acts more like a barrier to expression rather than its medium; the singer seems to stand apart from her own song, detached from its lyricism. Thus, while there are emotions flickering in and out of the piece—anger, sadness, weariness, etc.—they seem to be barred as they are expressed, and the piece as a whole is given over to its strange aesthetic effect.

The same goes for the second cut of the day, "Wandering Boy," which is written from a more traditional maternal perspective.[38] Here, the speed of the song creates some marvelous effects, forcing Sara to break up the fluid melody of the lyric and work with shorter, more intense juxtapositions of tone and rhythm. Avoiding the lush melodic style that marked ballad performance in the most immediate past, Sara's rendition alternates between sped-up clusters of syllables and long drawn-out notes, low sobbing slips down the scale and startling leaps back up again. It's a marvelous piece of vocal drama, and yet it comes across as remarkably anti-lyrical, sounding as if the voice itself is struggling against the emotional depth of the song, trying to rise above it and maintain composure. Here, I'm reminded of Shane Vogel's excellent account of the impersonality of Lena Horne's performances.[39] For Vogel, Horne manipulates the linguistic sign as defined by Saussure, emphasizing the "sound" of the "sound/image" complex that determines linguistic meaning. "Horne did not express or represent a sexual subjectivity in performance," Vogel writes, "even if her audience insisted on discovering one. Rather, her performance worked to unperform the sexual subjectivity that her audience expected of her." Similarly, Sara Carter did not offer an alternative version of southern womanhood in her songs, but, rather, she used her voice to break up the surfaces of traditional song and destroy its expressive function; she "offered sound in place of subjectivity," and, so, when working through traditional country materials in country music settings, adopted "a psychic stance that withholds, rather than makes accessible, a sexualized and racialized subjectivity" (24).

As we know, it was Sara's voice that originally fascinated A. P. and then Ralph Peer, and then legions of fans in the years following those first Bristol recordings. Her singing, with its quick, compact delivery, its abstract lines of flight, and flat, emotionless tones, sounded like nothing heard in the region before, and audiences at once felt and acknowledged its keen modernity.[40] But even as Sara's voice contradicted the pathos of her source material, such material continued to haunt her performances. The bits and pieces of rural life may have been unmoored by her vocal style, but they continued to circulate within and around each piece, signaling, in their own obscure ways, the underlying life of the region. Similarly, lyrically, the landscapes of these songs are tortured not only by what has departed, but also by what remains. While their protagonists try to bury the pain of the past, or transform it into clean, crystalline forms (as in Sara's singing), it returns again and again. Daily life is plagued by presences as well as absences, not just old servants and faithful dogs, but also parting lovers and ancestral ghosts. In "Bury Me Under the Weeping Willow," for example, a dying bride requests a prominent burial site in hopes of attracting a future lover. In "Will You Miss Me When I'm Gone," the bride pleads for a planted rose, a symbol that as much reveals as it covers over her own decaying body.[41] With their morbid imagery, these songs deny as they embrace the ravages of time; they bury the pain of loss and yet still imagine some possible reconciliation, some future moment of homecoming or restoration. In this, we seem to return to romance, an image of regional culture embalmed—lost, yet untainted by time. Or, worse, a ritual of burial and return, an obsessive reenactment of traumatic loss, gothic horror as the return of the regionally repressed. But if these songs, like A. P.'s wifty wanderings or Sara's detached lyricism, straddle two impossible realms, they also contain within themselves the possibility of another region entirely: the space and time of song as the space and time of regional change.

Given the losses of World War I, massive migration to the North, the Dust Bowl and Depression, the Carters' South appears as no gentle homestead, but as a vast limbo of the forgotten, the outcast, and the shut-in. The region's recent history of unrest and displacement raises grave doubts about its actual existence, let alone its possible restoration. Slowly, painfully, the South ceases to exist as an actual place to become, as in William Faulkner's *Absalom, Absalom!* or Walker Evans and James Agee's *Let Us Now Praise Famous Men*, a series of bewildering reflections. Does home exist in the soil, like a dead body awaiting its lost lover? Is it any more than a memory, ghostly, immaterial, haunting the minds of its betrayers? Or perhaps home is the pain that arises from this giant chasm, the cry of song that must always repeat the rift it hopes to heal? In "Can the Circle Be Unbroken," one finds all three possibilities at work.[42] The mother's body, spiritual salvation, song itself—each makes its appeal, promises some sense of belonging or restitution. But the narrator trails behind each—as she trails behind the hearse—and we feel her bewilderment with every step. One by one, her hopes fade, and we are left with only a sad chorus, the mournful image in the last verse of "brothers, sisters crying." But if we see this final image as an ironic reference to the Carters themselves, who sing beautifully about their mother's death, we can begin to see the value of their own wavering and ultimate detachment. In other words, there's a connection to be made here between the structure of regional loss and the formal structure of song itself, as they each provide a kind of pleasure and release.

Barbara Ching usefully draws our attention to the song's attenuated sadness: "Rather than seeking closure," she writes, "the singer begs the undertaker to move slowly. The bereaved family wants to keep the corpse. The unbroken circle amounts to keeping company with this deathly image" (208). Similarly, the song itself feeds off of its own sadness, its own emptiness, as if this emotion alone could sustain an otherwise doomed life. Its attenuated sadness becomes, in the form of song itself, a kind of presence, a form of strength and persistence, and, more importantly, the origin of a remarkable emptiness, an ultimate—and ultimately exhilarating—sense of detachment and freedom. Sara's singing is distinctly flat, listless at first, but soon picks up speed and energy, as if she were leading a revivalist meeting. At the same time, Maybelle's remarkably bouncy guitar scratch rises to the fore of the song; her bright picking seems to lead us beyond the scene of mourning, beyond the empty house, and toward another place altogether. Thus, while the lyrics tend toward the grave, the group itself is strangely vital, at once singing, strumming, scratching all the way home—gleefully engaged in their own music making. By the end, the song seems both unbearably deep and lightly detached, heavy with feeling and utterly indifferent in form, somehow lightened by, if not fully released from, its own pain.

In this, the song points beyond mere nostalgia, beyond its own necrophilia, toward the active work of mourning. The split between its emotional fullness and formal detachment distinctly recalls Sigmund Freud's original theory of mourning, which was written to account for his patients' similarly modern feelings of loss.[43] For Freud, the "work" of mourning entails an imaginary "introjection" of the lost or missing person. The mourner's love is slowly returned to the ego, as, bit by bit, "Each single one of the memories and hopes which bound the libido to the object is brought up and hyper-cathected and the detachment of the libido [from the other person] is accomplished" (154). Thus mourning first produces an internal fullness, as the mourner becomes engorged with various memories and sentiments. But the mimetic work of internalizing the past (like the mimetic work of phonography discussed in the last chapter) ultimately leads to purgation and release. The mourner "works through" these more or less imaginary forms by testing them against the reality of loss, until the process is complete, the loss final, and he or she can find a new investment for the libido. The Carters' "lament" performs precisely this function, at first binding and then dissolving the pain of loss via abstract sound and style, correlating the heavy sadness of death with the unreal lightness of song. The indifference of the performance, then, is not simply the indifference of modern life, but also the release of the mourner, whose intense love for the mother, for the region at large, is transmuted into the pleasure of song.

But, as Freud knew, mourning always threatens to become melancholia, a seemingly endless "lament" in which the bereaved remains ambivalently caught in his or her loss. Freud here describes an unconscious impasse of love and hate (grief and guilt) that preserves not simply the lost person, but also the moment of death as something both desired and feared: "The self-torments of melancholiacs, which are without doubt pleasurable, signify . . . gratification of sadistic tendencies and of hate" (162–63). Arguably, in the Carters' song, the mother (and the South she represents) figures as a significant source of resentment; she is yet another corpse pleading for return, haunting the region's youth, threatening to drag them down into her own grave. Moreover, her death itself is a significant betrayal, a kind of domestic abandonment, one that forces the child singer to take her place in a lonely home. Thus, if the song refuses to let the mother go, it also seems committed to her continual death and the repetition of her burial, replaying it over and over again in more or less "pleasurable" ways. The odd liveliness of the performance could then be attributed to either the manic need to oust these guilty feelings or, simply, the affective charge occasioned by the fantasy of matricide. Either way, the song hauls around a corpse it can neither simply bury nor revive. It enacts an apparently endless cycle of disembodiment and reembodiment, repeating the mother's death (with each rendition) only to restore it again. Or, to take our cue from the title of the song, it breaks the circle over and over again in order to experience the pleasure of repairing it. But is this mourning, or melancholia? Does country music ever actually heal the region, or does it only reproduce regional trauma within a single sonic loop? In a way, it depends on the voice and the airy detachment of song itself.

Mourning often manifests itself in symbolic forms—church eulogies, commemorative toasts, poetic elegies, and stone monuments. As Tammy Clewell explains, each abstract sign "emerges as a consoling substitute for the lost one," establishing a comforting distance from the dead as it transcends death itself in the form of an immortal aesthetic artifact.[44] As Freud argued, however, the mourner originally uses the voice—a voice like Sara's, both withdrawn and exclamatory, listless and swollen—to manage loss. Freud reminds us that the work of mourning recalls the "oral or cannibalistic stage" of childhood development, a period when the infant's mouth becomes the center of a profound struggle for mastery (160). In a similar vein, the mouth of the mourner pours out "laments," constant "plaints," a "discharge" of words that suggests a purging of, if not a specific defense against, painful feelings (165). Perhaps, then, the Carter lament serves to spew out all the pained images of the past, the very tradition that nurtured it, that it had been forced to swallow, weaning the self off of its regional pap in order to sing of something new. In fact, Clewell argues that the loss of the mother establishes an empty space in the bereaved from which speech and language begin to emerge. More precisely, the loss of the maternal breast results in the opening of the mouth and thus allows a kind of "vocal self-fulfillment" that perhaps also signals a new maturity (50–51). Ultimately, then, as the mouth of mourner purges itself of the old, it also, in its very emptiness, announces the new. This voice is still perhaps torn between two moments, the past and the present, and between two kinds of speech, between the intensity of its sentiment and the blankness of its delivery, but its emergence as voice is always irrevocably severed from its source. Whatever therapy it might have provided for the Carters, this voice detaches itself from the scene of mourning to produce other kinds of emotions and new kinds of investments for the South, and indeed the nation, at large.

Here, we might look back to the traumatic repetitions of the blues, but country music confronts a crisis that is more explicitly generational and broadly collective. Moreover, unlike the blues, which negotiates the specific features and experiences of the Delta landscape, country music works through a kind of aesthetic detachment that is further removed from everyday life and its various patterns. The Carters' songs are never simply biographical—they don't sing about Neal's Store, Sara's affair, or broadcasting for XERA. They don't even play the kind of music that might be heard at a barn dance, a corn shucking, or a country fair. Their song is radically dis-oriented, dis-placed, and, in this aesthetic trick, pushes country music beyond the work of mourning. The empty yodel in "Sweet Fern"; the crowded, shifting vocal echoes of "Little Log Cabin by the Sea"; even the bratty razz of "Chewing Gum"—these soon become part of the listener's own repertoire; they are made available for everyday use, more or less surreptitious or simply alternative patterns of abstract stylization and affective exchange. Even in narrative-based songs such as "My Clinch Mountain Home" or "Can the Circle Be Unbroken," the emotional currents of sound and rhythm work over the discursive logic of the lyrics and thus over the symbolic structures of everyday life. But this influence is realized, paradoxically, only in detachment. No way but through—alienation upon alienation precedes the possibility of wholeness, and not the reverse. Each song lifts the South away from itself, rebraids its various strands, and hangs it high above the hearth, a new husky vortex within the old homestead.

In other words, each Carter song always entails a certain "Carterness," by which I mean a certain stylized way of being, a highly specific way of making and listening to music. Their blankness, their indifference, their very deathliness lifts each song out of the morass of southern history, propelling the listener beyond any immediate present, into what can only be called the stylish realm of "Carterdom." A musical space, sure, but no less compelling or transformative. So, despite all I've said about country music and its historical situation, the Carters' music—as an aesthetic abstraction of the ballad form—proves valuable precisely because it loosens us from any immediate historical consideration. As we'll find, it anticipates the pop of the later decades insofar as it gives us a style, a way of being that is firstly musical, and thus it lingers, suggesting, persuading, guiding in contexts that are neither musical nor unworldly (see chapter four). Again, though, the musical moment is split in two directions, pointing two ways. *In song*, the South is at once preserved and transformed, incorporated and dissolved; the region as a whole is *suspended*, at once mired and released from its own past, its own image. But, also, *as song*, as the dynamic act of songmaking, of singing, the South becomes its own activity, its own enactment, free to create itself again and again (we'll see Guthrie work this logic for political ends in the next chapter). Thus, for a moment at least, in the space and time of a song, the region slips free of its material restraints and, at once flexible and free, grows—for better or worse—into the living dream of itself.

So Let There Be Radio . . .

The popularity of country music was no doubt bound to the availability and widespread appeal of cheap country radio. The music's presumed directness and communal spirit seemed to thrive on the airwaves, as it was transmitted across hill and dale right into the home of the farmer, the widow, the shut-in, the tenement dweller, and the factory worker. Indeed, almost every tiny radio operation that cropped up in the 1920s tells the same story: smug station manager allows hillbilly on air to save money, phones start ringing, telegrams fly in, mail piles up—within days, the whole studio goes country, broadcasting nothing but fiddlers, banjoists, and straw-beaters. Given the evolution of southern life in the early twentieth century and the dire economic conditions of the Depression, radio seemed to draw a magic circle around the region. Suddenly, with a simple turn of the dial, the South was alive again, sounding once more in all its faded glory, uniting each listener in spirit, if not actual flesh. In order to see the unique appeal of early radio, though, we need to address two paradoxes concerning its reception. First, we need to understand why the region's traditionalism played so well through the snaky wires and alien tubes of a radio set. Secondly, we must consider what it must have felt like when the familiar experience of rural culture coincided with the potentially awkward intrusion of modern technology. Again, though, we'll find that the moment is split in two directions, pointing two ways. With radio, with the ritual transmission of southern song, the region is both preserved and imperiled, disembodied and reconstituted. It is at once lost and found in radio sound, transcending its material contingencies only to reemerge, changed, on the other side of its reception.

For here, we're talking about the emotional patterning of an entire region. Radio is indeed a unique medium of communication. Unlike bare speech or text, it more easily radiates, effloresces, casting its sentiments widely, simultaneously, over and across an otherwise fragmented region and thus immediately conjures up ideas of community and space. Unlike a journal or a newspaper, it does not easily lend itself to a seemingly rational exchange of ideas and arguments; rather, it emits—in real time—a series of shifting, overlapping currents of public sentiment, forging, in its own rushed and contradictory ways, a dynamic public of distracted listeners. As disembodied emotion, as feeling from afar, it does not so much inform its audience, but charges and shapes it, amplifying or dampening its affective potentials, re-animating each body as it goes about its common chores and rituals within an abstract whole. As Michele Hilmes explains in *Radio Voices: American Broadcasting, 1922–1952*, for many listeners, early radio represented a unique form of cultural experience and exchange.[45] The device offered citizens a new way to imagine and project themselves as part of a greater social order, one reminiscent of Benedict Anderson's theory of "imagined community": "And in such an 'imagined relationship,'" Hilmes states, "based on nothing so tangible as concrete geographic boundaries, common ethnic heritage, or linguistic homogenization, but instead on assumptions, images, feelings, consciousness, it is not only the technical means of communication, but the central narratives, representations, and 'memories'—and strategic forgetfulness—that they circulate that tie the nation together" (12).

In this, no doubt, the evolution of radio in the modern era gave rise to heated, and often conflicted, feelings about its potential uses and values. For the modernist intelligentsia—F. T. Marinetti, Bertolt Brecht, Ezra Pound—it signaled an alternative mode of cultural transmission, a more direct and efficient means of spreading cultural values and forging deep communal bonds. Paradoxically, the new technology suggested a healthy return to primitive culture, one in which the radio tower would serve as tribal drum, sending out a subliminal or infra-human signal to the otherwise isolated inhabitants of the modern jungle. As Aaron Jaffe explains, the moderns' radiophilia was informed by a spiritual vision of history in which "radiant cosmos becomes cosmopolitan radiation," as if radio could restore an increasingly fragmented culture, rounding the splintered world once more and making it fit for human habitation.[46] At the same time, though, many early commentators believed that radio technology signaled potential danger, if not complete catastrophe, some final turning from everything that grounded human consciousness and experience. The device implied a radical dematerialization, one that began with the loss of traditional coordinates of space and time and led to a complete dissolution of personal and regional identity. As Jeffrey Sconce explains, the radio signal could seem both fearfully close and painfully distant. Some experienced it as an invasion of personal life, while others felt that it generated a sense of foreignness and alienation. Thus, Sconce writes, the "tribal magic" of the medium, its potential to effect cultural revival as a "form of electronically disembodied consciousness," appeared in a darker light, as a one-way means of cultural degeneration, or, worse, a form of manipulation and mind-control.[47]

Given these general associations with loss, death, and catastrophe, it is perhaps not surprising that early radio programmers were able to tap and exploit the melancholic spirit of the New South. While the device itself seemed to signal regional demise, its most popular programming worked to revive immaterial, and thus seemingly immortal, forms of cultural authority. According to Timothy Campbell, the transit of the radio voice, as it disappears into the ether only to reappear again in the home, seems to enact a ritual of death and transubstantiation. As in the songs of the Carters, loss precedes wholeness and signals, for better or worse, the restoration of a more transcendent authority. Campbell writes, "the wireless transmission is invested with an authority precisely because of its wireless (and not wired) materiality" (19); spirits, not bodies, speak through the radio—their voices are "distilled," "supreme"—attaining presence and power in their very disembodiment (7–9). In the South, of course, almost all the spirits roaming the airwaves were domestic. Listeners were by turns haunted and relieved by the transmission of Mother's tender songs or Father's authoritative voice, which now seemed to be echoing eternally in the barn, the parlor, or right next to the bed. But while, for some, the broken circle of regional identity was made whole again with a simple turn of the dial, for others that dial became the means of actually expanding the magic sphere of regional identity and pushing against the traditional borders of southern life and culture.

Early on, there seemed to be no great anxiety about rural radio. The format was mostly practical, commercial, and quickly institutionalized. Listeners were busy and distracted, and programs offered either some genuinely useful aid (weather reports, stock quotes, farming advice) or easy cultural fare (religious sermons, comedy skits, and sporting events). Most listeners were comfortable with the radio performing the kinds of cultural work that were previously bound to local folkways.[48] As Bill Randle argues, "Rather than fragmenting and breaking up the established local and regional folk traditions in America, the mechanical and techno- logical innovations of the 1920's presented those minoritarian cultures an opportunity for revival and reinterpretation."[49] In fact, with the addition of local cultural broadcasting—mostly songs and skits—the homemade radio ousted Mother as the singing preserver of domestic life and reorganized family, furniture, and routine around its miniature dials.[50] At bedside, in the parlor, or even the barn, the device amplified and augmented the most basic sentiments of home, a fact charmingly expressed by Carmen Malone in an ode published in a 1938 issue of *Rural Radio*:

> When dusk has fallen, daily tasks
>   Have passed away with setting sun,
> We sit around and sew and read—
>   The children get their home-work done—
> While music floats about the room
>   And soothes our weary bodies, minds,
> While friendly voices come to us
>   And serve us as a tie that binds
> Our family in happiness.
>   The sweetest hour that I know
> Is that when we together sit
>   And listen to our radio.[51]

Listeners also celebrated radio broadcasting as a source of neighborly spirit. As one fan recalled, "In the summertime, Daddy'd open up that window there and turn that horn around to the outside and the whole neighborhood would come around."[52] Another explains, "The select few who had these first radio receiver sets entertained the whole town. . . . We would gather there in the evening to listen to all the music and talk beamed to us from Pittsburgh. . . . It was entertaining, inspiring, and full of the

IMAGE 2 The milkman tunes in at milking time, circa 1923. Courtesy of the Library of Congress, Prints and Photographs Division.

friendliness of our town of Wagener, South Carolina" (Barfield 4). Thus, despite its newness, radio—in its programming and technology—provided a significant sense of regional stability and renewal. Many households left it on all day long, linked up with their neighbors through the grapevine system of connected receivers. Travelers, too, could find a steady home in the clear-channel signals that cut across towns and states. In this way, the region quickly re-bound itself in sound, stuffed station mailbags attesting to listeners' deeply felt connections to the radio community

As mentioned, station managers everywhere realized the revenue potential of these new bonds and quickly set to work rusticating their broadcasts, corralling local talent and dressing it up in suspenders, patches, and clothespins. The most successful broadcasts were geared toward family, emphasizing stable community relations, old-time fun and games, and age-old virtues. At barn dances, specifically—Nashville's WSM Barn Dance, the WWVA Jamboree in Wheeling, the Renfro Valley Barn Dance in Kentucky, the WKH Louisiana Hayride, the Tennessee Jamboree, and the Ozark Jubilee—the evening's entertainment was served up cozy and sweet. Listeners were "welcomed" to the program by a friendly, honey-toned voice, while cast and crewmembers were introduced as longtime friends and relations. Throughout the show, stars casually dropped in to say howdy and play the latest hits, while listeners were encouraged to sing and dance along, to join the frolic by staying tuned, writing letters, and holding parties. As suggested by the promotional department of Sears' Chicago station, the Barn Dance programs were meant to be natural, authentic, and collective: "WLS is very human and friendly, and is at its best when it expresses personality in the most natural way. You hear a friendly voice in your home that comes to you out of the air. When the song is ending you wish to know the singer because you warm in response to the personality that beckons to you in friendship so naturally. It is not the act of the play actor so culturally correct, but the heart and emotion of the unseen singer that gives out to you in the song."[53]

And yet, apart from the comforts occasioned by the Barn Dance, many rural listeners turned to the radio as a distinctly modern device, and many tuned in for the new worlds it could reveal rather than the old one it might affirm. As one listener from Nebraska suggested, the radio provided an antidote to cultural isolation and boredom:

> As the result of the dearth of "culture," my father was always seeking out some "touch of civilization." Somehow he must have read about a thing called a "Radio." I'm not sure where he got the idea to have one made, but a young fellow put together a crystal set and put it in our din-ing room. . . . My father would sit hunched over the set, straining to hear something—anything. (Barfield 5)

Similarly, a listener from Mississippi explained that radio provided his family with a significant sense of worldliness and cultural otherness:

> The sounds which came from it were truly magic to a family in Greenville, Mississippi, who thought that Memphis was somewhere on the other side of the globe. . . . I can't recall what was being broadcast, which is unimportant. The all-engrossing attention was to the fact that we could pull unseen voices out of the air and into the living room from all over the world, or at least as far as the world extended to St. Louis and Detroit. (Barfield 7)

For many listeners, radio came to represent universal culture and a more expansive present. With a simple flick of the dial, the mind of the rural listener was freed from habit to travel the airwaves, sampling cultures and voices from abroad in a *detached* way. According to Bob Coltman, "Radio's gift to Depression listeners of distant visions of culture and confidence proved especially fascinating to country people, changing their lives, their understanding of the world, their tastes, among other things, in music." In other words, as we saw with records in the last chapter, the radio, as commodity form, initiated a dynamic process of cultural exchange and sensual discovery, doubling the region in relation to other times and places. "People," Coltman writes, "were forced to look outward, to develop double vision that blended their prized rural understanding with growing awareness of the cosmopolitanism that poured in daily over the radio. . . . They began to want something different of their own to listen to."[54]

At the same time, the promotional material for country radio (published alongside promotional material for bands like the Delmores and the Vagabonds) emphasized technology as much as tradition. Souvenir programs took listeners into the studio, providing pictures of stars, directors, technicians, and sound engineers. Spreads and pictorials featured the "completely modern studio" and provided illustrations of control panels, amplification tubes, and high-voltage rectifiers.[55] Throughout, the rural listener was depicted as modern, progressive, and techno-literate. A May 1938 issue of *Rural Radio*, for example, printed the results of a write-in contest on "What Radio Means to My Family." The winning entries all linked rural know-how with urban consciousness and repeatedly affirmed the curiosity and expansiveness of the country mind. For example,

> We are busy farm folk. You might think us uninformed . . . isolated . . . but we're not! Radio makes the whole world our neighbor—brings us "company" every day! Also, it is a teacher, counselor, forum. Entertainment, information, inspiration, enlightened understanding, broadened minds, enriched lives! That's what RADIO means to us!
>
> Mrs. H.H. Golay R.R. 2, Hopkinsville, Ky.

> RADIO in our home assumes a MULTIPLE PERSONALITY. As-
> Physician, it brings us health hints;
> Chef, it teaches modern cooking methods;
> Humorist, it inspires good cheer with its comedy;
> Mathematician, it adds happiness, subtracts gloom;
> Magician, it gives us the STARS in our living room,
> with the world's finest entertainment.
>
> W. H. Fletcher, Carrollton, Georgia

Radio gives us an up-front view in the arena of world events, a desk in
the library of world knowledge and a box seat in the world's theater of
finest entertainment – right in the comfort of our living room at a cost
of but a few cents daily.

Frank G. Davis, P.O. Box 911, Springfield, OH[56]

Considering the relative newness of regional radio, it is interesting here
how quickly southern values become aligned with modern values. Hard
work, hardiness, authenticity, self-reliance—radio seems to cultivate these
virtues and thus, as universal medium, brings together, in its single transmission, the otherwise estranged halves of the nation.

Most astoundingly, many listeners tried to link up the otherworld-
liness of the radio signal with the physical realities of their own lives.
Partially out of anxiety, but also out of hope, pride, and even playfulness,
they sought to re-materialize the de-materialized sound on the air and
adopted strategies to reconcile the broadcasted *voice* of the South with
actual *life* in the South. They avidly collected pictures of stars, announc-
ers, and station personnel. They pored over "Rural Radio Roundup," a
monthly photo spread, to find images of performers as "they look when
they broadcast." They flipped through "Family Gossip" to gather physical
information about their idols; they were reassured that, yes, the Preston
Trio of WFAA "wear ten-gallon hats, fancy cowboy shirts and black ties,"
and "Texas Daisy is 23 and single, and is very pretty, having long black curls
and brown eyes."[57] Some fans attached pictures of their favorite stars to
the radio when their voices came on the air. Some would doctor pictures
to suit their own visions of how the stars should look, adding cigarettes,
lovers, and clothing to otherwise disappointing images.[58] In all this, the
logic of mimetic culture, as defined in chapter one, takes another leap
forward, as fans reorganized their listening environment according to
rituals of copy and contact. Many tried to attain or touch the objects
associated with radio broadcasts and their performers. Others sought
connection with the airwaves by collecting curios, clothing, autographs,
and handbills, or, conversely, by sending out their personal objects to the
stars, accompanied with requests to hold them while they sang on air.[59]
The most eager listeners would restage radio barn dances at home as they
occurred on the radio, occasionally entreating performers to come to town
themselves and sing the songs exactly as they were sung in the studio.[60]
Overwhelmingly, these gestures suggest a need to reconcile the alluring
but immaterial sounds of the air with the tangible facts of everyday life. If
the radio projected an idealized image of southern culture, listeners sought

to ground or embody that promise in reality and perhaps make good on the device's aura by remaking the world in its form. Here, again, we find that *discontinuity* becomes a significant form of *continuity*, part of daily ritual and a more dynamic negotiation of personal and public life.

With this in mind, let's turn to John Lair, one of the era's most important radio innovators, to show how he interpreted this fatal encounter with radio-modernity and used the barn-dance format itself to modernize one very small corner of the South. John Lair's passion was mountain music, and he worked tirelessly for its preservation. He performed mountain music, promoted mountain music, staged mountain-music concerts, and published mountain-music guidebooks; he even constructed a mountain-music library and then finally built a real mountain-music town in the real mountains of eastern Kentucky. To be truthful, though, Lair sought to preserve his *entire* past, to bring everything he knew and loved as a country boy into the present. As a youth, growing up on his grandfather's Renfro farm, Lair developed a deep love of southern history and became, in time, a Civil War buff, American frontier historian, and Abe Lincoln fanatic. When he was drafted for World War I, he served willingly and ably, even finding time to write a book of nostalgic Americana titled *Lest We Forget*. But upon his return to the peaceful valley, Lair was disturbed by the number of automobiles and electric lights in the region, and he quickly realized that everything he had trusted as a youth was starting to fade.[61] In fact, even as Lair began to launch plans for restoring the valley, modernity seemed to sweep him out of the region all over again. A series of work opportunities—as teacher, advertiser, claims adjustor—took him to Louisville, Boston, and then Chicago. His nostalgic dream, however, found new life in the middle of the city, where he discovered the value of radio. Paradoxically, his furthest point from home contained some stranger promise of return, and the radio heralded the future as well as the past.

Lair easily ingratiated himself at WLS in Chicago and soon found himself serving the station in a promotional capacity. In 1930, his attention was divided among recruiting performers, writing advertising copy, composing songs for the barn-dance program, and playing the jug in his own stringband, the Cumberland Ridge Runners. Soon he developed his own show, the *Alladin Barndance Frolic*, and became famous for a song that neatly summarized his nostalgic vision, "Take Me Back to Renfro Valley." But Lair was clearly uncomfortable in the city, and he objected to the canned nature of WLS's programming. As he later described his misgivings in *Renfro Valley Keepsake*, "he wasn't satisfied. The barn dance type of program which he had helped to develop didn't ring true, somehow. It didn't remind him enough of the real things he had known in the good old days in Renfro Valley. He felt that what radio needed was a little realism—a little less 'showmanship' and a little more heart-felt sincerity."[62] Specifically, Lair dreamed of a program that resembled the "community gatherings" of his youth, weekly events during which neighbors would meet to share news, plan for the future, and celebrate their cultural traditions (*Then and Now* 18). He did not reject radio, but sought to ground its power within the heart of the country. He planned to relocate his operation to Renfro and then broadcast real events across the region—a quilting bee, a shucking party, a fish fry; hopefully, by bringing sonic form together with material reality, he could remake Renfro Valley into a truly vital community, rather than a merely sentimental one.

So Lair set out to build not just a barn, but a *radio barn*, from which he would broadcast not just a barn dance, but a *radio barn dance*. After a brief detour at Cincinnati's WLW, he and his loyal coterie of musicians moved on to Renfro and took to the airwaves on November 4, 1939. Lair introduced the first show by emphasizing both its novelty and its roots: "This is the Renfro Valley Barn Dance, coming to you direct from a big barn in Renfro Valley, Kentucky—the first and only barn dance on the air presented by the actual residents of an actual community."[63] As the show grew more popular, Lair continued to reassure listeners that transmission and event would serve each other, and the show would proceed "with the resolve to actually do what we told folks on the air we were doing" (*Then and Now* 43). Yet the program's effect and significance changed over time. The very success of the Renfro show transformed the reality of Renfro itself, the copy slowly reshaping its original. As the radio tower emitted its genial message of community, the town itself began to grow beneath it, in both size and wealth. Over time, the small-town studio became a town-size studio, with its own gristmill, music library, museum, restaurant, candy shop, gift shop, U.S. post office, and walnut-cracking plant. The original site was meant to be an inspirational setting for the broadcast, but it had now become its own stunning effect. The airy transmission had generated a powerful feedback loop; sound and ground (copy and contact) amplified each other, pushing the entire culture in a new, but still recognizable, direction. Lair, in turn, had realized his original dream of moving backward by moving forward, and yet he also came to accept its unexpected twists and turns. "Always we have kept one thought before us," he remarked, "the ambition to retain for coming generations a picture of America in the making. Our highest aim has been to keep alive the friendly, neighborly spirit of the plain folks who made America what it is today, and whose children will make it what it is tomorrow" (*Then and Now* 44).

In the end, Lair's interests in live broadcasting and "mountain music" mirror each other. Both forms exploit the detachment of sound in order to generate emotional patterns and thereby negotiate cultural continuity alongside change. In a 1930 interview, for example, Lair explicitly connects his love of country song with his interest in sonic transmission, with the detached ways in which songs cross time and space: "[M]ost of the mountain ballads can be traced back to some of the old English and Scotch ballads that the settlers brought with them hundreds of years ago. . . . All the old songs were passed from person to person, from memory."[64] A similar logic lies behind Lair's embrace of radio and the modernity it represented. Lair often defended radio's imposing otherness, its radical detachment, as a creative and often progressive source of regional identity. For example, in a testimony before the Federal Communications Commission, he expressed support for the expansive clear-channel system on the basis of its necessity on a regional level:

> There has been very little change in the mountain homes in the last 10 years. In the more remote sections we can say that what change there has been is due to radio. Radio being their only means of communication with the outside, they are more dependent upon it than any other people in America and are more the result of what is given to them by radio. Being inarticulate they themselves cannot ask for what they need—it is up to radio to take to them what they should have—that is what the Renfro Valley Program over WHAS does and I find them very grateful.[65]

Lair's comments here suggest that rural culture persists precisely in its discontinuity; it sustains itself through and within the changes brought about by technology and other forms of modernization. He privileges radio insofar as it works both to maintain and transform the affective dimensions of rural life. As he defines the regional audience, he also imagines an "outside" that implies neither a celebration nor a critique of its existence. Rather, this "outside" is the detachment of modernity itself, which, in the form of radio and radio song, does not oppose or threaten rural life, but gives it a future. In this, he asks listeners to abandon the logic of regional trauma, to think of detachment not as a kind of death or even a new birth, but as the very means of continuity, the possibility of stability amid change.

* * *

I must admit that while I reject the romance of country music authenticity, I am quite smitten by the kinds of public exchange that country music culture once seemed to sustain. I am particularly invested in the way that country music, as a form of rural modernity, suggests an alternative to the "public sphere" maintained by the urban middle classes of the same era. The work of Jürgen Habermas, for example, defines the modern public sphere as both a real space, or series of spaces, and the seemingly open-ended process of debate and discussion that occurs within them.[66] Habermas emphasizes the significant role that print played in the formation of this sphere, for he claims that the formal anonymity of print, bound up with the anonymity of public life in general, allowed seemingly rational citizens to state concerns and criticisms without fear of infamy or punishment. While I appreciate the liberal ideals that lie behind this version of public life, I am, like many contemporary scholars, suspicious of its economic exclusivity (the very costs of anonymity) and its blindness to the ways that other publics might wrestle with similar issues. For me, country music mediates the experiences of a significantly different class, a significantly poorer and less literate class, and it works via the looser affective currents of song rather than the presumably rational qualities of speech and text. Moreover, its chosen medium—radio—implies not the anonymity of abstract thought or the presumed universality of the Western mind, but the generality of a voice that is still embodied—charged with feelings, traces of regional identity, and material events.

Michael Warner alludes to something like this other public sphere in an essay titled "The Mass Public and the Mass Subject."[67] For Warner, the seeming universality of the bourgeois public sphere was always highly particularized, sustained by the privilege of a specific kind of body. He writes, "The subject who could master this [abstract] rhetoric in the bourgeois public sphere was implicitly—even explicitly—white, male, literate, and propertied. These traits could go unmarked, though, even grammatically, while the features of other bodies could only be acknowledged in discourse as the humiliating positivity of the particular" (239). Looking elsewhere, Warner distinguishes this exclusive public sphere from what he calls the "mass-cultural public sphere," an equally modern formation founded upon the efforts of minoritized bodies to enter public life. Warner dwells on the mass-cultural spheres of consumer culture and visual culture, pointing out how minority populations use these forms to negotiate their embodiment alongside promises of disembodiment (think corporate logos, star culture, and graffiti). Warner further suggests that the mass-cultural public sphere finds expression in reports and images of public disaster. He argues that the spectacle of mass death (think plane crashes and earthquakes) affirms both the particularity of the mass body and its nearly spiritual transubstantiation into a public; witnessing its own destruction, the mass public affirms its own materiality as well as its abstract significance (250).

This seems to be the body—the public body—that is destroyed and redeemed over and over again in country song. The death of the mother, the home, the South, the old faithful dog—each disaster allows the double pleasure of particularity and transcendence, regional embodiment and release. And, in the end, radio carried this regional rite to a whole other level, enacting it via the very technology of transmission and thus formally extending it as a historical principle. Overall, though, this double gesture—in its endless overturning—brings rural modernity closer to the critical function of the bourgeois public sphere; like the boy who murdered his way from home or the little girl frozen at the doorstep of the South, this culture upends its own romances as it moves persistently—via its own cultural forms—toward some vision of future wholeness. Again, though, I insist that this dynamic is mediated, most powerfully, by sound. Warner focuses on visual culture; he considers the mass-produced images and icons that mark the public life of minority populations and makes a compelling case for how these representations shape an alternative public sphere. For me, though, country song, like country radio, exposes the potential of a specifically sonic public sphere, one in which the struggling body finds not simply expression, but a decisively affective movement between places, times, and identities. Thus, whether in Carson's appropriation of consumer technology, the Carters' massive reorganization of the ballad tradition, or the radiophonic development of Renfro Valley, the modern South appears less as a static set of marginal representations than a dynamic series of overlapping modalities, at once affective, productive, and open-ended.

So, again, how far back do you want to go for a little bit of country? How far back for some real pain? And what drives us on this wayward course? What myth of heroic identity burdens the heart and causes it to lament the past? Perhaps, though, we need consider not just the causes, but the effects—the uses—of emotion. Perhaps the sentiments of country song not only hold us back, but can also push us forward, carry us to other times and places. If the country music star always destroys the thing he loves, he is also creating another possible future for himself. While he sings of the past, as the past, as an impossible ideal, his song detaches itself from home and moves forward in time, beyond its own sad start. As in Carson's original hit—perhaps the first and last country song—there's no going back, and no easy way forward; with obstacles at every turn, sometimes all a feller can do is sing:

> Now the footpath is growed up that led us 'round the hill,
> The fences all gone to decay.
> The pond it's done dried up where we once did go to mill,
> Things have turned its course another way.

Yes, times have changed—"things have turned its course another way." But those country paths were carved by people looking for something better. And this song, too, carries us away, elsewhere, toward something better down the lane. In the end, such music isn't just about going back, but also about moving ahead, and its pain is not just the pain of leaving, but also the pain of arriving.

CHAPTER THREE

A Rambling Funny Streak

*Woody Guthrie, Revolutionary Folk Song,
and the Migrant Art of the Refrain*

Man Fights Nazis, Fuels Car with Song

The nearly miraculous climax of Woody Guthrie's *Bound for Glory* takes place at the Ace High bar, where a down-and-out Guthrie and his partner Cisco Houston are playing for chips in front of a "pretty low" crowd. After surveying the rather grim mood at the bar, the two musicians launch into a set of comic verses about the brave boys fighting the good fight abroad:

> Lord, it's stormy on that ocean
> Windy on th' deep blue sea
> I'm gonna bake them Nazis a chicken
> Loaded full of TNT![1]

The music stirs the weary listeners to laughter and then clapping, singing, and dancing. As Woody and Cisco toss off their giddy rhymes, the act quickly dissolves the boundaries between performer and audience, singer and soldier, art and war: "Everyone was wheeling and whirling, waving their hands and shuffling along like a gang of circus clowns dancing in the sawdust" (264). This frolic is nothing, though, compared to the scene that soon ensues outside the club. The Ace High performance is interrupted first by an angry voice and then by the sound of breaking glass. Woody and the patrons rush outside to find a mob bent on lynching a Japanese family that runs a nearby saloon. Sides are quickly drawn in the street, and Guthrie's happy song is lost in a sonic welter of threats and curses.

A shard of glass cuts one of Cisco's strings, and then a thug threatens to bust Woody's music box over his head. Wasting no time at all, though, Woody aims his guitar at these homegrown fascists and urges his pals to sing along:

> We will fight together
> We shall not be moved
> Just like a tree
> That's planted by the water
> We
> Shall not
> Be moved.

And it works. The thugs' angry curse words crash into a sound "as loud and as clear and as rough-sounding as a war factory hammering." The song, despite its airiness, proves to be a real material force, strenuous, moving, effective—the basis of significant power and change. It hits the mob of rioters "like a cyclone tearing into a haystack." The fascists stop and stagger backward, spitting out teeth and raking their eyes—"I thought the battle was on," Woody claims, "but nobody touched each other" (268).

Guthrie's *Seeds of Man: An Experience Lived and Dreamed* provides a more humdrum, but no less astounding, example of song's motivational power.[2] Here, a younger Woody is driving his family down to New Mexico, chasing a vague dream of finding his grandfather's hidden goldmine. Riding the hills out of Texas, the Model T—already burdened with travelers, luggage, and moonshine—runs into a blizzard and, as the wind turns against its front end, loses the necessary momentum to gain the next incline. Quickly, Guthrie and his kin turn to the only resource they have left—song—and launch into a little ditty about the car and its uphill battle. First, the father sings defiantly into the wind. Then, accompanied by guitar and mandolin, all the travelers join in:

> You better run, little T truck,
> You better run, little T truck,
> You better run, little T truck,
> Oh, wello, you better run. (110)

Woody explains to his girlfriend that their song is a "worksong holler" and it's "a-keepin' this old engine flippin' over right now." In fact, he says, singing is no different than pushing your foot down on the gas: "Yer song's a-suckin' in around through that there motor. . . . I can hear it a-siftin' an' a-poundin' down around in them there manifolds, an' all down around amongst them there cylinder walls, an' a-soakin' inta ever' one o' them there pistons, an a-blowin' fiery blazes in around them there dern-gone old spark plugs" (112). Again, miraculously, the song *works*; the car slowly gains momentum up the hill, defying all the laws of physics. Yet, in a sly twist, Woody looks back to find that his companions, inspired by the song, have left the car to push it up the hill. The joke's on Woody, of course, but he laughs gleefully, marveling at the idea that song, singer, and machine can form a single productive assemblage. Later, when the group is again coasting along, and most of the passengers have fallen asleep, Woody muses, "Our dreams are pushing the wheels along. Our hopes are shoving the bearings and sparkplugs along. Our songs have already pushed our hopes along against the weight and the whipping of the high wind" (119–20).

If Woody Guthrie was a socialist, it was because he lived by the labor of his song and he believed music was a natural resource akin to coal, steam, or oil. He confronted the events of his troubled era—from the Dust Bowl to the Depression to World War II and the Cold War—with a belief in song as a public utility, a common property, and thus as the basis of an alternative economy. Today, perhaps, we tend to resist the idea that popular music has much practical significance, let alone any direct political power.[3] Simon Frith provides one of the most generous statements on the issue, but even his careful argument limits song's potential effects: all we can expect from any particular pop song is that it may "provide people with the means to articulate the feelings associated" with their political positions. For Frith, songs are belated when it comes to values and actions; as performance, as rhetoric, they do not so much convince, but show listeners how to inhabit established choices: "The most significant effect of a pop song is not on how people vote or organize, but on how they speak."[4] But Guthrie had something more radical in mind, a kind of song that—as fuel, as labor power—moved beyond performance to something like economics and then politics. Here, we might recall that the Latin etymology of "emotion" is "ex" (outer)+ "movere" (moving, stirring). For Guthrie, song is emotive and thus always also "motive" or "motivated"—part of a much larger set of dynamic forces and forms called the "nation," capable of setting citizens, machinery, and natural resources into productive relation. It is not just a taking stock, but an actual stock, a reserve of energy or power that can be harnessed and wielded toward other ends—like building dams, fighting Nazis, or driving cars.

So we need to work through Guthrie's peculiar materialism before we can appreciate his politics. At the start of *Bound for Glory*, Guthrie defends his music before a group of laborers by showing them the blisters on his hands (20). Later, when a young girl teasingly asks him why he only sings about work, he responds, "Time ya sing six hours or eight or ten, right straight hand runnin', in some of these saloons or places, like I do, you'll say music runs inta work" (273). At his most blunt, in an article titled "America Singing," Guthrie proclaims, "Singing and working and fighting are so close together you can't hardly tell where one quits and the other one begins." He then launches into an explanation of the famous slogan on his guitar:

> I got picked up by a man in Washington not so long ago and he asked me: "What's that there label say there on yer music box?"
>
> "This machine kills fascists," I told him.
>
> "How'dya figger that?" he asked me.
>
> And I says: "Well, you see this guitar makes me feel like beatin' the Fascists, an' then that makes me sing how much I hate 'em."
>
> "Yeh?"
>
> "Then, well, I sing fer a bunch of folks, folks workin', fer soldiers, sailors, seamen, that sort of makes all of us whip it up a little—then we all get ta feelin' a little more like beatin' 'em, an' 'course if a Fascist then just sort of happens to git in our way, he just naturally comes out loser, that's all."
>
> And the man stopped and let me out. He drove through a gate into a big orchard, yelling back, "Kinda like my plow, by God!"[5]

Here, the emphasis is not on "fascists," but on the "machine," not on the political struggle, but on the economic one. For Guthrie, all song is political because it is always already a kind of labor—a specifically industrial labor. His guitar is a "factory machine," just as the human being is a "hoping machine" (*Pastures* 60, 247). Every song is less an expression of identity or even a statement of fact than an affective motor in its own right, harnessing and augmenting the energy of the nation for progressive ends.

But Guthrie's chosen form of "work" complicates his materialism in interesting ways. If anything, his economy is founded on song's immateriality, its undeniable airiness. It was precisely the emptiness of his "music box" that made it such a radical alternative, as if the difference between the immateriality of song and the materiality of its effect defied the market's own logic of value and expenditure. For Guthrie, song was freely accessible, infinitely renewable, and cheaply reproducible; its airy forms remained undiminished in exchange and only grew more valuable in their use or consumption. The "refrain" itself was a nearly worthless scrap of popular discourse but capable—in its easy circulation—of producing "something out of nothing," and thus—like wind or waterpower—opposed the economics of scarcity with something like the plentitude of nature itself (*Bound* 158). This logic shaped not only Guthrie's carefree, rambling compositional style, but also his commitment to quasi-socialist singing unions such as the Almanac Singers and, later, People's Songs. Guthrie and his singing comrades worked as hired hands, cheaply producing songs piecemeal, assembling standardized verses on the spot, creating affectively charged motors of progressive sentiment according to the needs of each audience. No doubt, Marx would have approved. The group's methods were rigorously industrial as well as defiantly anti-industrial: collectively, they aimed "to organize all of us that write songs for the labor movement, to put all our collections of songs into one big cabinet, and to send to any union local any kind of song, any kind of a historical material about anything they might need, and to shoot it out poco pronto, in today and out tonight" (*Pastures* 157).

Guthrie was clearly not alone in his efforts to construct a socially viable art, and his music of the 1930s and 1940s reflects a much larger transformation in both the understanding and production of popular culture. Together, the artists and writers of the Depression era can be characterized not just by their leftist leanings, but also by their "cultural turn," by their self-conscious efforts to rethink artistic labor in relation to the forms and symbols of everyday life. Responding to Roosevelt's New Deal administration, as well as the Communist Party's own shift to a Popular Front, they tended to reject the elitism of the modernist avant-garde in order to reshape public life from the ground up, using public art to counter—on a mass scale—the increasing threats of capitalism, on the one hand, and fascism, on the other. As Michael Denning clarifies, Guthrie worked alongside artists such as Dorothea Lange, James Agee, and Ben Shahn as part of a loosely defined "proletarian avant-garde" waging war on a specifically "cultural front." His song was part of a much wider, ad hoc effort—including plays, radio broadcasts, murals, dance, and photography—to revolutionize "labor" as well as the "laboring of culture."[6] To be sure, Guthrie was no simple folk artist or even a dependable propagandist, for he worked a much more general cultural terrain—setting his sights on the culture industry itself—for the larger national good. As he wrote in the *Sunday Worker*, "When the workers own and control their own movie sets and studios, own their theatres and radios, then we can have real facts of life played and acted for us by artists even more capable, more social conscious than the ones we got now" (*Pastures* 189).

And yet, of all the musicians discussed in this book, Guthrie—the self-proclaimed "dustiest of the dust bowlers"—also identified with the high-modernist intelligentsia. For all his time spent riding the rails and working the jungle camps, his rambling also brought him into contact with the likes of Nicholas Ray, Martha Graham, Thomas Mann, Charles Olson, Bertolt Brecht, and Jackson Pollock, and, like many of these artists, his proposed renovation of the *world* began with a revolution of the *word*, a focus on aesthetic forms over explicit political contents. Indeed, while Guthrie worked with the basic DNA of the folk song and drew from the efforts of earlier "protest" singers, he pushed his own music toward new structuralist ends.[7] By focusing on the form of the folk song, particularly the unique properties of the refrain, rather than its presumed authenticity or expressiveness, he set the terms—common, migrant, progressive—for a counterculture that eluded typical political categories. In other words, Guthrie's complex cultural allegiances pushed his music beyond the cultural divide entirely. As I hope to show here, his cheap, derelict song represents not just a new vernacular modernism, but also the first *pop counterculture*—one that, in its rambling approach to art, proved more supple and more productive than either the political counterculture of the left or the idealized aesthetic counterculture of high modernism.

We cannot underestimate Guthrie's role in pushing the regional traditions of his past toward the kinds of rock and pop music that emerged in the 1950s and 1960s. As both composer and performer, Guthrie used song to radicalize popular culture and its political dimensions on a level that exceeded all local ties. As Peter La Chapelle explains, the singer mobilized a whole range of genres—not just folk songs, but also printed broadsides, Tin Pan Alley tunes, minstrelsy songs, cowboy songs, and commercial hillbilly music—to advance a "liberal-populist political commentary and even radical social critique."[8] In what follows, though, I'll show that Guthrie's unique blend of popular song and populist politics was shaped in and through his sense of the national economy and its relation to the growing migrant classes of the 1930s. If his craft represents the loosening up of regional traditions and the burgeoning of a new national pop culture, such was accomplished through a sense of song as a specifically *migrant* form fit for a *migrant* people. La Chapelle continues, "Guthrie in his songs and writings began to associate refugee Dust Bowlers with larger, more politically focused struggles with fascism . . . . By outlining how others shared migrants' status as refugees and informing readers and listeners about these other conflicts, Guthrie worked to mobilize migrants and other listeners as supporters of the antifascist left" (65). Again, my commitments are more formal. As I'd like to emphasize, sonic deterritorialization everywhere overlaps with and exceeds regional deterritorialization. If, with Guthrie, hillbilly culture gives way to popular culture, and regionalism makes way for nationalism, this slippage is everywhere driven by changes at the level of form itself, within the airy space and time of song and through the migrant art of the refrain.

The first section of this chapter, then, explores Guthrie's youthful encounters with modernity, specifically the boom-and-bust cycles of the 1920s, and considers his adolescent embrace of *dereliction*—poverty, rambling, and idleness—as a dynamic alternative to the static forms of identity and property enforced by the modern economy. The second section outlines Guthrie's work as a member of the "proletarian avant-garde" of the 1930s and tracks his efforts to remake folk song as a progressively motivated art, one that foregrounds the migrant form of the "refrain" in order to set the political machinery of the nation into motion. The next section tracks Guthrie's postwar songwriting as it evolves into a fully *comic* mode, one that laughs away the symbolic limits of modern life in order to mobilize other, more radical kinds of values and definitions. In the final section, I'll outline the vision of deterritorialized citizenship and nationhood that is suggested by Guthrie's art, specifically as it prepares the way for pop culture more generally. As we'll find, Guthrie was a committed activist, but only ever loosely affiliated with any specific party, region, or doctrine. His greatest contribution to the cause was the quasi-Marxist dialectic he performed within song itself, using his voice to mobilize and dissolve the categories of modern life and thus establish a suppler, more common mode of revolutionary praxis—a pop politics for the people. By and large, Guthrie's migrant song pushes the processes of regional deterritorialization at work in country and blues to its logical breaking point. His "rambling funny streak" allowed him to move beyond the limited stances and attitudes of his age and establish the possibility of counterculture on a national level, one that was by turns "left wing, right wing, chicken wing," always rambling, always revisable, giddy, ecstatic, and democratic.

Tornado Sweeps through Town, Freeing Millions

Guthrie's music—laughing, rollicking, persistent, and proud—owes everything to the blustery forces of modernity that blew across the southwestern plains during his youth. Its migrant spirit emerged out of the boom-and-bust cycles of the 1920s and reflects, in its own rambling way, the violently whipsawing economy that created and destroyed the little towns and cities of Arkansas, Oklahoma, Texas, and New Mexico. *Bound for Glory*, Guthrie's semi-autobiographical novel, provides the best starting point, as it tracks a triple evolution of nation, singer, and song in response to these economic upheavals. Here, Guthrie's modernity is a violent, complex affair, linked with the cyclones that bang and twist across the plains, overturning not just chicken coops and wheelbarrows, but the traditional relations and values of the past. As I hope to show, this violent energy both intrigued and frightened Guthrie; as it reorganized the structures of his life, it also ultimately served him as a model of creativity, an art that is not only engaged and motivated, but also spontaneous, fitful, and errant. The famous first chapter of the book, for example, focuses on a boxcar crowded with jobless men. As the storm outside grows wilder, the workers in the car grow violent, answering fear and confusion with aggression. Guthrie himself, sitting atop the car, exposed to the rain and thunder, faces a series of difficult questions: "Who's all of these crazy men down there howling at each other like hyenas? Are these men? Who am I? How come them here? How the hell come me here? What am I to do here?" (35). Guthrie here conflates natural, economic, and psychological disasters into a single apocalyptic scenario, the boxcar figuring as a metaphorical ship of state facing historical catastrophe.[9] Yet, in a radical twist, Guthrie gives up any claim to coherent selfhood, shakes his fist at the skies, and calls down all the chaos of the age upon himself and his fellow travelers. He yells, "Strike, lightning, strike!" recalling not just an enraged King Lear, but also Karl Marx, linking the creative violence of nature to the very forces of labor roiling below. Somehow, within the chaos of the moment, lies a certain revolutionary potential. Guthrie claims that the "sky ain't never as crazy as the world," yet he imagines some kind of promise in this mad destruction (36). In fact, as the chapter ends, the men below break out in song, insisting—powerfully, madly—that this crazy train is bound, in all its tumult and chaos, for glory.

Cyclones appear throughout the novel—some real, some imagined, some metaphorical. In fact, Guthrie's most potent memories all involve a certain whirling or twisting: watching his sister's hair swing in circles as she dances, climbing to the top of a tree as it sways in the wind, trying to rein in a pair of bolting horses on his cousins' farm. Throughout, Guthrie links this wild energy to the instability of the national economy in the 1920s. In a chapter titled "Mister Cyclome" [sic], his father explains his fear of cyclones in purely economic terms: "What do you know about cyclones? You've never even seen one yet! Quit popping off at your mouth! Everything that I've been working and fighting for in my whole life is tied up right here in this old London Place!" (83). When the formidable Mister Cyclome finally arrives, all brusque and businesslike, Guthrie focuses on its indiscriminate destruction of property. The cyclone upturns whole houses and all their contents, liquidating everything in its path, leading the young narrator to pity "all of the people in the world that have worked hard and had somebody else come along and take their life away from them" (88). The connection is pressed, metaphorically, in a later chapter, "Boomchasers," which depicts the discovery of oil in the area and Okemah's transformation from a sleepy frontier town to a wild industrial city (40). Nearly overnight, Okemah becomes the site of a constant, dizzying revolution. Both property and population are constantly overturned: "Folks called them boom chasers. A great big rolling army of hard-hitting men and their hard-hitting families. Stores throwed their keys away and stayed open twenty-four hours a day. When one army jumped out of bed another army jumped in. When one army jumped out of a café, another one marched in" (98). As Marx famously proclaimed, with capitalism, "All that is solid melts into air."[10] Here, too, the city's very boundaries seem to dissolve, swept up in its own creative destruction, and Guthrie responds with characteristic awe and fear; the rough spectacle of modern life—men who "work and heave and cuss and sweat and laugh and talk" (95)—both seduces and scares him. "This was a pretty mixed up mess," he declares, returning to the cyclone motif, "the wild spinning of all these things had the men whipped up to a fever heat, jumpy, jittery, wild and reckless" (96, 99).

For Guthrie, the inspiring artist, the boomtown is also defined by a chaos of speech. The streets are crowded with signs and slogans. Preachers, politicians, and bosses shout each other down from opposite corners, while newsboys scream out the latest headlines and merchants loudly tout their wares. Everyone is "pushing, talking, arguing, and trying to read," and this racket ultimately troubles Guthrie's own prose, which, with its long, rambling lists and increased fragmentation, seems barely able to rise above the sonic tumult:

> The first people to hit town was the rig builders, cement men, carpenters, teamskinners, wild tribes of horse traders and gypsy wagons loaded full, and wheels breaking down; crooked gamblers, pimps, whores, dope fiends, and peddlers, stray musicians and street singers, preachers cussing about love and begging for tips on the street corners . . . . Thousands of folk come to town to work, eat, sleep, celebrate, pray, cry, sing, talk, argue, and fight with the old settlers. (96)

Guthrie's modernity is marked by discursive chaos. All that is solid in Okemah melts into a whirlwind of voices, one loaded with conflicting powers and authorities. In fact, in *Bound for Glory*, America at large appears as a set of bewildering commands and directives, scattering people and populations this way and that. Traveling westward, Guthrie describes Los Angeles as a city made of signs, a landscape perverted by manic signification. He writes, "Red and green neon flickering for eats, sleeps, sprees, salvation, money made, lent, blowed, spent. There was an electric sign for dirty clothes, clean clothes, honky tonky tonks, no clothes, floor shows, gyp-joints, furniture in and out of homes" (224). The rambling absurdity of this report gives way to genuine angst when Guthrie comes across signs that bar access to work and food. These signs, and—by extension— the modern economy, appear opposed to both natural order and natural rights: "Fruit is on the ground," Guthrie writes, "and it looks like the trees have been just too glad to grow it, and give it to you. The tree likes to grow and you like to eat it; and there is a sign between you and the tree saying: 'Beware The Mean Dog's Master'" (223). However, despite Guthrie's anger here, we'll find that this cyclone of voices and violence came to define his work as a songwriter and performer. His early experiences of modernity provided him with a sense of song as a force of both territorialization and its opposite. The vibrant suppleness of this sonic public sphere, its cheap and disposable signage, becomes the precondition for a rambling, fluid style, a comic, helter-skelter performance of humility and openness within a constantly changing world.

First, though, this modernity—in all its wild, well-oiled distraction, its whipsaw twists of bounty and bitterness—inspired Guthrie's embrace of the migrant life. For it is precisely in response to such chaos that Guthrie presents himself as a reckless and ultimately radical citizen, mobile and motivated. With the desolation of his family home and then the boomtown itself, Guthrie slowly loses his personal bearings but thus gains the ability to rethink his identity on a national level. After a brief sojourn in Oklahoma City, the family returns to Okemah to find the city deserted, the oil dried up, and the boomchasers gone. Woody wanders the empty streets, seeking out old friends and other comforting markers of the past, but he quickly attracts the attention of a gang of bullies and earns himself a vicious beating. Afterward, busted up and broke down, he sees his reflection in the plate-glass window of an abandoned shop and stares in wonder:

> Hello there, me. What the hell are you walking along so slow for? Who are you? Woody who? Huh? You've walked along looking at yourself in these windows when they was all lit up with bright lights and hung full of

> pretty things for pretty women, tough stuff for tough men, fighting clothes
> for fighting people. And now look. Look, you lonesome outfit. Don't you
> look lost flogging along there in that glass window? (148)

This monologue recalls Guthrie's thoughts atop the boxcar, but here the
loss of identity is explicitly linked to the emptiness of the economy. With
the destruction of the marketplace that once shaped his ideal childhood
reflection, Guthrie comes to confront the falseness of its underlying principles regarding selfhood as property and possession. Unable to forge a
productive relationship between himself and his environment, his mind
starts to spin out of control and the world around him turns into an open
trash heap, full of rot and disease.

In the chapter titled "Junking Sack," Guthrie rambles aimlessly through
the empty town, picking through piles of rubbish for scraps of food and
shelter. At one point, stricken with a delirious fever, he loses consciousness
and imagines himself as a "junk man" and then a persecuted "Jew" and a
"Nigger." In his delirium, though, he is at once pleasured and persecuted;
loss of selfhood figures as terrifying death and glorious release, the violent ecstasy of collective being (160–61). This psychological unraveling is
visually depicted in the novel by a series of dusty self-portraits. In these,
identity appears blurry, incomplete, aimless, but also grandiose, mythic,
inclusive. Guthrie himself appears as a cyclone—wandering and lost, but
always in motion, active, his form charged by twisting lines of force, engorged and extended by a rush of forms and feelings.[11] Tellingly, then,
when his fever breaks, he asks for a new "junkin' sack" and takes to the
road again. As if reborn, reconstituted in his very dereliction, he decides
to embrace his self-impoverishment as an ethos. As Guthrie explained
elsewhere, "I had a crazy notion in me that I wanted to stay down and out
for a good long spell, so's I could get to live with every different kind of a
person I could, to learn about all kinds of jobs they do, and to live with
them for a long enough time to find out it was time to move on." With this
dereliction, then, Guthrie begins to cultivate not only a more expansive
vision of selfhood, but also "a great sympathy for folks along our roads
that are all down and out," for a counterpublic of impoverished, but also
ultimately mobile and motivated, Americans.[12]

Simply put, Guthrie *goes down*, and in the slow dissolution of selfhood, he begins to cultivate a new model of citizenship and community.
He pursues the loss of identity—familial, economic, and regional—with
a vengeance, divesting himself of all relations, property, and even coordinates. In fact, his movement westward, into an increasingly featureless

geography, figures as a slow negation of all false categories, until at the moment of near annihilation, he humbly declares, "I was just there" (194). At each step, his body exhibits a new and oddly inverted economy—a *via negativa*, if we want to be spiritual about it—one in which every loss figures as new gain, each crushing moment of humiliation augments a growing pride and conviction in the value of his life:

> I kept getting weaker and emptier. . . . I kept shaking and looking blanker and blanker. Just got into a stupor of some kind, and sat there on the main line of the fast railroad, forgetting about even being there . . . and thinking of homes, with ice boxes, cook stoves, tables, hot meals, cold lunches, with hot coffee, ice-beer, homemade wine—and friends and relatives. And I swore to pay more attention to the hungry people that I would meet from there on down the line. (201)

As this expanding list suggests, the migrant Guthrie at once loses himself and gains the world. Later, hanging from the back end of a train, anonymous to all the world, Guthrie realizes that he could slip and die, unnoticed and unmourned. Yet here, precisely at the moment of near extinction, thinking of all the anonymous corpses that litter the sides of the rail tracks, he gains his greatest reward—complete identification: "And no doubt my line of politics took on quite a change right then and there, even though I didn't know I was getting educated at the time" (228).

Bound for Glory romanticizes this open, loafing life and thus perhaps serves as the missing literary link between the national poetic visions of Whitman and the postmodern picaresques of Kerouac and Pynchon. As Eric Lott suggests, slumming narratives of this sort, despite their implicit exoticism, contain, in their "clumsy courtship" of the underclass, a "utopian or emancipatory moment."[13] Guthrie, in his delirious identification with African Americans and Jews, and then in his cross-country act of class abdication, appropriates as he celebrates the critical pleasures of otherness as the basis of a renewed national culture (50–51). But his narrative is saved, it seems to me, by its active commitment to identity as a dynamic process; it avoids any easy opposition between motion and stasis, freedom and property, individual and nation, and offers, instead, a more supple modality in which these categories are continually adopted and overturned (in comic fashion, as we'll find). In other words, Guthrie's dereliction is neither opposed to identity as such nor represents merely an exchange of one identity for another. Rather, it allows for a more open process of identity formation, one that recognizes the self in provisional relation to others, and thus as part of a larger mobile collective. At one point, a depleted Guthrie finds a compelling reflection of himself in another hungry man's form. As in the earlier scene with the plate-glass window, Guthrie here glances from the other man's face and clothes to his own, remarking, "For the first time I stood there and thought to myself just what a funny-looking thing I was—that is, to other people walking along the streets." Guthrie both loses and finds himself in this comic self-image; he comes to himself as estranged, as a changing, dynamic other, and thus remains in a state of non-coincidence, at once present and open, assured and active. Indeed, the exchange is mirrored on both ends and thus proves oddly productive; as the two men converse, their ideals and values begin to echo each other's, and, by the end of the conversation, they together construct a mutual sense of pride and self-respect, and so move on, renewed in their search for work and food (206–8).

This novel sense of identity—as provisional form—also comes to shape Guthrie's sense of habitation and community. Roaming the countryside, the young Woody begins to admire the shifting populations that wander into and out of the jungle camps and housing projects, the casual friends and families that can easily inhabit these spaces because they never own them. As Janet Lyon explains, many modern artists and writers were drawn to gypsy life not so much for its exotic otherness, but for its ability to slip in and out of standard categories. The patterns of motion and stasis that define gypsy life suggest a specific kind of engagement with modernity, one that erodes as it inhabits the latter's economic structures and symbolic coordinates. "Gypsy mobility could not be categorized as a species of agricultural migrancy, nor indeed as any form of migrancy," Lyons writes, "which entails a fixed and regulated territorial trajectory; instead the very flexibility of Gypsy mobility resembled a kind of deterritorialization that was produced moment-to-moment by local conditions."[14] Toward the end of the novel, Guthrie stumbles upon a jungle camp close to Redding, California, where a growing horde has been waiting for work on a new dam site. The camp is little more than a structured junk heap, built out of the scraps of cars, old blankets, and packing crates. Its inhabitants are poor, lost, and hungry, yet eager to work and respectful of each other, bound by hardship into loose but affectionate clusters. As in his description of the Oklahoma boomtown, Guthrie can here do little more than list the things and people that inhabit this mixed-up town—all is a confusing but genuinely warm welter of human life, defiant of typical categories and structures. In this, the jungle camp figures as neither premodern ideal nor postmodern cultural jumble, but something like a countermodernity within modernity, perhaps even a modernist bohemia:

You've seen a million people like this already. Maybe you saw them down on the crowded side of your big city; the back side, that's jammed and packed, the hard section to drive through. . . . These people have had a house and a home just about like your own, settled down and had a job of work just about like you. Then something hit them and they lost all of that. They've been pushed out onto the high lonesome highway, and they've gone down it, from coast to coast, from Canada to Mexico, looking for that home again. . . . These are migrants now. They don't just set along in the sun—they go by the sun, and it lights up the country that they know is theirs. (249)

Guthrie here celebrates not simply the underside—the "back side"—of the national economic order, but also the way in which it inhabits and appropriates the very forms of economic exploitation. In this migrant mirror image of American stability, all is inverted, so that widespread loss becomes a massive gain and the production of value depends on the production of waste. The very refuse of modern life—all that has literally been *refused*—becomes the precondition for a more inclusive embrace.

In other words, Guthrie does not simply replace form with flow, property lines with boundless poverty, stability with mobility. Rather, in his wanderings, he inhabits a more fluid structure, a kind of derelict code, one that weakly coheres and quickly dissolves across traditional lines. In this, too, he begins to pursue a more radical formulation of song, as a code that upends all codes, or, as we'll see, a "motivated" discourse that claims and dissolves the symbolic structures of everyday life. As presented in *Bound for Glory*, Guthrie's music evolves from a simple truth-telling medium to a more gleeful, rambling, and somewhat surreal corrective to the official language of economics and politics. At first, Guthrie sees all art as a simple act of clarification, a way of naming problems in order to correct or, as we saw with the blues as *nommo*, master them. One day, a disgruntled laborer shows up at his door, mistaking him for a fortune-teller and demanding answers to life's great problems. Bemused by the mix-up, Guthrie obliges and, after making a few sensible observations about the worker's condition, decides to go into the business himself. With characteristic humility, he describes himself not as a mystic, but a simple truth-teller, offering clarity to the otherwise confused and vexed lives of his fellow citizens—"People lost. People sick. People wondering" (188). But, slowly, as local conditions worsen, Guthrie realizes that truth-telling isn't enough. One of his clients ends up in an insane asylum, and then a group of angry, inconsolable workers shows up at his door asking about

Hitler and Mussolini. At this moment, Guthrie shifts his emphasis from truth to hope. His advice, like his song, turns propagandistic, proffering earnest but somewhat simplistic visions of socialist redemption. "We got to all git together an' find some way to build this country up," he tells the men; "We gotta find a job an' put ever' single livin' one of us ta work" (189). Songmaking appears here as a kind of prayer, one that has value precisely in its contrast to everyday life. But Guthrie errs again with this more willful approach. The laborers scoff at his quasi-Marxist message. "You ain't no prophet!" one of them shouts. "Hell, any of us coulda say the same thing! You're a dam fake!" (189–90).

At this point in the novel, Guthrie's songmaking appears caught between a direct, but ultimately fatal, objectivity and an unworldly, perhaps ungrounded, idealism, a tension that plagued not only many blues and country musicians, but also—as we'll find—many Depression-era artists with similar political commitments. Yet Guthrie's book offers another alternative, one that more closely adheres to the specific qualities of music and his own rambling style as a musician. At a pivotal moment, Guthrie gives up a budding interest in painting for singing. His decision is guided by finances but also implies a new aesthetic ethos. "[C]anvas is too high priced," he claims, "and so is paint and costly oils, and brushes that you've got to chase a camel or a seal or a Russian red sable forty miles to get." Singing, on the other hand, is cheap, and its very cheapness, its immateriality, lends it a more expansive range: "A picture—you buy it once, and it bothers you for forty years: but with a song, you sing it out, and it soaks in people's ears and they all jump up and down and sing it with you, and then when you quit singing it, it's gone, and you get a job singing it, again" (178). With this, Guthrie redefines song in terms of its sonic promiscuity, as a form of cultural dereliction, and thus as part of the migrant economy outlined above. Its very cheapness proves its greatest strength, making it expandable and adaptable; its empty airiness gives it a power to span, to survive, to insinuate itself across great distances and otherwise rigid boundaries. Thus, once he leaves home, Guthrie starts to produce a constant supply of cheap and often silly songs, translating every incident of daily life—driving a car, picking apricots, cleaning dishes, waiting for work, walking down the street—into a loose, rambling music. By turns political, amorous, spiritual, and humorous, this music is never expressive or explicitly political; rather, it is only always a "little song," lightly floating over everyday life, casually shaping its affective dimensions and thus, like some secret saboteur or tricky shadow, eroding its rigid boundaries and categories.

The novel ends with Guthrie's account of his failed audition for the Rainbow Room. Bucking against the class dynamics of the swanky restaurant scene and the potential commodification of his Dust Bowl identity, Guthrie looks out the window of the restaurant and stares longingly at the "living and breathing and cussing and laughing" city below (294). He notes specifically the scraps of paper spinning, cyclone-like, in the wind, and, in a moment of artistic epiphany worthy of James Joyce, reaffirms his commitment to a cheap, derelict art:

> Limp papers whipped and beat upwards, rose into the air and fell head over heels, curving over backwards and sideways, over and over, loose sheets of newspaper with pictures of people and stories of people printed somewhere on them, turning loops in the air. And it was blow little paper blow! Twist and turn and stay up as long as you can, and when you come down, come down on a pent-house porch, come down easy so's not to hurt yourself. Come down and lay there in the rain and the wind and the soot and smoke and the grit that gets in your eyes in the big city—and lay there in the sun and get faded and rotten. But keep on trying to tell your message, and keep on trying to be a picture of a man, because without that story and without that message printed on you there, you wouldn't be much. Remember, it's just maybe, someday, some time, somebody will pick you up and look at your picture and read your message, and carry you in his pocket, and lay you on his shelf, and burn you in his stove. But he'll have your message in his head and he'll talk it and it'll get around. (295)

Like these scraps of printed material, Guthrie's song is nearly worthless, almost weightless. It proves powerful in its very disavowal of power, in its constant fading, its near obscurity, slipping past the borders of proper society (the propriety of the Rainbow Room) and generating a certain friction, a small heat, a humble, nearly silent or surreptitious protest. Inspired by this image of circulating garbage, Guthrie himself slips out of the restaurant, down to the lobby and out the building, singing all the while. He fills himself full of "free air"—a phrase that beautifully links his economic and musical aspirations—and sings for the workers of the city, "not singing because he was hired and told what to sing, but just walking through there thinking about the world and singing about it" (296). And he sings his way across the city, toward its "slummy edges," attracting a growing, shifting crowd of men, women, children, workers and idlers, bums, soldiers, and cops. He sings for everyone and everything "that ain't all slicked up and starched and imitation," everything poor and open and free. "And I knew," he writes, "that I was glad to be loose from that sentimental and dreamy trash, and gladder to be edging my way along here singing with the people, singing something with fight and guts and belly laughs and power and dynamite to it" (299).

Socialists Abandon Documentary Realism for Motivated Forms

But with this turn to "the people"—migrant, shifting, disorganized—we're dealing with an "authenticity" of a different sort. As is well known, the folk movement of the 1930s entailed an unprecedented exchange between the intellectual left and grassroots labor movements. As the strikes in Gastonia, North Carolina, and Harlan County, Kentucky, caught national attention, and the protest songs of Aunt Molly Jackson, Ella May Wiggins, and Sarah Ogan Gunning began to circulate up north, urban thinkers and labor leaders began to consider a new, more dynamic approach to class warfare. Distancing themselves from the political avant-garde of the past, they linked their otherwise abstract program of class revolution to a specific vision of folk authenticity, one rooted in traditional song and regional customs. "Real folks music" or, better, "real living song," became not just a source of aesthetic pleasure or even cultural fetishism, but also, possibly, a "great weapon" of dissent, a way beyond the class politics of the past and the foundation of a new national solidarity.[15] Of course, as Shelly Romalis notes, terms such as "folk," "tradition," and "authenticity" have no apparent or essential meaning. Rather, they appear in our discourse as troublesome sites of social contention, and the struggle over their meanings is deeply political.[16] The left of the 1930s embraced a highly particularized version of folk tradition, one that rested on a mythic and indeed homogenous vision of the underclass. The most celebrated songs of the day—Aunt Molly's "I Am a Union Woman," Wiggins's "The Mill Mother's Song," Sarah Gunning's "I Hate the Capitalist System"—seemed to express the "real" needs of the "real" people, even though they represented only a fraction of lower-class life and were often built upon commercial forms. Still, we must admit that, in this case, the category of "tradition" came to inform a powerful program of *change* rather than *stasis*, giving a certain weight and force to the party's otherwise abstract discourse. Indeed, of all the ways in which the category of "tradition" has been applied over the last century, the left's appropriation is perhaps most in line with contemporary notions that it is an active and indeed negotiable form—a tool to be used in the present rather than a static image or ideal of the past.[17]

Nonetheless, this collusion of leftist thought and grassroots music tended to emphasize certain features of folk song over others and perhaps placed an undue attention on contents over forms. The strike song of the late 1920s was typically a first-person account of work-related hardships, interspersed—via its refrain—with direct calls for solidarity or action. It was essentially documentary in approach, using personal facts and public events to bond with the listener and then generate a common emotional response, such as sadness, anger, or hope. The intelligentsia picked up on these features and celebrated their presumed immediacy, specifically in opposition to the formalism of high modernism. As Romalis points out, once groups like the Composers Collective and the Workers Music League heard the music of Aunt Molly Jackson, they quickly abandoned their efforts to develop experimental music for the working class and instead adopted folk song as a more direct mode of political expression (161–62). And yet, as we'll find, Guthrie and his coterie turned their sights precisely on this music's formal properties—the very abstraction and impersonality of the folk song—and thus, paradoxically, ventured a more fluid vision of class identity. Guthrie's specific experience of modernity—as tracked in *Bound for Glory*—led him to emphasize, beyond folk music's expressive or documentary features, the properties of the refrain as it harnessed, in its very repetition, established social forces and generated a looser, more open-ended collective. Thus, in a way, while Guthrie borrowed from former folk artists such as Jackson and Gunning, he exploited the formal dimensions of their songs and thus pushed "protest" music beyond the very category of the "folk" itself. His song, as "real living song," as motivated discourse, united form and feeling both, art and activism, into a single, moving whole, and thus became a way of not simply naming or even binding "the people," but reopening the political field as such.

For really, the art of the 1930s was anything but stable or unified. Proletarian artists were not solely committed to the documentary and its presumed authenticity; their work veered wildly between genres and strategies—from snapshot to mural to ballet, and then, in terms of mode, from realism to surrealism to what some even called "superrealism." Photographers like Dorothea Lange and Walker Evans worked alongside muralists like Diego Rivera and José Clemente Orozco; angsty expressionist paintings by James Guy and Louis Guglielmo were hung next to the mythic iconography of John Steuart Curry and Thomas Hart Benton.[18] And though we could organize these efforts along a continuum from objectivity to abstraction, they all share, more than anything else, some anxious preoccupation with issues of *motivation* and *form*. While intellectuals on the left wrestled with their detachment from the "people," the artists and writers of this period were questioning the potential violence of representation itself. In *Let Us Now Praise Famous Men*, for example, James Agee fretted endlessly about his role as social investigator and the ways in which his language might distort the lives of the sharecropping families it was meant to explain:

> [C]ommunication is not by any means so simple. . . . I am liable seriously, and perhaps irretrievably, to obscure what would at best be hard enough to give its appropriate clarity and intensity, and what seems to me most important of all: namely, that these I will write of are human beings, living in this world, innocent of such twistings as these which are taking place over their heads; and that they were dwelt among, investigated, spied on, revered, and loved, by other quite monstrously alien human beings, in the employment of still others still more alien; and that they are now being looked into by still others, who have picked up their living as casually as if it were a book.[19]

"Twistings"—the term immediately recalls the cyclone imagery that Guthrie uses to represent the linguistic storms of modernity. More importantly, though, this crisis of representation is both aesthetic and ethical; all expressive forms are shot through with willful and excessive demands, unsettling motivational forces, either within or around the frame of vision itself. In this, I'm reminded of Kenneth Burke's characterization of the "grotesque" in modern art. As Burke argues in his 1937 study *Attitudes towards History*, "poetic forms are . . . designed to equip us for confronting given historical or personal situations," but the "grotesque" is an uncertain "mode," one that exposes the anxiety and distortion that attends any representational act. By way of example, Burke turns to the complicated forms of high modernism—the overwrought symbolism of Joyce and Lawrence and the distorted landscapes of Dalí and Ernst. In these works, he explains, an overflow of "subjective elements" distorts the "objective, or public, elements," thereby displaying the artist's own failure to attain coherent form.[20] In a way, all the art of this fraught era—both high and low—seems unsure about motives, and yet, as I'd like to show, its very ugliness maintained something like a critical potential. As it shifts wildly among forms and styles, and everywhere exposes its own uneasy intentions, it imbeds itself in a series of public and private energies, and pushes the collective as a whole beyond mere representation toward a more active and open-ended exchange.

First, then, we should note that, for all his offhand "folksiness," Guthrie shared his contemporaries' frustrations with the logic of representation. In fact, he suffered from a nearly debilitating graphomania and wrestled his whole life to match up words to the people and objects around him. As he wandered back and forth across the country, he scribbled on everything he saw—papers, walls, desktops, guitars, menus, and cars. Many friends noticed his frequent bouts with "binge writing," marveling at the sheer quantity and velocity of his prose, his seemingly interminable list making, and his compulsion to invent nicknames for everyone around him.[21] Certainly, Guthrie's long-flowing syntax and compulsive punning place him in the company of Rabelais, Joyce, and Pynchon, and, in this, we can award him a significant place in the great modern tradition of the literary carnivalesque.[22] But his wayward prose also suggests (if not the onset of Huntington's chorea) a frustrated relation to language as a medium of personal and public expression. In a piece titled "My People," for example, Guthrie explicitly frames the problem of writing as an ethical dilemma centered around issues of representation and its motivation:

> My people
> Are not quaint
> They're not colorful
> They ain't odd nor funny nor picturesque,
> Nor strange,
> Nor humorous,
> And they're not strangers
> You introduce with big long words.

After this series of negations, Guthrie rails against speeches and books and "you big long-haired writers" who "whack away at my people." But if his poem exposes the motivated nature of public discourse, it also—in its own motivatedness—ends with a compelling sense of humility and inconclusiveness:

> I don't know
> And won't say what my people are
> Just folks
> Just like me
> All messed up and tangled up
> And all worried
> And all screwed up.[23]

Grotesque, sure—but only as a compelling representational problem, one in which the very effort to name his "people" sets the category of the "people" into dynamic motion. As usual, Guthrie writes here with both commitment and indecision, purpose and openness. But his diction is freed by its own motivated nature, as if all such assertions only reveal their utter provisionality. If anything, his people need—more than representation or even commitment—an open, flexible discourse, one that, like the song he sings outside the Rainbow Room, "ain't all slicked up and starched and imitation." And it is precisely with this assertion, here coming from his own motivated folk-heart, that he offers a speech that is full of urgency and gloriously incomplete.

Guthrie most successfully pursued this motive language in song, using the formal properties of both sound and performance to heighten its possibilities. Sure, here, too, he always begins with the facts. In a letter to Alan Lomax, he defines a good folk song in terms of simplicity and directness: "A folk song ought to be pretty well satisfied just to tell the facts and let it go at that" (*Pastures* 47). Subject matter should come from everyday life, and style should hew closely to the speech of the people: "I hear so many people coming around me and going on about where you get your words and your tunes. Well I get my words and tunes off of the hungry folks and they get the credit for all I pause to scribble down" (*Pastures* 48). In this, Guthrie presents folk song as a living document, a little bit of the folk-real broadcasted into the ether. As a member of the Almanacs, for example, he imagined himself performing a "singing newspaper," translating recent news and events into musical form. Later, working for Moses Asch, he drew upon history books and newspaper clippings for material, thought of recording a monthly "musical newspaper," and then later put together a singing "American Documentary."[24]

Yet, as we saw in *Bound for Glory*, Guthrie was dissatisfied with the passivity of the merely documentary. He also often insisted that song should have a clear sense of purpose, a motivation that makes it more than a simple factual account. As he once claimed, apparently in contradiction to his own materialist leanings, song is "working up the news to the point where you can sing about it" (*Born to Win* 73). If the news needs to be sung, then song is always somewhat supplemental, emphatic; the songwriter defines his craft precisely in its difference from material reality, in its ability to generate and sustain moods and feelings that are not bound to any immediate fact or circumstance. Always, Guthrie's song displays this remarkable doubleness, resounding somewhere between fact and form, meaning and motive, between the day's news and the future's hope. Its value rests not just in its authenticity, its self-proclaimed realism, but also in its difference, its performative excess, its nearly miraculous pattern of style and affect. In this, moreover, Guthrie's song does not align itself with some easy fantasy of "the folk," or even any obvious political position, but nonetheless establishes countercultural patterns and possibilities. As I'd like to show, here and throughout the rest of this chapter, this formal excess—especially in the form of the refrain—at once provides song with its motive force and then leads beyond it, both establishes a significant position or stance and then prepares the way for its own eventual overturning.

To varying degrees, then, almost all of Guthrie's "protest" songs fore-ground the intentionality of expression and its open-ended consequences. First, we recognize a certain intentionality *within the frame of each song*. Guthrie typically charges the heavy weight of factual evidence with deci-sively human perspectives and motives. In his gripping account of "Ludlow Massacre," for example, he sings from a worker's perspective, depicting his life as a series of charged relations (work, family, religion, and politics) and emotional investments (pride, fear, despair, apathy). After Guthrie establishes this motivational complexity, he focuses on the reciprocal vio-lence brought on by the strike, the moment when motivation becomes material effect and creates a seemingly static knot that goes by the name of history:

> We took some cement and walled that cave up
> Where you killed those thirteen children inside.
> I said, "God bless the Mine Workers' Union"
> And then I hung my head and cried.[25]

At the same time, though, Guthrie emphasizes the intentions that circu-late *outside the frame of song*. Guthrie often structures his material from the perspective of the present, establishing an intensive relation between the document at hand and his audience's own responses. While he draws upon a shared set of contemporary feelings and current expectations, he also tests out his listeners' motives with verbal asides, direct addresses, and challenging questions. For example, Guthrie struggled for weeks on a commemoration for the 115 sailors who died when the *Reuben James* was torpedoed in the north Atlantic. First, Guthrie tried to compose a song that included all 115 names of the dead in rhyming form. This docu-mentary approach, though, proved "unsingable and unlistenable," and so the songwriter took a more dynamic approach, first setting the tale in more commonplace terms, and then demanding, via questions, an active response from the listener:

> Tell me what were their names? Tell me what was their names?
> Did you have a friend on the good *Reuben James*?

What was their names? Tell me, what was their names?
Did you have a friend on that good *Reuben James?*[26]

Finally, then, Guthrie also and most interestingly plays with the intentionality of *the framing act of songmaking itself.* As both songwriter and performer, he foregrounds the work of singing and playing, not to mention listening, as forms of community building and ethical representation. According to his biographer, the formative moment of Guthrie's career occurred when he was asked to perform at a Communist Party rally for labor organizer Tom Mooney. Warned that it would be a committed left-wing affair, Guthrie replied, "Left wing, right wing, chicken wing—it's the same thing to me. I sing my songs wherever I can sing 'em." That evening, in fact, Woody slept through most of the proceedings, bored by "the sloganeering, [the] wooden phony language that grew up in the party." Yet when his turn at the podium arrived, he stepped up with a rousing song about Mooney and his recent pardon. The song, like most of his political work, provided few facts and absolutely no policy. Rather, by turns exclamatory and interrogative, it established a mood, an attitude, a stance that was both charged and free:

How does it feel to be FREE?
How does it feel to be FREE?
How does it feel to be out of jail
Since Olson has given you liberty?

Here, raucous emotion meets up with open-ended questions, and so the song provides both a way in and a way out for each individual listener. The piece is riddled with intention, a certain affective force, but all its passion is left free and available for other kinds of investment.[27] As Guthrie himself claimed, "Our song is our meeting and our music is our union."[28] He consistently tapped song's formal features—its dynamism, repetition, and vocality—as a means of building community, often above and beyond any immediate political cause.

Here, in relation to motivation and motivational form, we begin to see the significance of the refrain. Take, for example, "Babe O' Mine," a protest song that perhaps best demonstrates Guthrie's formalist approach and its open-ended nature.[29] The song, in fact, has multiple versions, all linked together by their astoundingly simple refrain. Guthrie, hoping to rally CIO trade unionists, based his 1941 version of the song on an earlier protest version by Sarah Ogan Gunning, who, before him, had based her own Harlan County strike version on the melody of an old popular version about courtship.[30] Gunning's song is explicitly political and largely realist. The title alone, "I'm Going to Organize," announces the singer's main intention, while the verses outline the personal feelings and experiences that inspired it. The lyrics are largely biographical, and, in the recorded version at least, they are sung in an open, expressive manner, full of honest emotion and passion. No doubt, the song's success as a "protest" song depended fully upon its perceived "authenticity"—of fact, feeling, and tradition. In the mining camps and strike lines of the late 1920s, it would have appealed to each worker's sense of shared injustice and any associations he or she might have had with the original melody. Guthrie's version, though, written a decade later for a larger, national scene, minimizes the song's political thrust and draws all attention to its catchy formal structure, thereby bringing it closer in line with its original popular form. Guthrie strips the song's title of any reference to the socialist cause but preserves the sentimental charge generated by the phrase "Babe O' Mine." Each verse consists of a single repeated intention, many of which are decisively apolitical; one by one, Guthrie outlines a series of everyday motives—*I'm gonna write you a letter, I'm a-goin' to California*, etc.—and then whips them up, via his quick strumming and vocal repetition, into a specifically sonic pattern. The song's intended listeners would have been caught up in this affective repetition as it led in each verse to the song's more explicit refrain—*I gotta keep organizing, babe o' mine*—and its later variation, *We gotta keep organizin', babe o' mine*. In this, then, the song's form overlaps with its intention, as, indeed, the disorganized rambling of the verses finds itself structured into a single motive force. In contrast to Gunning's version, the song does not list the reasons for organization, or even declare an intent to organize, but organizes itself, generically, as a sonic union of sorts, moving toward both common and uncommon ends.

The little phrase "babe o' mine" has made quite a journey from its place in nineteenth-century courting rituals to this new collective form of protest. But its slightness is precisely what allows it to survive in the pop ether. It is essentially an empty form, a little bit of pop detritus—much like the scraps of paper floating about at the end of *Bound for Glory*—defined precisely by its lack of definition, its sheer re-usability or re-iterability. Like any useful sign, it would be nothing without its capacity for repetition in different contexts for different ends, even as it might be charged with the affective weight of the past. Here, even in this brief history, the little phrase seems to wander freely from line to line, song to song, place to place, filled out in each case by a different set of meanings and intentions. In this, it is an essentially migrant form, a tiny sonic cog capable of being inserted into any number of songs and thus mobilized for a range of different causes. It's a fit form for a migrant community—cheap and empty, like a piece of cultural refuse—to be picked up as a momentary shelter or dwelling or perhaps for some immediate stance or battle. Most importantly, the power of the refrain at once grows and diminishes with each iteration. Every cheap rendition at once refills and empties the phrase all over again, as if to prepare it to accomplish something new—steal a kiss, attack private property, kill fascists, please a crowd. It accumulates cultural power over time, but only as it also grows more cliché, more inconsequential or worthless. "You sing it out," Guthrie writes in *Bound for Glory*, "and it soaks in people's ears and they all jump up and down and sing it with you, and then when you quit singing it, it's gone, and you get a job singing it, again" (178). And, so, "Babe O' Mine!"—what a powerful, sincere, tender, empty, useless, annoying phrase. And all of these features are rolled up together in its very enunciation. Singing "Babe O' Mine" consolidates a place, a time, a history, only to disperse it all over again, release it, decenter it—into the past, over at the next mine, the cotton mill, at a New York salon, the future. Thus "Babe O' Mine"—the phrase and its singing—reveals something about all motive forms, which are always both symbolic and practical, empty and charged, bound to context and yet incredibly, thankfully, virtual, ideal, open-ended.

Again, Guthrie is far from toeing the party line with any of these songs. He consistently refuses to provide easy answers, working instead to stir up difficult emotional complexes and forcing listeners to examine their own values and motivations. He seems, moreover, to recognize that motives are never organic or even consistent; rather, they are inherently abstract; they function more like a flexible vocabulary or repertoire of stances than a set of deeply held or entrenched positions. Indeed, in this music, the very concept of "motive" appears both symbolic and practical, determined by language or form as it leads toward immediate action. Similarly, from amid the culture industry of 1940, sociologist C. Wright Mills rejected the notion that motives are innate or essential "springs of action," as if they emerged from some authentic place within the self and automatically produced certain behaviors and actions. Rather, for Mills, motives are open and ultimately adaptable forms, at once general and situated—"typical vocabularies having ascertainable functions in delimited social situations." In fact, for Mills, motives are indistinguishable from talk about motives. They exist *formally*, as part of social "conversation"; each is an "answer" to a social "question," a "name" for "consequential situations and surrogates for actions leading to them."[31] More bluntly,

Kenneth Burke opens *Attitudes toward History* with the assertion that "Action requires programs—programs require vocabulary" (2). Guthrie's most powerful performances are most often defined by a similar abstraction. His best songs are framed as open questions and provisional answers, and their specific formal qualities—particularly the repetition of chorus and refrain—expose their provisional nature. When Guthrie sings "I'm stickin' with the Union," for example, he at once names and enacts his commitment to a specific union, but he also performs his commitment to his own song, to his own performance, to himself and to his audience, and thus exposes the inherent transposability of the motive form. As Mills explains, "Motives are common grounds for mediated behaviors" (443–44). For Guthrie, too, song—as a *mediated* behavior—at once sets language to work and leaves it open, creates as it releases the statement into a dynamic field. His song frees its own chorus—"I'm stickin' to the Union"—for use in a range of social practices, both those named in the song (marriage, labor, politics, etc.) and those surrounding the scene of performance (congregating, marching, listening, etc.). This simple sonic gesture could be picked up elsewhere, in other places and times, and it could also just as easily be dropped, abandoned, removed from the social repertoire. In other words, intentional language always seems to expose the possibility of other intentions, other engagements and investments, and perhaps suggests the possibility of another union, one more responsive and flexible than any shaped by party policy or doctrine.

Guthrie, then, pushed for a new "vocabulary of motives" as the basis of a more flexible public exchange. His most powerful work foregrounds the motive power of sound and song in order to expose and revise the political collusion of power and symbol, as if only a more radical intentionality can restore something like a truly democratic state. Take, for example, his late collection *Ballads of Sacco and Vanzetti* (1947), which, for almost all listeners, seems to fail on the level of straight documentary.[32] The idea of covering the Sacco and Vanzetti case was suggested to Guthrie by Folkways founder Moses Asch, many years after the case had been closed, and Guthrie approached his research with diligence, carefully consulting articles and pamphlets to flesh out the details of the case.[33] In making the album, though, the songwriter worked to juxtapose hard facts with subjective vision, presenting each facet of the trial from a differently motivated angle. His approach was designed to address the complexly motivated nature of this material: given the political misuse of evidence and testimony that marked the trials, the technique of shifting perspectives—no matter how "grotesque"—served to reopen the motivated terms of judgment and establish a more "rounded" response to an otherwise closed history.

Thus Guthrie first embeds Sacco and Vanzetti in a larger and more common motivational network—a more expansive "vocabulary of motives." In songs such as "Two Good Men" and "Suassos Lane," he counters formal court evidence with affective evidence from Sacco and Vanzetti's private lives. The men are seen inhabiting many different roles and relations—as friends and neighbors, as husbands and fathers, as Italians and Italian Americans, as dreamers and readers, and, of course, as workers. "Suassos Lane" is particularly successful in this regard. With its rushed, nearly frantic rhythm and episodic verse structure, it defends the two men by summoning a long line of neighbors and clients who interacted with them on the day of the murder—Joseph Rosen the peddler, Alphonsine Brini the housewife, Melvin Corl the fisherman. For Guthrie, this social suppleness seems defense enough, freeing the two men (if not from the crime itself) from their rigid politicization by both the left and the right. At the very least, it provides a significant response to the abstract machinery of the judicial system, presenting an open network of intention and exchange against the rigid logic of the judicial system. At the same time, Guthrie works through the provided evidence and witness accounts to interrogate the motivated nature of legal discourse. In "Red Wine," for example, he exposes the heated intentionality of public testimony and thereby grants the two men a set of imaginary reprieves. The song begins with what seems like objective reportage but ends with a violent fantasy that upends the validity of the "official" record and reverses the trial's "official" verdict:

> I hoped they'd pull Judge Thayer on down
> From off of his bench and they'd chase him around.
> Hoped they'd run him around this stump
> And stick him with a devil's tail about every jump.

To return to Mills, not one of these songs, as "the vocalized expectation of the act," can truly reverse the case, but they each set its seemingly final terms into motion again. Motive, as an abstract form, does not simply negate or overturn factual evidence, but opens up judgment itself, releasing it into a dynamic field of possibilities—so many other motive forms and operating milieus.

Thus, throughout Guthrie's collection, singing itself embodies the fluidity of motive; voice becomes a continual enactment, with the power to undo its own judgment and "change things around." Guthrie's music offers itself up as a model for motivated language—at once symbolic and active—and thus as a powerful tool to be used by a migrant community in opposition to the mythic language of the law. Guthrie, for one, resists Sacco and Vanzetti's transformation into mere signs or symbols, and he uses the specific qualities of his craft to reopen political discourse and thus the political process. At the end of "Two Good Men," for example, he reminds listeners that song is a "living" art and urges us all to "jump in" and continue the common, open-ended work of singing the political. In a later song, "Vanzetti's Rock," he claims that song, of all the arts, provides the most fitting memorial for these two men, as it can at once record, enflame, and disseminate its message. In this regard, "I Just Want to Sing Your Name" may be the most avant-garde moment of the collection, if not Guthrie's entire career. Here, the folksinger strips away all politics, all ideology, and almost all signification. He croons, moans, and whispers the sounds "Sacco" and "Vanzetti," smoothing away the distinction between intention and form. Each repetition becomes the product and affirmation of a deliriously unrestrained commitment to sound itself. By the end, the barest semantic trace gives way to a committed non-sense, the purely sensual fullness of noise itself, one single, empty, airy, and utterly affirmative hum:

> Nicola Sacco, Bart Vanzetti,
> I just want to sing your name.
> Oh, ho, ho, ho, ho, ho, ho . . . Ho, ho, ho, ho, ho, ho . . .
> Yes, yes, yes, yes, yes, yes . . . Yes, yes, yes, yes, yes, yes . . .

Is there even a "cause" here? Is there expression or representation? Can we say that intention is still aligned with politics at this moment? Or has it drifted off into own carefree, even careless art? Indeed, here, motivation, in its own abstraction, its sheer virtuality, seems free to extend itself in other creative ways. This song is neither propagandistic nor grotesque, neither stern, pessimistic, nor ugly; it follows no program or teleology, no myth or historic fatality, and yet it totally compels us to sing along. As it pushes its own intentionality beyond itself toward something like pleasure, it opens up into another dimension entirely—the space of pop proper—one that is neither simply committed nor entirely detached from social reality, but affective and transformative nonetheless. As I want to show next, this is the song of Guthrie's counterpublic—cheap, endless, explosive, and giddy; motivated song becomes comic critique, laughing its way through the rigid categories of personal and political identity, and thus through history at large.

Folksinger Busts Up Economy with Bellylaughs

In *Attitudes toward History*, Burke defines comedy as a way of maneuvering from one-sided, oppositional discourses toward more open-ended, more dynamic "frames of acceptance." It all comes down to naming, he claims, the intentional forms by which we confront and describe our historical situation: "Call a man a villain, and you have the choice of either attacking or cringing. Call him mistaken, and you invite yourself to attempt setting him right. . . . The choice must be weighed with reference to the results we would obtain, and the resistances to those results" (3). Unlike the one-sided frames of epic and tragedy, Burke argues, the comic mode is inherently flexible. It laughs its way through all absolutes, and, so, in a process of continual negation, even self-negation, it is always "moving towards something better" (4). In this, Burke takes his dialectic from Marx, and his meliorism from FDR, but his comedy is all Henri Bergson. Bergson famously defined "laughter" as liberation from an increasingly mechanical world. We laugh, he claimed, at humans behaving like things and thus in order to relieve ourselves of our own potential thingliness. Laughter, as a "sort of *social gesture*," works to "soften down whatever the surface of the social body may retain of mechanical inelasticity." Thus a good guffaw restores the human body as well as the social body: it dissolves the "rigidity of body, mind, and character that society would like to get rid of in order to obtain from its members the greatest possible degree of elasticity and sociability."[34] Again, though, for Burke, the comic is a form, a rhetoric; comic negation is accomplished through and against the machinery of language. He explains, "abstractions are but fossilized metaphors," often guarding rigid property relations, and comic language works through free imagery, open-ended adjectives, and affective connotations to reopen the social terrain (13, 18). Thus, as Burke contends, comedy is the "most civilized form of art." It enacts a "progress of humane enlightenment" by working through linguistic biases and returning them to the flux of history and time (50–52).

First, then, humility—an embrace of poverty and even dereliction in opposition to the structures of pride and power. Secondly, the dialectic—a movement through social forms, rising and falling with each category, inhabiting in order to erode each abstraction. Finally, optimism—reclaiming and redistributing all accumulated value, poaching the well-guarded stock of cultural forms, restoring wealth to the common. In the end, comedy becomes a revolutionary praxis—dissolving, negating all claims in order to level the social field, redistributing value and wealth in relation to the whole. Like Marx, Burke accepts the necessity of capitalism itself, but only as the occasion for revolutionary laughter. Capitalism—or, rather, "the *capitalist* vocabulary of behavior"—cannot be simply discarded; rather, it must be met head-on by the wider frame of the comic, "actively, positively," so that it can be more humanely advanced within a broader discourse of need and progress (122, 132). Comic representation entails a public appropriation of private value; it approaches man and property as neither universal categories nor historical contingencies, but willful constructions that can be reconceived in more humane terms. Again, everywhere, motive seeps into discourse and, like some migrant energy, appropriates its forms and sets them into motion. In fact, Burke concludes his study by linking the comic mode with "folk" culture in general. Folk art is always, he writes, "folk criticism," a "collective philosophy of motivation, arising to name the relationships, or social situations, which people have found so pivotal and so constantly recurring as to need names for them." As comedy, folk culture considers human life as "a project in 'composition,' where the poet works with the materials of social relationships," trying not just to dissolve economic or political inequity, but to restore, in the end, an "ecological balance" (223–24).

Unlike Burke, though, Guthrie is actually funny, and his song helps us laugh our way toward something like social justice. Increasingly, he embraced comedy as a critical praxis, slyly exposing and eroding the vocabularies of power that perverted the communities through which he traveled. More specifically, Guthrie practiced a bumpkin version of "worried humor," affecting a simple inbred innocence and unnerving humility against all manner of sophisticated cons and corruptions. More partisan than the witty quips of Will Rogers and more explosive than the charming slapstick of Charlie Chaplin, his seemingly humble shtick provided a laughing release from the pretentions of politicians, businessmen, and the media: "There is a stage of hard luck," he writes in *Bound for Glory*, "that turns into fun, and a stage of poverty that turns into pride, and a place in laughing that turns into fight" (235).[35] Guthrie's prose is a marvel of categorical humor. Through puns, exaggeration, overstatement, understatement, irony, satire, and burlesque, he turns public language and then the public sphere on its head. Take, for example, the following riff from his "Woody Sez" column:

> Broke this morning, ain't got a dime. Everybody hit a little hard luck
> sometime. Boy, when I just sit here and imagine how much money they

got in the world I just wonder how everybody's got to be broke. Windy as the dickens where I'm writing this morning, so don't get excited if I blow a little. I guess there's plenty of stuff here in Washington that they never air. Oh, well, read the Daily Worker, you'll get wind of it. Woman and a dog a going across the grass. Dont know which is leading. Woman wanted to stop but the dog wouldn't let her. I think maybe she checks the dogs blood pressure before she votes, and then hires three doctors to check up again to see if the election went to suit the pooch.[36]

Guthrie's criticism takes shape subtly and indirectly. He begins with the seeming innocence of everyday words and categories, but ultimately exposes their manipulations and distortions. These words are nothing without the power that backs them up, he seems to be saying; it all could go a different way—*society ladies taking blood pressure, dogs voting at the polls, socialists winning the election.* Guthrie himself is just "blowing," using his own cheap art to mock the grandest of pretentions, and his "windy" discourse sets the discourse of modernity into comic motion, upturning its sureties and sanctities. But—and this is the kicker—even though his language exposes the absurdity of the modern world, it never completely abandons established categories and values; even in the midst of irony, in the midst of his deepest bellylaugh, Guthrie's speech maintains a deep sense of all the common and deeply held American values—truth, pleasure, reason, democracy—that have been perverted along the way.

Guthrie more successfully, more gracefully taps this laughing, rambling streak in song, where the affectively motivated phenomena of voice, rhythm, and melody literally set language into motion. In fact, all music, at a certain point, asks us to laugh at its own intensity, its own intense passion and fleeting commitment. What an absolutely silly and amazing thing to do—pluck strings, bang drums, blow into pipes—as if the entire world depended on it! Song is always raising ideals and promises it could never possibly keep, but also, in its own implacable motion, allows us to laugh at its pretention, to release ourselves from its own pained impossibility—and to preserve that promise intact even in its failure. So, at the end of *Bound for Glory*, after his audition at the Rainbow Room, Guthrie declares his commitment to music "with fight and guts and belly laughs and power and dynamite to it" (299). Similarly, in a letter to Lomax, he claims that his saddest songs are also his funniest: "Lots of songs I make up when I'm laughing and celebrating make folks cry and songs I make up when I'm feeling down and out makes people laugh" (*Pastures* 48). Ultimately, Guthrie offers song itself as a *via negativa*, a creative mode of dereliction, both destructive and restorative, and thus inherently "comic," working dialectically to soften and level an uneven discursive terrain, to dissolve false claims and promises in order to create a more "just" society. As he writes in his introduction to *Hard Hitting Songs for Hard-Hit People*, "These songs will echo that song of starvation till the world looks level—till the world is level—and there ain't no rich men, and there ain't no poor men, and every man on earth is at work and his family is living as human beings instead of like a nest of rats."[37]

Guthrie's talking blues, for example, may be his most lasting legacy to American popular music, and their success is no doubt due to the fact that their critical activity takes form as a freewheeling romp through a familiar American landscape. These blues work though a casual and apparently common dialectic; as Guthrie's rubes seek out all the formal markers of mainstream success and happiness, the pileup of mistakes, accidents, and frustrations produces a new critical stance—what Burke would call a more "rounded" frame. In "Talking Dust Bowl Blues," for example, Guthrie's hapless migrant follows the American dream way out west on a journey that is at once physical, moral, and totally hilarious.[38] He chases farm, family, money, car, gasoline, all in hopes of finding a bit of peace, but each promise raises only another set of problems, pushing him farther along on a seemingly endless trek. Ultimately, all his dreams are overturned, but not necessarily abandoned; rather, they are patched together and held in place as an entirely different strategy is applied, one that counters entrepreneurial spirit with a greater humility and the possibility of collective action. Forced to give up his pretensions, the rube emerges at the end of the song as a flexible survivor with both a greater critical eye and a genuine point of view. In the same way, Guthrie's own performance works over the discourses of modernity. Indeed, his greatest comic device is his own voice, with which he here slides and slurs across this proprietary landscape, using it to mock a range of professionalized languages, from psychoanalysis to engineering to politics. He changes "breakdown" to "bustdown," turning a joke about man as machine into a commentary on the disciplinary language of psychotherapy. He mangles "gasoline" and "engine," reversing the implicit insult that informs the language of professional expertise. He also holds the first syllable of "politicians" for an extra beat, drawing attention to a legal language defined by its own incredible stubbornness. Beyond these specific instances, though, Guthrie's overall lazy, drifting singsongy style wields its own subtle power. Here, Guthrie inflects everyday speech—"talk"—as song, as a loosely motivated performance of identity and sociality. His slanted speech slurs the habitual forms of communication and thus turns them into objects of critical attention and perhaps alternative investment. In other words, he sets everyday speech (or at least his fabricated version of it) back into motion, sings it in it order to reveal its flexibility, leaving the listener with the possibility of some other way of voicing life and thus some other way of living it.

But if Guthrie's comedy is always political, then his most important social collection is also deeply "comic." *Dust Bowl Ballads* exploits all the dusty, derelict glee of Guthrie's modernity and thus pushes the category of the nation toward something like its pop apotheosis. In his notes for the piece, Guthrie declares himself the "Dustiest of the Dust Bowlers" and then goes on to celebrate, in his own negative way, all the devastating "twistings" of the "migratious" experience. As Denning points out, Guthrie's collection rejects the epic symbolism of Steinbeck's classic take on the subject, *The Grapes of Wrath*, and adopts instead an ironic, picaresque approach. His method is migrant rather than mythic, intentionally episodic, itinerant, open-ended, and perhaps boundless in its hopefulness (270–75). In this, Guthrie fully exploits the migrant qualities of his medium. Laughing his way through a range of styles, voices, and attitudes, he presents each song as a usable but ultimately cheap and disposable response to an otherwise overwhelming situation. The collection opener, "The Great Dust Storm Disaster," is straightforward documentary, a nearly spoken list of dates and places with only a droning guitar for accompaniment. But Guthrie shifts tone and tempo with each new song, offering, in turn, a jokey talking blues ("Talking Dust Bowl Blues"), a politically inflected folktale ("Pretty Boy Floyd"), a rousing choral number ("Dusty Old Dust [So Long, It's Been Good to Know You]"), a weary blues ("Dust Bowl Blues"), and a sprawling seventeen-verse synopsis of a Steinbeck novel ("Tom Joad"). The songs veer wildly from historical fact to subjective reverie, from vicious social commentary to intimate expressions of hope and pleasure. They unfurl in the air like some dusty kaleidoscope of human moods and attitudes—anxiety, despair, horror, rage, humor, wonder, joy. In fact, Guthrie gives us an entire population of victims and survivors—farmers, preachers, cops, hobos, alcoholics, housewives, children, chickens, cows, and roosters. Each is given momentary due within the great sprawling collage of the whole, each an affective engine in its own right, motoring, motivated, pushing the entire delirious, giddy social whirligig beyond itself. Throughout, comedy—as the airy movement of song itself, the very motion of motivated form—laughs away at all narrow ideologies and rigid political positions, opening and closing upon itself as a kind of mocking counterdemocracy within an otherwise failed American democracy.

Tellingly, this is a fully elemental collection—a comedy of crazy cross-winds and dusty drafts. "The wild and windy actions of this great mysterious storm" becomes, for Guthrie, the model for human agency at large, in all its unsettled urgency and potential. Each human action is motivated and thus bound to a vast and ultimately open-ended system of force; a dusty proliferation of intentions becomes the exponentially increasing potential of connection and community. In this, Guthrie deepens the paradoxical economy of loss and gain outlined in *Bound for Glory*. Here, every failure is also always a bewildering beginning, a new opening, a new path; every desolation or alienation leads to some more alluring possibility or perspective, some new clearing in the landscape, in the national imaginary. By a kind of dust-borne ascesis or purgation, in the forceful erosion of custom and habit, all these migrant workers come to a new vitality and connectedness. Thus "The Great Dust Storm" ends—with the actual passing of the storm—in a state of stunned openness, a complete break with the past that is also an empty new day. Elsewhere, the crushing violence of the storm results in a new sense of personal value, a certain survivor's pride. In "Blowin' Down the Road (I ain't going to be treated this way)," the migrant worker cuts his own path across the dusty landscape, marking his own values and distinctions in the newly open terrain:

> I'm a-lookin' for a job at honest pay,
> I'm a-lookin' for a job at honest pay,
> I'm a-lookin' for a job at honest pay, lord, lord,
> An' I ain't a-gonna be treated this way.[39]

And so the comedy of dust spreads across the land, dissolving, leveling all in its path, washing away the romantic abstractions of modern life, the egotism and entrepreneurial violence of the market, forcing, enabling, inspiring its victims to pursue new paths across the terrain, to mark it in more useful, more satisfying ways. The empty air becomes the place to sing the self and thus the nation, to drift in both deed and voice, to wander, to waver, to laugh, always, toward something better.

Again, though, in this comedy, form is never abandoned, but made flexible, and, in this, we can fully clarify Guthrie's use of the refrain, which, as the encapsulation of Guthrie's "vocabulary of motives," reflects the dynamic migrant ethos of pop at large. On *Dust Bowl Ballads*, Guthrie's refrains are both bleak and defiant, faltering and assertive, and thus they enact a comic dialectic in miniature, affirming, again and again, the inherent openness of motivational discourse. Indeed, whether the message is proud ("I ain't gonna be treated this way") or weary ("I ain't got no home in this world anymore") or even wry ("So long, it's been good to know you"), the refrain seems to persist in the face of its own emptiness, establishing itself precisely as it empties itself of value and significance. This is not simply an issue of lyrical content, but also a wonderfully formal effect; each refrain at once appears and dissolves in its own voicing, drifts away with each rendition, as if clearing the air for its return, for some new and equally forceful declaration of intent. Each verse in "Dusty Old Dust (So Long, It's Been Good to Know You)," for example, describes another dusty end, but the chorus returns with a rousing jocular fever. In fact, the chorus consists of quoted and thus repeatable speech; it is basically a witty, black retort, utterly negative and apocalyptic, but it is adopted again and again in slightly varying ways—as defiance, detachment, and evasion—in the face of complete catastrophe:

> We talked of the end of the world, and then
> We'd sing a song an' then sing it again.
> We'd sit for an hour an' not say a word,
> And then these words would be heard:
>> "So long, it's been good to know you.
>> So long, it's been good to know you.
>> So long, it's been good to know you.
>> This dusty old dust is a-gettin' my home,
>> And I got to be driftin' along."[40]

At once warm and ironic, sympathetic and wry, this chorus generates a most peculiar affective position. Audience and singer assert as they deny any further communion, establish as they dismiss all future commitment. In this, perhaps, it is the most fitting mantra of a migrant community and the best expression of its attempt to turn forced displacement into a genuine way of belonging. But it is also what we all experience as the comedic pleasure of pop. Drifting along the dusty highways of modernity, such refrains—recycled in our own headspace—became at once our glorious release and consistent salvation, territorialization and deterritorialization both.

Finally, then, while we might not laugh at Guthrie's most famous political anthems, their appeal lies mostly in their comic reversal of mythic nationhood and all its discourses. In "Pastures of Plenty," for example, Guthrie confronts the rigid categories of the modern world only to open and disperse their contents.[41] He organizes the song around a not-so-subtle distinction between the dynamic ethos of the laboring class and the static propriety of the owners. The lyrics quickly fall into a syntactical pattern, linking laborers with active verbs and owners with possessives, so that history itself appears as the constant creation and erosion of economic forms. Importantly, though, the song never questions the need for structure and appropriation; in fact, it does not question any of the virtues that seem to underlie America's capitalist spirit (liberty, property, the pursuit of labor, etc.), but it redistributes them along new class lines. The paradox is implied, if not fully explained, in the song's last few lines:

> Well, it's always we rambled, that river and I.
> All along your green valley, I will work till I die.
> My land I'll defend with my life if it be,
> 'Cause my pastures of plenty must always be free.

Here, Guthrie defends property—"my land"—to the death, but only in the name of freedom and equality. Instead of denying capital's organizing power, he wants to preserve it in the name of access, of renewal and increase, of potential and potential transformation, imagining a fluid continuum between human effort and natural bounty. The migrant— who comes and goes with the dust and wind—preserves the categories that currently define his dereliction, but seeks to mobilize them in more humane ways, in accord with the natural order and in respect of shifting human needs. In this, Guthrie's song proffers a truly dialectic, and, again, "comic," vision of America, one that retains the virtues of capitalism as it moves toward a more fluid redistribution of wealth and resource. In fact, the song not only projects, but enacts this vision; here, with Guthrie's own flat voice, form and force flow together in a single motivational continuum, one that intends to create—in its own intentional sound—the very America it describes.

"This Land Is Your Land" goes even further, demonstrating how song, and particularly song's refrain, implies proper land use and thus proper nationhood.[42] Once again, Guthrie outlines a tension between the human desire to possess the land and the fullness of the natural landscape. Here, though, he has no illusions about the latter—there is no prediscursive terrain, no unwritten land: nature is always already a sign, always already its own beautiful speech, and thus, in a way, it essentially belongs to the human. In fact, the land appears here specifically as a "voice" and chants its own open song, at once naming itself and calling the listener to claim its potential. Thus the issue is not necessarily possession, but ethical possession, a form of appropriation that preserves natural bounty and accessibility. The song demands a more ethical mode of representation, one that allows nature to be re-presented, to be used/sung again and again without perversion or restriction. In an earlier version of the song, Guthrie explicitly addresses the improper marking of the land. Natural rights of ownership are contrasted with perverse land claims, by rigid signs cut into the ground, creating impossible barriers between bounty and its rightful—in effect, collective—heirs:

> Was a big high wall that tried to stop me.
> A sign was painted said, "Private Property,"
> But on the back side it didn't say nothing—
> God Blessed America for me.

As is well known, Guthrie originally composed the song as a rejoinder to Irving Berlin's conservative drumbeater "God Bless America." With these lines and the original refrain intact, "This Land Is Your Land" both signals the discursive warfare that carves up the nation and itself becomes a key weapon against misappropriations of American identity. The blank back side of the sign becomes the collective openness of the song's own imagined nation; Guthrie sings of an America that is both marked and free, defined but not restricted, and his own open song is offered up—in its collective transmission—as its most fitting expression. In fact, the sign that appears here is just one instance of re-presentation and re-appropriation. The lyrics work through a number of discursive registers—economic, religious, and cultural—adapting prior significations for new uses. With the more famous second refrain—"This land was made for you and me"—the song recodes the language of industry and ownership in terms of community and cooperation. Similarly, with the earlier, deleted refrain—"God blessed America for me"—it mimes religious discourse in order to challenge its authority and moral exclusiveness.

But the actual history of the song suggests that the power of the refrain is affirmed only in its various uses, beyond the initial act of composition. Its most famous line, when set apart from Guthrie's more aggressive protest verses, has attained a certain neutrality in our culture, capable of wandering from voice to voice, place to place, eroding, on a whole other level, the most basic markers of class and—with the civil rights movement—race. It has come to serve—in its airy transmission—as both a kind of national chorus and a counter-chorus, and thus further presses the song's humble case, making of it a common property—a common wealth—available for a range of voices and uses, in classrooms, at stadiums and rallies, on commercials, campuses, courthouse steps, and churches. Ultimately, the song's decisively popular history realizes what Guthrie always ultimately sought in political music: a language at once motivated, mobile, and provisional, drawing its power not from any explicit message or expression, but from its collective appeal and contextual uses. Yes, the song is marked by a specific analysis of property relations and human rights, but it ultimately works its political cause in its actual singing, as the floating refrain becomes both the matter and means by which alternative exchanges and communities may be enacted. The song, in other words, itself stands in for the missing commonwealth, holding its place in pop consciousness with each rendition, with each new context, even as wealth and property continue to assert an entirely different set of relations.

Studies Show Phenomenal Growth in Migrant Traffic

It all begins with a simple air. The migrant's little tune establishes a shelter, a center amid the chaos, a territory, a sense of space and time in an otherwise boundless terrain. But as Gilles Deleuze and Félix Guattari explain, that song itself remains fluid, dynamic, abstract, and so, even in its work of territorialization, it effects the opposite—deterritorialization, the decoding of both tradition and identity, the release of all social form and value, the liberation of the nation at large:

> Every milieu is coded, a code being defined by periodic repetition; but each code is in a perpetual state of transcoding or transduction. Transcoding or transduction is the manner in which one milieu serves as the basis for another, or conversely is established atop another milieu, dissipates in it or is constituted in it. The notion of the milieu is not unitary: not only does the living thing continually pass from one milieu to another, but the milieus pass into one another; they are essentially communicating.[43]

So many refrains, so many milieus: constant form and constant chaos, one in and through the other. The overlapping modes of Guthrie's music demonstrate this complex process and its incredible openness. First, the refrain as rhythmic code provisionally makes and unmakes the immediate milieu in which it sounds. It is both a movement and a pattern, a gesture physical and abstract, motivated and repeatable. It is not dogmatic, like meter, but active and critical, marking continuity through and as discontinuity; as form, as repeated form, it exists, despite any uses, precisely in its uses, as it momentarily gathers space and time about it. As in a *talking blues*, then, the refrain allows and sustains lines of flight; its repetition is also always break from repetition, from some other code, and so directs the wanderer on a journey that is by turns anxious, errant, and giddy. But, soon, the milieu ceases to be directional and becomes dimensional, its parts communicating with each other, maintaining balance and consistency, expressive consistency, even a style. The milieu, in becoming a territory, assigns qualities and functions to its various parts and participants, and so stable meanings and values are communicated between them; everything in it is marked for a specific use, rendered proper and thus as a kind of property, at once opening certain doors and closing others. As in a *national anthem*, as in "This Land Is Your Land," the refrain becomes expressive; it names a space and thereby claims it, establishing its internal and external relations, and thereby produces both a homeland and a people. But, then, always, the refrain, as autonomous form, as abstract relation, works over other refrains, other codes, freeing them from their intended purposes. The refrain absorbs the codes that define the territory, re-arranges them, re-patterns them, in sound, and thus is always also accompanied by a certain chaos, a potential openness. One code decodes another, strips it of its meaning, its inevitability, and so makes of it a certain resource to be used otherwise. In this, the refrain—"So long, it's been good to know you"—also always signals departure, a movement away from the territory. As in a *dust bowl ballad*, the refrain at once catches up the chaos of the world and pulverizes it, reduces it to dust, the chaotic. And, so, in their proliferation, all refrains ultimately "rejoin the songs of the Molecules, the newborn wailing of the fundamental elements . . . . They cease to be territorial, becoming cosmic . . . The Cosmos as an immense deterritorialized refrain" (327). A laughing, comic refrain.

Territorialization is deterritorialization; the nation, as rhythmic refrain, makes itself over and over again in giddy sonic spasms. But why sound? Why music? What is the art of the refrain, and how does it relate to politics, to a people? Certainly, sound and song already suggest a certain abstraction, the transcoding of everyday life into a looser, immaterial set of relations. A song is capable of attracting and binding otherwise disparate forms and forces to its own sonic code; it is a flimsy mechanism—light and detached—yet only thus more powerful, a remarkably strong machine capable of cutting into an established territory and carving out new spaces and times within it. Indeed, color clings too closely to the objects in the territory, too closely to the economy, but sound carries all away with it, it has its own "phylogenetic line" or "continuity," and this abstraction places it at the cutting edge of territorialization and deterritorialization both:

> Sound invades us, impels us, drags us, transpierces us. It takes leave of the earth, as much in order to drop us into a black hole as to open up to

a cosmos. It makes us want to die. Since its force of deterritorialization is the strongest, it also effects the most massive of reterritorializations, the most numbing, the most redundant. . . . That is why the musician has a different relation to the people, machines, and the established powers than does the painter. In particular, the established powers feel a keen need to control the distribution of black holes and lines of deterritorialization in this phylum of sounds, in order to ward off or appropriate the effects of musical mechanism. (348)

Song, as sonic machine, builds nations and kills fascists—often at the same time. It is never simply expressive or representational, for its form, as we've seen throughout these first three chapters, inevitably effects new patterns and relays in the world about it, at once linking up or shutting down other assemblages and machines (333–34). But song always ultimately points beyond its own productions toward other possible productions and thereby slips past any specific political uses. As Deleuze and Guattari explain, "The artist opens up to the Cosmos in order to harness forces in a 'work,'" and this "work," as work, reveals the "trace of creation in the created," shows us that "this world has had different aspects, will have still others, and that there are already others on other planets" (337). The songmaker is one who, in singing to the people, "lets loose molecular populations in hopes that this will sow the seeds of, or even engender, the people to come, that these populations will pass into a people to come, open a cosmos" (345). For Deleuze and Guattari, the songs in the air, even the very cheapest, mass-produced, and totalizing ones, always supersede the machines that produce them—industrial machines, political machines, human machines. Indeed, they conclude their study of the refrain with an idea I'd like to take seriously in the next two chapters: "the sound molecules of pop music are at this very moment implanting here and there a people of a new type, singularly indifferent to the orders of the radio, to computer safeguards, to the threat of atomic bomb" (346).

To conclude, though, let's bring this all back down to earth. Guthrie's art emerged out of specific class experiences and economic challenges. His own enforced poverty allowed him to see himself as a member of a new migrant community. Similarly, his song's value lies in its lack of value, its seeming worthlessness. Unlike painting and poetry, song is easily made and freely mobilized in the empty air. Weightless, formless, it can extend over seemingly unbridgeable chasms of time and space, seep across both public and private boundaries, and generate new affective currents within and across a divided populace. In this, Guthrie's music extended the mobility and detachment that defined blues and country music. With its cheap formalism, it points beyond regional and political propaganda, beyond even the grotesque contortions of the Popular Front, toward an airy, giddy, and childlike sense of laughter and play. Tellingly, most of his work in the 1940s, such as the quirky collection of children songs or his Technicolor lyrics about Coney Island, reveals a vibrant absurdist streak, a more complete embrace of song's essential emptiness. In "Mermaid's Avenue," for example, class experiences of loss and negation support a new surrealist collectivity, a ragtag bottoms-up kitchen-sink democracy of everyone who's nobody in a nation that is not—fast and slow folks, hot and cold ones, rich and poor, wolves and haybags, hags and wags and witches.[44] "But," the refrain goes, "there's never been a mermaid here / On Mermaid Avenue." The star of the street never arrives—she doesn't exist—but her alluring promise, her song, in its very absence, attracts and sustains a giddy counterrepublic-cum-amusement-park—a specifically "cosmic" people. All the promise of the original republic returns here, but only in its utter failure, in its refusal to define itself, and thus critically, as an open republic, a free republic—at once ethnic, culinary, kinky, and trashy. In fact, there's no song here, either; Guthrie never recorded his own version of "Mermaid's Avenue." These are just lyrics, tossed-off refrains, free to be picked up here and there by an equally scruffy collective of musicians—Wilco, the Klezmatics, Jonatha Brooke—who now re-create this cosmic America in purely sonic terms, over and over again in the empty air. Thus the derelict space and time of Mermaid Avenue becomes the derelict space and time of pop itself, where feelings and forms wander aimlessly, mingle freely, more freely than they ever did on the immigrant streets of New York or in the ranks of the socialist movement.

No doubt, if Guthrie had avoided the disorder that claimed his life, his art would have moved further and further toward this absurdist mode, designed not so much to evade social reality, but to provide a whimsical challenge to its ruling economies. Again, his folksy avant-gardism of the 1940s anticipates the world of pop itself, which was just then poised to take over the nation's folkways in a major way. As the next two chapters show, singers like Elvis Presley and Buddy Holly were soon pursuing their own derelict art in the empty space of the studio, without much anxiety about region or politics, playing with forms like blues and country to thrill a nation of lonely teens and lost consumers. Michel de Certeau's midcentury study *The Practice of Everyday Life* best explains this transition from "folk" to "pop" and the kind of "people" or "nation" it presupposes.[45] Certeau celebrates the modern "user" as part consumer and part migrant, one whose activity in relation to the economy is defined by procedures over products and selections over expressions. The user's activity is notable for its sheer provisionality and ultimate abandonment and thus suggests a cunning alternative to the capitalist logic of authority, ownership, and accumulation; it is decisively "not directed toward profit" and thus casts a shadow, like pop culture in general, over the official economy (25). Guthrie, as migrant worker, folk singer, and modernist artist, only ever made *use* of the forms—the "refrains"—around him, and thereby established alternative patterns and values in an otherwise well-policed world. But with the growth of the consumer marketplace, this migrant activity came to be stitched into the economy itself and became the purview of a significant underclass. Thus, as we'll see, we move from regional expression and political songmaking to pop culture at large—or, rather, fan culture, as a form of social protest by way of fashion, taste, style, and gesture.

Ultimately, this transitional or hybrid formation—between folk and pop—suggests a different approach to the public sphere and nationhood. Certeau further distinguishes between a "strategy," which marks off a territory in order to control its use, and a "tactic," a more or less spontaneous seizure of opportunity within a field or milieu. The former begins with a proprietary claim, both a property and a proper mode of behavior, whereas the latter is inherently ad hoc, dynamic, and circumstantial, responsive to the specific features of the environment. Thus, as Certeau explains, the user-tactician pursues his livelihood through a kind of cultural poaching; he slips, like Patton and Carson, like Guthrie, across a prefabricated world, appropriating geographic, economic, and discursive structures for his own needs, and thus introduces a certain drift—"wandering lines" and "indeterminate trajectories"—into an otherwise stable and rigidly guarded system (38, 34). His dusty flight creates a series of counterrhythms and refrains, new ways of wandering-working-singing the land, opening it all up again, bit by bit, for his fellow travelers. Guthrie's song is nothing if not tactical in this way—contextual, provisional, subversive; it never stops rambling—"on the wing"—moving through established landscapes and property lines, taking what it can, where it can. Over time, with each repetition, the entire land is claimed or, rather, *re*claimed for a very different kind of economy and a different kind of politics. As Josh Kun explains, the migrant spaces and times of pop music everywhere overlap with the migrant spaces of the nation: "Music does not respect places because it is capable of inhabiting them while moving across them—of arriving while leaving. Through music, space is constructed and deconstructed, filled up and hollowed out. Music creates spaces in which cultures get both contested and consolidated and both sounded and silenced—double acts of delinquency that question both the geopolitical boundaries of the modern nation-state and the disciplinary boundaries that govern its study in the academy."[46]

Certeau specifically links wandering with song. He defines both as an emphatic reuse of space and time, not necessarily creating, but re-emphasizing, re-distributing, re-amplifying the forms and forces of everyday life. He writes, "All the modalities sing a part in this chorus, changing form step to step, stepping in through proportions, sequences, and intensities which vary according to the time, the path taken and the walker. These enunciatory operations are of an unlimited diversity" (101). Similarly, Guthrie's voice sings and re-sings the landscape through which he wanders, marking it with his own motives, without necessarily changing it in substance or even form. He does this through a song that is itself neither a place nor a thing, but a discourse, a virtual movement, with no weight, no capital, no stock, free to move precisely because it carries no baggage. Indeed, for Certeau, singing—like walking—means "to lack a place. It is the indefinite process of being absent and in search of a proper." Guthrie's music moves across the land like "a passer-by, a network of residences temporarily appropriated by pedestrian traffic, a shuffling among pretenses of the proper, a universe of rented spaces haunted by a nowhere or by dreamed-of places" (103). We have visited these deterritorialized spaces—Patton's bird nest, Carson's log cabin, Lair's Renfro—but Guthrie's song is distinguished, from both blues and country, by its collectivism, its cheap and open virtuality, and all its deep, gutsy laughter. In this, in its constant ramblin', it moves us toward another country entirely, the giddy and indifferent spaces and times of rock and pop, where a tossed-off song is itself a form of transgressive pleasure, a sensual reoccupation of a prefabricated and well-policed world. Guthrie claimed the entire land with his voice, or, rather, he *de*claimed it—he sang it in order to free it, in an open, vital process, one that asserted, with each refrain, the utterly provisional and ultimately ridiculous nature of all such claims.

CHAPTER FOUR

Four Elvises

On the Dada Possibilities of
Midcentury Rock and Roll
and Modern Fan Culture

So the artist goes shopping. With his belly full of wine and sandwiches, he heads down Fifth Avenue and enters the showroom of the J. L. Mott Iron Works. He wanders over to the bath section and eyes the fixtures on display—sinks, tubs, toilets. He fingers the white rims, notes the play of light and shadow, looks cautiously into a pipe. There, at the end of the aisle, he spies the one he wants, a flat-back "Bedfordshire" urinal—smutty and sleek. His friends help him haul it back to Fourteenth Street and lift it onto a pedestal. They play with its positioning and lighting, shifting it until they find the best angle, and then, *voila!*, he signs it—*R. Mutt*—and sends it off to the Independents Hall with his $6.00 entry fee. A few days later, the exhibition committee opens the box; they glare at the thing lying quietly on the ground and start shouting at each other. "It's indecent!" "It's art!" "We can't show it!" "He paid his fee!" One member of the committee tries to defend the work on the basis of purposeless beauty. "A lovely form has been revealed," he claims, "freed from its functional purpose; therefore a man has clearly made an aesthetic contribution." But his peers won't listen—not here, not this time. Someone threatens to smash the hideous thing and then agrees to hide it behind a screen. The work is never exhibited, but a few days later it shows up at the studio of a famous photographer and eventually becomes a masterpiece of pop art.[1]

Thirty years later, a teen shops for art. He walks into a Memphis beauty salon and asks for the Duck's Ass—Tony Curtis–style. He then heads over to Beale Street and enters Lansky's. He eyes a neat pile of slacks and picks out a pair of shiny black gabardines—pleated up top, pegged down below. No, not the solid black, the pair with the green stripe on the side—yeah, that's the one. He takes a suede belt, too, and then the "gab" shirt, with the rolled collar like Billy Eckstine's. He heads home, changes, and checks himself in the mirror. Something's missing. He opens his mother's drawer, fingers the scarves, and picks the pink one—no questions asked. The next day, the teen walks into shop class, turns on the wood sander, and tries to drown out the insults. "Hey, squirrel!" "Hey, freak!" Later, in the hall, the boys push him against the wall, threaten to cut his locks, and punch him in the balls. A muscular senior appears on the scene, defends the teen's choice, and makes a fairly convincing case for stylized dissent: "There ain't no need for this. If he likes his hair that way, well, no sense in hassling him." The teen wriggles away, tears in his eyes; he runs down the hall, home, into his bedroom, fixes himself again in the mirror. A few weeks later, he shows up at a recording studio on Union Avenue and becomes a pop star.[2]

Mechanical standardization, mass production, consumer desire, cheapness, indifference—these are the founding principles of pop counterculture. Somewhere between Marcel Duchamp's arty toss-off and Elvis Presley's tossed-off art, everything changes—modern art gives in to modernity and becomes a matter of daily life. Iconoclasm is made available to the masses via the marketplace, put in the service of an everyday rebellion, against both the elite taste of the avant-garde and the conventional tastes of Ma and Pa. This is at least partially a matter of class politics. Duchamp's fanciful experiment in "readymade" art becomes a form of stylized dissent for Elvis and his disaffected fans. What the avant-garde prankster casually demonstrated from the comfort of his atelier turns into a desperate way of life for the hooligan underclass. But it is also a matter of economic history. By the time Elvis arrived on the scene, all the avant-garde possibilities of chance and indifference were built into the commodity form itself, made available to any teenybopper with a little bit of cash, a ride to the mall, and a sense of fun. Everywhere, a certain "tastelessness"—the complete leveling of aesthetic value affected by the marketplace and industrial technology—turned the ordinary into the extraordinary, translated trash into art, and raised the possibility of another modernity altogether: pop modernity.

As I'm sure you can guess, I have no romance for Elvis authenticity. There is no real King, no pure Elvis, who fell to the likes of Steve Allen, Colonel Parker, or Nipper the RCA dog. There is no Elvis before his own repeated humility; he was never anything more than his own grubby groping toward fame, a series of commodified poses and gestures—on records, film, television, posters. His convulsive performances—all tics and spasms, jerky poses and juxtaposed styles—express neither the authenticity of region nor the immediacy of race, but the giddy mediation of all identity in the modern era. In other words, when it comes to Elvis culture, repetition precedes renewal, and self-estrangement implies self-renewal. Thus this chapter presents Elvis as a product of modernity at its most violent and frenetic, and it explores early rock and roll as a gloriously cheap exchange between self-stylized fans and the often cheap objects of their affection. Here, the themes of previous chapters—dereliction, detachment, indifference, abstraction, repetition—come together to present Elvis as neither folk hero nor artist-genius, but a charged commercial form, one that, because of its emptiness, gripped the body of the fan in a number of ecstatic ways. But first, quickly, we must do away with the overlapping myths of authenticity that continue to circulate around the King's body.

First, *the authenticity of region.* Elvis's popularity has always been linked—vaguely, but effectively—to his southern roots. In a 1958 article for *Harper's Magazine*, for example, James and Annette Baxter frame the King's compelling "primitivism" as a reflection of "authentic Southernness." Here, Elvis represents the South as a "more enticing realm," a cultural backwater that yet "retains a comparable aura of mystery, of romantic removal from the concerns of a steadily urbanized and cosmopolized America." If Elvis speaks to American teens, the Baxters contend, it's because his "backwoods heterodoxies"—his casual sexiness, his working-class roughness, his suggestive "blackness"—signal an "instinctive rebellion" from modern life.[3] Later, with civil rights and the cultural revolution of the 1960s, this discourse would shift slightly in relation to the south but remain bound to it nonetheless. In the work of Nick Tosches and Greil Marcus, Elvis the rebel is a decisively *redneck* rebel, a hell-bent hillbilly with a social agenda, and thus a figure who both reflects and resists his southern roots.[4] Most famously, in *Mystery Train*, Marcus locates Elvis's authenticity in his instinctive otherness; he is unassimilated and therefore resistant to both regional and national ideology—the masculine embodiment of democracy as "a world of risk, will, passion, and natural nobility" (127). Here, again, authenticity hinges on a manufactured difference. Elvis's roots are affirmed, paradoxically, by his desire to escape them, and so the reality of both performer and region fall into hazy romance and myth-making.[5] The real issue, though, remains commerce and commodification, for in all such accounts, the authenticity of region is opposed to the falseness of the marketplace. Again and again, the consolidation of the culture industry is lamented as a moment of cultural betrayal, the death of traditional music and regional expression. Even in the most celebratory accounts—by, say, Marcus and Peter Guralnick—the arc of Elvis's career represents the stale packaging of an otherwise defiant folk culture and, in the final image of a bloated, drug-addled King dying on his throne, remains a cautionary tale about the manipulations and depredations of the culture industry.[6] This all seems a bit paranoid to me, and when all is said and done, the pleasure of popular music—in and beyond the South—cannot be divorced from the very real pleasures of the national marketplace. As I hope to show here, the Elvis phenomenon was from the start nothing without its connection to the expanding consumer economy; its revolutionary power cannot be distinguished from the technologies of a marketplace that radicalized the experience of music and created new and more thrilling possibilities of exchange for listeners, all of which in themselves seemed very "authentic."

Secondly, *the authenticity of desire.* For many, the Elvis revolution began with a pelvic rumble and culminated in an explosion of raw sexual energy. Here, the frankness of "the Pelvis" comes to defy 1950s conventionalism and, especially, the frustrated adolescence of the female bobbysoxer. Elvis comes swinging onto the scene dripping with the markers of illicit desire—as a hunk of inaccessible but arousing working-class and slightly racialized love. Barbara Ehrenreich, for example, argues that sexual development in this era entailed a fretful balancing act between giving and withholding, a deferred dream of romantic courtship that, in the end, proved less than satisfying. Here, though, Elvis emerges less as a radical form of desire than a conventional figure of fantasy: "Part of the appeal of the male star," Ehrenreich writes, "was that you would *never* marry him. . . . Adulation of the male star was a way to express sexual yearnings that would normally be pressed into the service of popularity or simply repressed."[7] Others argue that the very structure of the Elvis spectacle gave fans an opportunity to try out novel or more fluid forms of sexual *identity.* Elvis as performer inverted the traditionally gendered coordinates of the gaze, presenting his own male body as a sexual object and thus opening up the libidinal field and the power dynamics contained within it. As David R. Shumway explains, "The visual relation between fan and star under these conditions is ambiguous. The star remains an object of the gaze and thus is vulnerable to her, but the fan's visible response is seemingly produced by the star and thus is in her control."[8] In a way, this emphasis on sexuality and desire reflects less the Elvis phenomenon than the sexual revolution of the 1960s and later academic debates about the performance of gender. While some of these accounts recognize how commodified forms might generate new forces of attraction and repulsion, they obscure the fact that Elvis's fans describe a much wider range of responses, many of which were more affectionate than desirous; the King's body was never merely the static object of fantasy or the amorous gaze, but an active site of emotional exchange, self-recreation, and social engagement. More specifically, as presented in these cases, the logic of desire—at once binary and static, both rigid and frustrated—tends to obscure the more eccentric play of drives that occurs within it. My Elvis is not only more commercial, but more sluttish than anyone likes to admit. If his stardom is processed by the technology of commerce, it is also more dynamic: through records, radio, television, and film, his body becomes the site of strange drives and even stranger tastes, a relay of spasms, tics, and thrusts that circulate through and beyond traditional gendered identities and the general logic of desire.

Finally, *the authenticity of race*. Turning to issues of race provides a more nuanced point of entry, but once again leads to issues of commodification. As Eric Lott points out, "Every time you hear an expansive white man drop into his version of black English, you are in the presence of blackface's unconscious return."[9] No doubt, Elvis, as latter-day minstrel, worked through a certain version of racialized masculinity—defined by "cool, virility, humility, abandon"—in order to manage the complex cultural desires of the civil-rights era. His song-and-dance act played with the "collective fears of a degraded and threatening Other," teetering on the brink of racial romance and identification, and thus earned him and his handlers a bunch of dough (52–55). In turn, fans like Marcus celebrate Elvis's adaptations of "black" styles insofar as they strip away the guilt of racialized culture. In *Mystery Train*, Marcus claims that Elvis "beat the black man at his own game" (142); his minstrel hits have "more power, verve, and skill" than their originals—"It's the blues, but free of all worry, all sin; a simple joy with no price to pay" (155, 147). Such comments, no doubt, construct authenticity through related fantasies of race and masculinity (we should recall here, with no small horror, Marcus's account of his own obscene dream about Elvis's uncircumcised penis [172]). However, even at their most gratuitous, Lott suggests, Elvis's performances tended to unsettle racial categories and circulate alternative forms of racialized identity. The King's act was always framed by a sense "ludic fun," one that, in its self-conscious commercialization, tended toward both mockery and subversion. In other words, Elvis's act worked to decode the styles and values of mainstream culture *and* its racial Other, exposing both as constructions dependent upon the act of performance itself. Born of working-class dereliction and adolescent fun (rather than bourgeois fear and loathing), and yet cultivated within commercialized forms such as records and posters, the Elvis spectacle tapped the genre's tendency toward absurdity, that "fascinating imaginary space of fun and license" in which the construction of difference becomes a pleasure in itself (51). Moreover, Lott claims, such performances inscribed racialized difference within the commodity form itself, so that "the blackface mask" ultimately appears as a "figuration of the commodity, a sort of trademark assigned to the 'black' images white people paid to see" (48–49). Simply put, Elvis's fans accessed race and blackness as the ludic pleasure of commercial form itself; as Lott's work implies, Elvis—whether on records, radios, film, or television—performed "an act of blackness as 'target and purse,' . . . Commodification is, in a sense, [his] *attraction*" (62).[10]

Ultimately, this chapter explores commerce and the commodity form as foundations for any future thinking about Elvis and issues of regionalism, gender, and race. It brings together a number of earlier points regarding music's relation to the culture industry in order to provide a more dynamic picture of the kind of "publics" created through the filter of the marketplace. The fragmentation of the body, the power of the fetish, the separation of event and copy, the circulation of forms—these marketplace effects come together here in an account of fan culture as an open-ended process of affective transformation rather than an anxious expression of personal identity. My argument is certainly informed by a Frankfurt School paradigm that regards the products of mass culture with deep suspicion, but it is also attuned to the unique forms of pleasure and agency that accompany the commodification of modern life. From the perspective of fan culture, the discussion ultimately shifts from the issue of "authenticity" toward the possibilities of "performance," "enactment," and "investment." As Lawrence Grossberg argues, rock introduces a certain noise into the otherwise boring, routinized structures of everyday life. Its sound, as commodified sound, has "a unique and striking relation to the human body, surrounding, enfolding, and even invading it within its own rhythms and textures." At once sloppy, invasive, and tasteless, this sound drowns out the middle-class ego and instead calls "forth people's investments, and hence their affective anchors in reality. . . . locates them in the world by constructing the rhythms of their stopping and going."[11] In other words, this music doesn't "mean" anything—it expresses nothing about the authentic self or its regional shaping; rather, it "matters" in the double sense of the term, as *the matter* of everyday life and *that which matters* in an ethical sense. For Grossberg, fandom is built not on expressions, nor even structured codes and meanings, but upon a fluid series of "affective alliances." Unlike the consumer, who relates to music in terms of acquisition, in terms of what it "means" for the ego (i.e., as fetish), the fan approaches music with an "affective sensibility," seeking it out as a mode of "investment," as a way of organizing and evaluating relations in an increasingly commodified world.[12]

So from Duchamp to Elvis to the bedroom bobbysoxer, fans seek objects that matter, impressively, in everyday life, in relation to their senses, needs, and hopes. And behind such mattering lies affect as a kind of embodied judgment, at once sensual and smart, errant and obsessive, and thus capable of generating and sustaining its own values. Affect, we'll find, as a dimension of the drive, implies a valencing or turning of the body, a charged mode of engagement with the forms of the world rather than a readymade logic of identity as presence and absence. Moreover, affect is a dynamic form of communication, one that tends to collapse stable boundaries of self and other and to transgress standard formulations of both place and history. Affect "reads," but not in terms of abstract difference; it is attuned to the markers of daily life, but each as a message without a code, each as a sensual and sensible object that "matters" on its own terms and thus takes us farther and farther away from standard ideologies. Again, though, all begins with dereliction, the economy of loss and gain that defines blues and country, not to mention Guthrie's folk, and ends with the commodity form and the slippery kind of indifference it introduces into modern public exchange. Whereas Duchamp lifts trash into a new context, and thus presents it as high art, Elvis lets everything fall out of context, and it all becomes low art. In the King's own dereliction, he asserts, vigorously, defiantly, that our relation to the world is affective, charged, and dynamic, full of pleasures that are not simply acquisitive or even structured, but nonetheless powerful and significant.[13]

Readymade Elvis

So chance, indifference, tastelessness—Marcel Duchamp's blueprint for readymade art implies not just a cunning attack on artistic pretention, but also the origin of fan culture and its attendant pleasures. Simply put, the random selection and indifferent regard of otherwise common, slightly raunchy things defines the logic of the culture industry, particularly in America, the first country to recognize the cheap genius of both the King of the avant-garde and the King of rock and roll.[14] In this, I'm interested in comparing not just Elvis and Duchamp, two brilliant artists of everyday

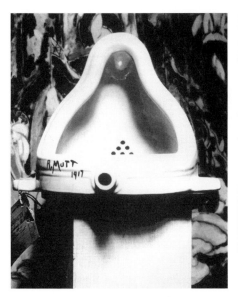

IMAGE 3 *Fountain*, Marcel Duchamp, 1917. (ARS)

IMAGE 4 Elvis Presley in *Jailhouse Rock*, Metro-Goldwyn-Mayer, 1957. (MPTVIMAGES.COM)

life, but also Elvis the star commodity and Duchamp's equally curvy pelvic *Fountain*—the King and the Throne, if you will (see images 3 and 4). On the one hand, a common industrial object—here, a urinal—is chosen by an idiosyncratic artist for its supple physical form, its suggestive curves and orifices, and thus appears endowed with an aura and uniqueness otherwise lost in the world of mass production and consumption. On the other, a grubby teen wanders into a Memphis studio and quickly, before the indifferent machinery of the industry, becomes the object of an entire culture's arrested gaze. If the juxtaposition seems cheap and dirty, it is necessarily so—I want to explore the collapse of identities and things brought about by consumer culture and the possibility of sensual renewal that it entails.

Before all else, Duchamp sought the renewal of everyday life through everyday things. By randomly selecting and displaying, say, a urinal, a shovel, or a clothes iron, the artist hoped to block conventional responses to these objects and thus open the way for new kinds of investment. In general, these are all easily overlooked objects, common objects of only habitual use, but their unnatural framing—as art, as waste—forces us to consider their purely sensual properties. By removing them from everyday contexts, Duchamp asserted the primacy of their shapes, textures, and colors, and so sanctioned the purposeless pleasure of just being near them.[15] Removed from the public bathroom, for example, the urinal becomes a gorgeous repository of aesthetic feeling. In its estrangement from mere use—its very transformation into waste—the work reveals a thoroughly modern "beauty of indifference" and affirms, for the perceiver, the "liberty of indifference."[16] Indeed, for all his headiness, the Dadaist most often defended his art in terms of the useless and even unnamable sensations that circulated in and around its framing. Tellingly, his attempts at clarification were charged, but nearly always incoherent, obtuse, expressing nothing more than his own pleasure and fascination. When pressed to explain the "meaning" behind his famous bicycle wheel, for example, he simply remarked, "I enjoyed looking at it, just as I enjoy looking at the flames dancing in a fireplace," and, later, "The curious thing about the Ready-Made is that I've never been able to arrive at a definition or explanation that fully satisfies me."[17] The enlightened press quickly followed suit. Early defenses of the *Fountain*, written under Duchamp's influence, emphasized the work's capacity to affect a nameless play of drives and affects. As we'll find with Elvis's own art, cries of "smuttiness" were countered with claims of "innocence," a return to sensual purity and bodily renewal. Some critics compared the *Fountain* to a Buddha and a Madonna, noting, with all seriousness, its "calm curves" and "chaste simplicity of line and color" (Camfield 38, 40).

That said, the influence of the readymade, at least as Duchamp himself suggested, was intended to be subtle, habitual. Its ability to transform human perception was merely an extension of what had already been going on—bodywise—for decades. According to Jean-François Lyotard, the readymade represents the culminating moment of the industrial revolution, one last step in a long historical process by which mechanical innovation—in factory work, transportation, communications, and media technology—pushed the human body beyond itself. For Lyotard, industrial labor led "to the demeasurement of what was human, to the toleration of situations that were thought to be intolerable. What was demanded was another body, in a different space, that of the mines and workshops, with different rhythms and postures, those commanded by the serving of the machines, on a different scale." Yes, industrial labor means exploitation and real violence, but also, in the end, a certain sensual revolution of the body's shape and capacity. Duchamp takes up this call with his art, turning the unintended consequences of industrial and technological modernity into the fortuitous pleasures of modern art. The readymade, as a surreal product of the modern art-factory, revels in the plasticity of the human form, uses the strange shapes and sizes of the modern world to tap the thrill of "the old European peasant-aristocrat body cracking and falling to pieces, according to the demands of a different mentality and a different sensorium."[18]

But we shouldn't underestimate the consumer side of things, and, in this, Duchamp's project corresponds to a world of photographic reproductions, wall-to-wall advertising, corporate branding, and window-shopping. As we've discussed in relation to the commodity-fetish, Duchamp's project allows the body to explore the wondrous surfaces of an artificially constructed world. It taps into the sensual experience of the consumer market as it reconstitutes both the object to be seen and the very act of looking. In the modern marketplace as in the modern art salon, nothing on the shelf is actually needed, no one thing is more necessary than any other, and so each, in its purposelessness, can become extraordinary. In fact, consumerism is always already a matter of sensuality. The consumer's gaze is inherently superficial, and this slight detachment, this plate-glass estrangement from the world of uses, raises the possibility of a purely sensual investment. In fact, the modern gaze—at once public and passionate, indifferent and erotic—restores art's potential to the very heart of the marketplace. Again, though, this possibility is stitched into the economy and its industrial technology. Unlike the commodity as fetish, which implies a locked relation of desire between one ego and one object, the commodity as readymade is essentially charged but indifferent; in its sleek standardization and sheer multiplicity, it decodes purposive responses and instead allows our pleasure to swerve and swirl freely across its surfaces.[19] As Dawn Ades explains, the readymade exploits and exposes the very real pleasures that lie on the fringes of all commodity fetishism; it shows that the consumer, as precursor to the "fan," subverts "the all-powerful system, by converting the ordinary commodity into his own pleasure-machine, by using it privately and even inappropriately, not according to the manufacturer's instructions" (155, 162).

Finally, in the marketplace of the readymade, which includes Elvis posters, photos, magazines, records, clothing, etc., renewal depends on a certain cheapness, even a certain raunchiness. For Duchamp, the man who turned a urinal into art, "tastelessness" refers not only to an absence of artistic hierarchy, but also to a positively trashy sense of the beautiful—any object will do, any useless object will do better. In its cheapness, its sheer worthlessness, the readymade/commodity becomes less and less an expression of individual identity, but makes itself available as a dynamic mode of engagement, a mode of investment that is, in its very cheapness, both ecstatic and indifferent, charged and blank. In turn, the sensual body, freed from the structured demands of the ego, and estranged from the established hierarchy of wealth and value, learns to swerve through a newly shining land of mass-produced forms, never claiming ownership, only always slipping from one to the next. In this, at heart, Duchamp's "tastelessness" also figures as the foundation for a new public body. The destruction of aesthetic hierarchy implied by "readymade" production implies the creation of a new smutty democracy, one founded not on a multiplicity of individual "expressions," but on the possibility of multiple engagements and affective alliances. The commodity's extraordinary ordinariness, its sheer worthlessness, sanctions an extra-indulgent pleasure and thus an extra-indulgent populace. No doubt, this possibility informs Guillaume Apollinaire's famous claim that "Perhaps it will be the task of an artist as detached from esthetic preoccupations, and as intent on the energetic as Marcel Duchamp, to reconcile art and the people" (Tomkins 121).

These very principles governed the studio that made Elvis a star. Sam Phillips's Sun Studio has been celebrated in American cultural history for capturing the raw emotions and social urgency of midcentury country and blues. If it weren't for Phillips's democratic ear, we might not have ever heard B. B. King, Howlin' Wolf, or Bobby "Blue" Bland, or any mind-blowing one-offs like Joe Hill Louis's "Gotta Let You Go." The Sun logo itself, emblazoned in rustic yellow on each single, suggested a new dawn for American culture; its motto—"We record anything, anywhere, anytime"—blazed forth as both an economic possibility and a social proposition for a disenfranchised community. As I want to show here, though, Phillips's studio—as a space designed for capturing the aesthetic dimensions of public expression—relocated the real on the other side of the recording. The democratic ethos of Sun was founded not just on its commitment to otherwise unheard voices, but in the abstraction of sound and voice it captured on tape, in the readymade production of sonic pleasure as the basis of a new fan culture. Ultimately, with Phillips, with Elvis, Duchamp's great indifference becomes a more common kind of cool, a rock-and-roll shrug, an everyday kiss-off—one that both frees and commits the public body to a more radical way of mattering.

Because, really, who needs Duchamp, or even Phillips, when machines can do it for you? Phillips's genius resided mostly in matching technology to feeling, opening the former to all the readymade subtleties and intensities of the latter. At Sun, seated between two Ampex 350 recorders, he became more or less a mimetic artist, letting the equipment work for him. "I saw myself as being the facilitator," Phillips explained, voicing the very ethos of the "cultural worker" in the age of mechanical reproduction.[20] First, sure, Phillips did all he could to inspire intimacy. He worked only with amateurs untainted by the business. He sat eye level with his artists and coached them to play freely. At once hillbilly therapist, social documentarian, and gimlet-eyed techie, he would counsel, "You're doing just fine. Now just relax. Let me hear something that really means something to you now" (Guralnick 85). At the same time, though, Phillips let the tapes roll freely. The gray steel console was always on—humming along, blank and indifferent—ready to catch the slightest gesture or cry. Again, chance, indifference, tastelessness, but all matched to the possibilities of mimetic technology (see chapters one and two) and the new availability of cheap tape. When Carl Perkins complained that a recent take was "just a big original mistake," Phillips replied, "That's what Sun Records is. That's what we are."[21] At Sun, mistakes became art and amateurs turned into stars, but only because of the machinery involved. You didn't need to be good all the time, just once; each take could just as easily lead to the dustbin or the charts; any old toss-off, once captured and released by the machine, could become the stuff of history.

But Phillips actively sought sounds that exceeded any obvious referent or expressive content. The slapback echo was perhaps his most famous intervention. By overdubbing two recordings, one with a slight delay, Phillips decentered the human voice within the mix and muddied its expressive purity. Similarly, by placing a mic below the bridge of the bass, he amplified its percussive slap and thereby disrupted the song's rhythmic flow and presumed immediacy.[22] In turn, his musicians started attacking their own instruments, deterritorializing their sounds from top to bottom—fuzzing out guitars, gluing tacks to the piano, putting drums in the hall, putting a sax in a cardboard box. In each case, the physical activity of soundmaking emerged at the center of the recording, becoming at once more primitive and more abstract.[23] Here, one recalls Duchamp's only sonic readymade, "With Hidden Noise" (see image 5). Duchamp instructed a friend to choose a small object and insert it into a ball of twine sealed on both ends by metal plates. When shaken, the work's "accidental noise"—created behind the artist's back, so to speak—refers to nothing beyond its own abstract sounding, and so binds the experience of listening to itself. Similarly, the music recorded at Sun, produced between steel walls, was defined by its own uneasy disarticulation, the way each noise—each abstract riff, shout, drum kick—threatened to derail

IMAGE 5 *With Hidden Noise*, Marcel Duchamp, 1916. (ARS)

the entire song. Here, sound drew all attention to its own manic sounding, carrying the listener, errantly, away from any obvious meaning or expression. Another way of saying this is that whereas the blues recalled the life of the jukes and cabaret, and country music echoed the space of the honky-tonk or barn dance, early rock recordings resounded in the utopian realm of the self-contained studio (see chapter five). Sun captured the audial dimension of an otherwise restricted musical tradition and gave it over to the ear as an apotheosis of musical experience and investment. As sound itself was distilled and decoded, it became an object of interest in itself, and listening grew both more abstract and more intense.[24]

Take "Rocket 88," for example, recorded by Jackie Brenston and Ike Turner at Sun Studio in 1951.[25] If anything, the song owes its distinction as the first rock-and-roll hit to both chance *and* indifference. As the story goes, Turner was racing to the studio when a sharp turn caused his amp to slide off the top of his car. Without a ready replacement, the group hastily repaired the busted device by stuffing paper into the speaker cone. According to Sam Phillips, "We had no way of getting it fixed, so we started to play around with the damn thing, stuffed a little paper in there and it sounded good" (Escott 24). The formula should be clear. Here, the amp, a practical device for producing loudness, became—in the hands of a few desperate teens—a significant means of aesthetic production. In the same way, the song's lyrics divest the titular car of any convenient uses, presenting it instead as a medium of aesthetic contemplation and sensual pleasure, blasting its riders beyond the tedium of the everyday world:

> V-8 motor and this modern design,
> Black convertible top and the gals don't mind
> Sportin' with me,
> Ridin' all around town for joy.

With joyriding, the readymade is set in motion along the highways and airwaves of town, thrilling to its own thrust and force. Movement trumps direction as well as destination, and the listener is carried along for a pleasurable swerving that is at once physical and aesthetic. In other words, this song is only superficially about the male ego or male desire—these guys already have a car and the chicks. Rather, it draws upon its own useless pleasure, gives itself over to the cheaper thrills of just coasting, mere transit—in sound, in song. It is nothing but its own egoless drive, its own inexpressive motion—rolling, twisting, bouncing, turning—an experience made literal when the listener finally arrives at the hop and starts to dance.

Similar forces were at work during the recording session that produced Elvis's first accidental hit—Sun #209 "That's All Right" / "Blue Moon of Kentucky."[26] Elvis had been playing with Scotty Moore and Bill Black for several weeks, searching for a new sound to cut through the airwaves. Urged by Phillips, they wanted to make a record greater than the sum of their very amateur parts, but the feeling was inchoate and the goal vague. "We were just looking for something," claimed Scotty; "we didn't quite know what it was, we would just sit there over coffee and say to each other, 'What is it? What should we do? How can we do it?'" (Guralnick 92). When Sam finally brought the band together in the studio, they worked through a few standards. Elvis tried each song from a number of angles, sometimes crooning, sometimes moaning, and sometimes just whistling his way along, trying to find a mood or vibe that made sense. Sam tried again and again to calm the boy, giving pep talks to "make him feel at home," but Elvis remained frustrated. Finally, late that evening, the boys realized they needed a break, and as they sipped Cokes, Elvis started goofing off, hamming up a version of Arthur Crudup's "That's All Right (Mama)."[27] As Scotty explained, "All of a sudden, Elvis just started singing this song, jumping around and acting the fool, and then Bill picked up his bass, and he started acting the fool, too, and I started playing with them. Sam, I think, had the door to the control booth open . . . and he stuck his head out and said, 'What are you doing?' And we said, 'We don't know,' 'Well, back up,' he said, 'try to find a place to start, and do it again.'"[28] The Ampex machines hummed into action and a late-night toss-off became the stuff of history.

The song's title is matched by its accidental, take-it-or-leave-it performance. While the cut begins a bit tentatively, the performance increases in confidence with each measure, as the band slowly discovers the pleasure of its own sound. Here, Elvis's voice proves perhaps the quintessential readymade. On its own, the refrain—"that's all right"—seems void of all content, a mere marker for any number of suggestive moods and attitudes. Elvis, as we saw with Guthrie, draws upon the phrase's essential emptiness, but ultimately uses it to express just how little he cares, or, better yet, to model the very pleasures of carelessness. At first, he delivers it in classic blues style, as a desperate moan, but, slowly, he begins to play with other variations, delivering it in turn as a cool kiss-off, an aggressive howl, a knowing joke, a mocking sneer, and a drunken murmur. With each verse, he performs the same process of investment and release. He starts off tentatively, rises in confidence on the high note, and then, in the end, shrugs it all off. By the end of the song, none of these declarations seem to matter anymore, because he's found his voice, his song, his hit. In fact, the lyrics fall away altogether, and Elvis, hooked by the groove, shouts out a string of scat syllables that signify little more than their own sweet sounding. What "Rocket 88" does for a car, then, "That's All Right" does for song itself, freeing it from any expressive need or purpose, giving it over to the play of chance and the slutty activity of the drives. For sure, Elvis fronts one of the most joyfully careless instrumental performances in the history of rock—just a bunch of spindly licks, jagged double stops, and sudden surges in tempo and volume. These tics or thrusts break up the traditional surface of the song, confounding any expectations about what it might mean—*is this a blues? a country wail? something they play on the negro station?* But that's all right, too—we hear each meaningless bit with a new attentiveness, carried on a purely sensual current from one to the next.

It's just too easy to say that Elvis "sexed" up or "blacked" up the original tune.[29] Sure, whereas Crudup's version seems tense and jittery, a prickly product of the jump-jive scene, Elvis's is all teases and taunts, notable for its sexy cat croon and overheated accompaniment. But something more interesting is going on here. First, Elvis proves himself to be a good mimic, as indifferent to his sources as the machine recording him. His vocal performance incorporates a wild range of styles—the bounce of the Western swing stars, the soft whine of the pop crooners, the jive talk of Memphis R & B, the gutsy grumble of the Delta bluesmen—some of which just happen to be sexy. Moreover, each one of these styles is picked up and dropped with ease; no single one matters any more than the others, any more than it mediates some immediate pleasure. Elvis burns through the entire archive—each style becomes its own cool sound, valuable only in its very sounding, as a momentary gesture or stance. According to Bill, "we couldn't believe it was us." Scotty, too, claimed, "It just sounded sort of raw and ragged. We thought it was exciting, but what was it?" (Guralnick 96). In fact, the very inarticulacy of all involved—singer, band, producer, and then DJ and the dozens of callers who contacted the station after its first spin—suggests that the impact of the record had little to do with what it meant or referenced. If anything, it was uncategorizable because it demanded a reconfiguration of any obvious categories, offering less any obvious *meaning* than a new way of *mattering*. As Sam Phillips laid it down, "they didn't give a fuck about classifying him in Memphis, Tennessee, *they liked what they heard*" (Guralnick 101).

In this, we can start to understand how the readymade process—in sound, but also in touch, smell, and vision—set the basic terms of countercultural investment in this era. Rockabilly, as it grew out of the hot musical seedbed of Memphis in the early 1950s, represents the first full flowering of rock-and-roll revolt. Singers such as Elvis Presley, Jerry Lee Lewis, Carl Perkins, and Gene Vincent tore through music as if the South were bursting into flames behind them. Theirs was a music for last days, propelled by a frothy mix of adolescent lust, rural rebellion, and working-class angst, and it used the very machinery of commercial domination in order to bust open the world of commerce. And yet, for all its rough hooks and angsty licks, this music was produced with a nearly catholic sense of precision. Each scrap of noise comes across cleanly, meticulously, a fascinating object of sonic perfection, something to follow, to ride, to grab and hold on to as it soars across the sonic scene. Here, the musical union of feeling and form—in its very defamiliarization—comes to sustain fan culture as a matter of affective judgment. The more fortuitous the sound, the more defiantly useless, the more likely it is to sustain extreme tastes. As with all fan culture, the most worthless thing becomes sacred; the cheapest commodity becomes a violent point of pride. To return to Grossberg, "By making certain things or practices matter, the fan 'authorizes' them to speak for him or her." But, with rock, this mattering is at once more extreme and more precise: "Because something matters, it must have an excess which explains the investment in it, an excess which ex post facto not only legitimates but demands the investment" ("Fandom" 58–59). Pop music matters emptily and excessively, tautologically. It matters because it matters, and it thrives in the extremity of its own feeling. In this, it allows us to experience, like Duchamp's Dada, difference as such, to feel difference and to cultivate those feelings excessively, exclusively, without needing to name or justify them. Fan culture entails the cultivation of difference in itself; it marks the empty but essential work of differentiation, or, rather, it exposes the work of mediation, and thus, as style, as self-stylization, marks out the investment of both the fan and his or her entire outcast society.

Dirty Elvis

Dirty Elvis stumbles onto the stage in the summer of 1956, at some dusty, overheated club or assembly hall in the South, perhaps Shreveport, or Jacksonville, or the air force base in Biloxi. He has three different kinds of grease in his hair. The seam on his left pants leg is split, and the cuffs on his jacket are worn thin. When he gets to center stage, he stops for a moment, taking it all in—the heat, the stink, the noise. His eyes are popping with a certain devilment; his mouth curls into a smirk. Then he shrugs, wipes his nose on his sleeve, and starts beating on his guitar. His body starts to shake—first his shoulders, and then his entire torso. His hair breaks its oily mold and flops over his brow. Each limb begins to wander—elbows pop, knees shake, his head falls to the left and dangles there for a spell. He shrugs again, spits a pink wad of gum into the crowd, and burps into the mic. He jumps forward and lands with his legs spread, cowboy-style, jumps to the side on his tippytoes, holds it, profile-shot, hair in his eyes, and then lets his thighs snap back and forth like pistons, carrying him across the stage. With Scotty's solo, he leaps backward, guitar in the air, strumming madly. "Fuck you very much," he shouts. Then, his turn again, he takes a few quick jerks forward, left, right, left, rumba-style, and thrusts crotch full forward into guitar for a few mindless pumps. Unsatisfied, he tosses the instrument behind his back and falls to the floor. He slithers over to Nipper, the RCA dog, and, sneering madly, humps the plastic canine icon, whose typically bemused expression seems to shift slightly toward gruff annoyance.[30]

Being Elvis was always a dirty business. It was down in the groove, in the tasteless play of the drives, that he established the pleasures of his art, and it was the frank libido of the fan that was exalted by his act. Indeed, it takes a radical lack of command to swagger with such grace, and this King everywhere asserted his power through humiliation. As a descendent of sharecroppers, a child of the Memphis projects, Elvis taps the readymade immediacy of the hopeless, the unprotected, and betrayed. With Daddy out of work and Mama at the laundry, he was left free to explore the only pleasures left to him—his voice, his posture, his moves, his attitude. His entire act followed the dumb topography of the body as it groped for the best available shape, the right hole or pipe or valve, to satisfy its own essential dissatisfaction. I mean it—when it comes to Dirty Elvis, we are in the world of drives, the dumb currents of attraction and repulsion that underlie the structures of desire. But, unlike desire, the drive knows nothing of lack, of absence and presence, of ownership or mastery. It knows nothing of language, of difference, of propriety. Always in motion, always moving on to the next best thing, it can name neither the pleasure it seeks nor the pleasure it finds. Dumb, yes, but all the more compelling—this drive serves not just Elvis culture, but all modern fan culture, and its obtuse movement is nothing less than revolutionary.

Commence coastin'! While the body's drives initially serve the body's needs (for nourishment, shelter, warmth), they are not structured by rigid difference and consistently elude the strict boundaries of self and other. Sure, each drive follows the path laid out by certain oppositions, between, say, the child and the parent, the mouth and the burger, but—as constant force, as continual thrust—it persists in excess of any immediate relation. The drive is always looking for a spin, a joyride, but it has no precise destination in mind, and so it is always capable of establishing multiple dynamic connections to the world, always linking up bodies and things in strange new ways. Thus Jacques Lacan, in his famous seminar on the drive, stresses the "extraordinary antinomy" between the satisfaction of desire and the motion of the drive. While desire fixates on some fetishized object in order to restore a sense of presence, the drive slips— imaginatively, loosely, endlessly—around the things on the horizon. Its pleasure resides in its own circuitous tour—a more or less meaningless ride out of the body, around the object, and back again. It swerves errantly, lustily, indifferently, seeking not acquisition, but the thrill of its own movement, its own escape and return.[31] Take a look at Lacan's famous

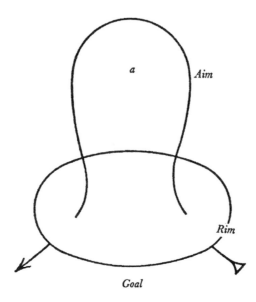

IMAGE 6 The Tour of the Drive, Jacques Lacan.
The Four Fundamental Concepts of Psychoanalysis,
originally published in French by Éditions du Seuil
and courtesy of Jacques-Alain Miller.

diagram of the drive (see image 6). It's as raunchy as any bit of bathroom graffiti from the 1950s, but it neatly captures the movements of Elvis and his fans. In terms of Elvis culture, "rim" could refer to any bodily surface (mouth, eyes, pelvis, shoulders, eyebrow, etc.); "a" is occupied by a range of cheap objects (suede shoes, a pink scarf, tailfins, poodle skirt, a new record, etc.); "goal" is something like a charged state—flippin', boppin', ridin' around the town for joy. Always, though, the drive's rimlike structure and dynamic motion suggest the incredibly plastic nature of being. The tour implies a movement both out of and into the self; presence is possible only in terms of its dynamic mediation, by circling someone or something else, and thus only in terms of its openness. In fact, above all else, the drives are associated with a kind of deathly pleasure, a loss of personal bearings that always entails a new and more thrilling sense of selfhood—not *meaning*, but *mattering*.

No doubt, Elvis was always twitching—his legs jumped, his hands flicked, his face smirked, winked, winced. He always needed something in his hands, something to fondle—a guitar, a piano, a water gun, a hamburger, a breast.[32] You can see it before and after his television perfor-mances, while he's desperately trying to banter with Milton Berle or Steve Allen. He stares blankly into space while his hands twist in the air and his legs snap in his pants like electric wires. As he explained to one of his early lovers, "I don't know, it's hard to explain. It's like your body gets goose bumps, but it's not goose bumps. It's not a chill either. It's like a surge of electricity going through you. It's almost like making love, but it's even stronger than that" (Guralnick 319). Not surprisingly, Elvis often sang of manic states. From "All Shook Up" to "Shake, Rattle, and Roll," his music depicts the body as it loses its everyday coordinates and finds itself caught in a series of ecstatic forms.[33] In fact, Elvis was comfortable only when performing, when all his energy could find—momentarily—a satisfying stance or pattern. When the band kicked up, his energy hooked into the rhythms and melodies of the music and strangely, thrillingly, fell into surreal, impossible form. Then his body, like the very song being played, became less a conditioned or even unified corpus than a series of intensi-ties seething into motion—sheer dilation and contraction—finding their own shape within the abstract patterns of sound. Pieces of the body shoot out, turning, touring, around a virtual space, feeling, fondling, evaluating new intensities, new pleasures, drawing us in against all better judgment, against all rational judgment.

But, again, for Elvis, the voice was the quintessential readymade, and his fame rose and fell on the tour of his vocal drive. As Lacan famously claimed, identity exists only in its negation, by way of some initial denial and restriction—an emphatic "No!" The self comes into being, anxiously, through someone else's restrictive demand, the voice of some other, more authoritative self—usually Daddy-o himself. Who I am depends on what I am not, what I am told I cannot have or do, and so I remain caught within an entire system of differences—in language itself—always denied and deferred, always only implied by some other term, some other lover, some new product or song, etc. But if desire seems forever caught up in a system of differences, the drive courses beneath it in a single, unbroken current, taking pleasure in its own constant thrust or motion in relation to its others. So, for Lacan, each drive is essentially a vocal drive, calling out, beseeching, appealing to the pleasure of another person in order to attain—reflexively—its own. In fact, the tour of the drive has three differ-ent "voices"—active, passive, and reflexive; it is essentially polyvocal, and, in its dance around the object—the little *objet a*—it calls out to the other, awaits response/recognition, and proclaims itself in its return (177). You've heard this one before—*I want you to want me to want you*—but you've also felt its power. Beneath the meaning of anything we might be saying, it is the very act of saying—in its doubling of need and demand—that establishes both presence and pleasure, and the pleasure and presence of the other. The humility of one's cry—its neediness, its emptiness—establishes a space for the cry of the other, and vice versa. Even when we talk to one another—about music, hairstyles, wine, etc.—we not only establish meanings, but also create new vectors of attraction and repulsion. Our speech is largely gestural, performative, and thus serves to nab the attention of another, to establish a charged relation between bodies that are always more than their own refined speech (182–83).

First, then, as drive, Elvis's voice is always doubled, at once opening and closing, losing and then finding itself in its own cheap performance. Take, for example, the first few measures of "Blue Moon of Kentucky."[34] The phrase "Blue Moon" bursts from Elvis's mouth three times in a row, like a giant gob of southern sentiment. It seems to represent not just lost love, but the entire damning tradition of southern song, and the singer can't decide whether he needs to spit it out or swallow it whole. Ultimately, though, he decides to play with it in his mouth—like a little sonic *objet a*—using it as a fulcrum around which his cheap voice can circle. Following Scotty and Bill's rhythm, Elvis rides his voice from one stance to another, abandoning the back-porch-crooner role for, in turn, the backwoods rebel, the Memphis jive talker, the needy teen, the pop star. At the same time, the lyrics outline a common southern despair—lost love, lonely nights—but, here, emptiness presages something like return, as if the very darkness of the southern night allows him to move freely through the landscape. The blue moon both outlines the barrenness of the region and signals a new, bright hope within it, and so the voice waxes and wanes with each repetition, both emptied and filled by its own demand, asserting everything and nothing. In contrast to Patton or Guthrie, Elvis is less interested in the viability of these poses than in their playful mediation. Love says goodbye again and again, as mere wish, as mere sound, but always returns again to the singer's conceit, as the circular pleasure of the vocal drive. And so the song—singing itself—comes to fill the gap between singer and lover, becomes, in its own constant thrust from one word to the next, as perfect and complete as a "wish blown high." Indeed, all of Elvis's performances work in this way—as dilation and contraction both, as a panting orifice of irrepressible drive. His dances too were by turns cocky and shy; he displayed his most outrageous moves when he was retreating from the audience, moving downstage, crouching low, looking away. Similarly, his voice was impossibly hurt as well as haughty—the entire act resounds at the borderline of absence and presence, demand and defeat, and thus, as it shifts from one empty pose to the next, attains—in its own mediation—both its compelling openness and significant allure.

Roland Barthes, in his famous essay on the "grain of the voice," notes the tension between body and language that marks lyrical performance. "Something is there," he writes, something "manifest and stubborn . . . beyond (or before) the meaning of the words . . . something which is directly the cantor's body, brought to your ears in one and the same movement from deep down in the cavities, the muscles, the membranes, the cartilages."[35] For Barthes, listening pleasure lies in this tension, in the mediation of the body in language and vice versa. The singer's drive falls into and away from certain preestablished forms, and, in this slippery process, the listener, too, is given over to the pleasure of mediation. The "grain," Barthes writes, "is the body in the voice as it sings, the hand as it writes, the limb as it performs." Its presence and pleasure exists neither before nor after expression, but within its very delivery, in the shifts and swerves of the phrase, in the cutting up of phonemes, in the expansion and contraction of the medium itself. In this dumb and dirty activity, Barthes writes, song emerges "as a space of pleasure, of thrill," one in which "I am determined to listen to my relation with the body of the man or woman singing or playing and that relation is erotic—but in no way 'subjective'" (185–87). There are no identities here, no expressions, just drives—shifts and swerves of attention, new vectors and valences of affective energy in relation to established forms. In fact, the entire process is more or less empty, abstract, governed by sounds that are themselves at once surging and fading, absent and present. The voice follows its errant course in a more or less virtual space; as listeners, we are drawn in by a play of forces that has no established referent, no discernible origin or endpoint—our pleasure is the pleasure of losing and finding ourselves in this intense but indifferent play, feeling within it the pleasure of our own careless mediation.

So, yes, you can hear Elvis's body in his voice. He sings with his legs, his guts, his hips, even his brow. Changes in timbre and tone and rhythm correspond, obviously, brutally, to the shakes and shivers of his entire corpus. But if vocal delivery exposes the continuity of body and language, pleasure and form, it also always disturbs its own authority, breaks its own law. Most critics, reading personal history into music, hear the voice of a torn man. For Richard Middleton, Elvis's early singles reveal a conflict of rebellion and conformity; his "desire for peace, escape, a dream-world" vies with "the irrational world of wild revolt and self-gratification."[36] Greil

Marcus, similarly, argues that the "respect Elvis felt for the limits and conventions of his family life, of his community, and ultimately of American life [was] captured in his country sides; and his refusal of those limits, of any limits, played out in his blues. This is a rhythm of acceptance and refusal. . . . It can dramatize our lives well enough" (*Mystery* 146–47). But the flow of Elvis's music was not nearly so dualistic. If Elvis seems to be struggling in his songs, it is because he is at every moment reaching for a satisfying fit or form. His voice is physically at work, groping for a certain satisfaction, turning around a set of preestablished patterns—blues, country, gospel, etc.—seeking the right shape, the right hook with which to catch something like presence. In this, Elvis's music does not necessarily represent or express his movement toward and away from home, as Marcus contends, but enacts it in the tour of his voice, as the sonic drive emerges from the body only to return once more. This voice is always at work on tradition, at once adopting and adapting the structures of the past, yet using them for some provisional pleasure and thereby emptying them of their authority. Each performance is utterly urgent and completely ridiculous—everywhere, psychic desperation is matched by ludic fun, sonic hooliganism. Ultimately, the King does not simply express any specific politics of rebellion, but calls into being, in his dirty voicing, an alternative, shadowy public sphere within the public sphere; the empty echo of his voice is the space of public mockery and personal indifference, the lawless voice within the law.

Indeed, within months of his first successes, Elvis had found his cow and milked it dry. "Baby, Let's Play House" is perhaps the most thrilling performance of his career.[37] As the King giggles and burps his way through the opening lines—"Whoah, baby, baby, baby, baby, bab-Y, b-b-b-b-baby baby bab-Y!"—he reveals a new vocal suppleness, one in which the slightest inflection of tone or timbre sends off affective sparks too quick to register. Again, all begins in loss. "Come back, baby, baby!"—he shouts it over and over again. But unlike "Blue Moon of Kentucky," this song conveys nothing but buoyancy, a lightness of touch; the hillbilly cat harnesses his dereliction and rides it at will as he travels toward new worlds of fast drives and cheap delights. Going, coming, love, and betrayal—all options matter precisely because they don't really matter at all, because they couldn't matter less to the vocal drive:

> Well, you may go to college,
> You may go to school.

> You may have a pink Cadillac,
> But don't you be nobody's fool.

As we can hear in his sly reference to the Cadillac, Elvis circles around these acquisitive pleasures only to shrug them off, trumping the value of each object on the commercial horizon with the motion of his own body and the indulgent flow of his own voice. Marcus writes, "If Elvis was looking down on his smart girl's Caddy from the vantage point of his own, he was implicitly presenting his new success as a target for his own resentments. . . . Somehow taking both sides, Elvis could show his listeners just how much, and how little, that Pink Cadillac was worth: more and less than anyone would have guessed" (*Mystery* 161). But the performance depends upon an entirely different economy than the one Marcus supposes. Houses? Colleges? Cadillacs? How can such mundane objects compete with the trashy pleasures of this very song? In fact, these objects only exist, only appear and disappear, for the sake of this voice, for the incredible pleasure that arises from the power of naming them. In fact, there's no car here, there's no girl here, no house, no car—nothing but the fleeting pleasures of voice itself, the invocatory drive and all the gorgeous plasticity of identity it implies. Like Guthrie's, Elvis's voice is inherently migrant—deterritorializing—but it drifts beyond (or is it below?) the sphere of economics proper into a hooligan realm of stylized fun.

As suggested, this is not merely an issue of body and pleasure, but of law and its glorious failure. The vocal drive makes its demands within and around the very structures of language. Born of a certain need, a certain powerlessness, the body raises its voice, makes its claims, but its sheer physicality is always in excess of its own language. It consistently exposes its own dirty drive, its own neediness and its own pleasure, within the more or less official operations of language, and thus exposes the sheer provisionality of language and law. As Mladen Dolar notes, drawing on Lacan, voice is at once physical and abstract, grainy and ideal, and so helps us connect matter and meaning into a single, living whole. But if voice holds the key to coherent identity, any sense of personal or political completion, it also always threatens to slip away from its own law, its own decree. Its doubleness is both its power and its danger, for it can always lose itself in an empty sign or, conversely, appear as purely sensual, leading toward decadence. This is especially true when it comes to music: "Up to a point, music is sublime and elevates the spirit; beyond a certain limit, however, it brings about decay, the decline of spiritual faculties, their disintegration in enjoyment."[38] No wonder Plato feared traveling musicians in his city. No wonder church leaders have traditionally banned certain modes and harmonies in their pews. No wonder every suburban dad insists on playing his own damn music in his own damn car. All rulers need to sing the law, to establish their need as the need of their subjects, their pleasure as the pleasure of the people—*I want you to want me*—but this exchange always threatens to expose its inherent neediness, its relative pleasure. As Dolar remarks, there is no law without the voice, and yet that voice "bears witness to that remainder of a presupposed and terrible Father's *jouissance* which could not be absorbed by the Law" (55).

But what kind of law intentionally exposes its own pleasure? What kind of voice revels in its own excess, its own inherent graininess? What kind of King promises good rockin' tonight and then gives it to us on the spot, in the very present of its promise? Well, that's all just rock and roll. For here we come upon a King who takes joy in his own decree, who exposes the empty *jouissance* of all vocalization. Here we come upon a derelict King who sings his own pleasure in order to win the pleasure of another, the fan, who, in turn, for a moment, recognizes this voice as the one he or she desperately needs to hear. As Dolar claims, the object voice—in its compulsiveness, its neediness—ties the speaker to the listener, and vice versa, "without belonging to either," but "this is the crucial point, the touchstone of morality: the voice is enunciation and we have to supply the statement ourselves. The moral law is like a suspended sentence, a sentence left in suspense, confined to pure enunciation, but a sentence demanding continuation, to be completed by the subject, by his or her moral decision, by the act. . . . The voice does not command or prohibit, but it nevertheless necessitates a continuation, it compels a sequel (98–99). As I hope to show now, this dirty voice, in its pleasure and its neediness, lies at the heart of modern fan culture and bears its social and ethical dimensions; this voice establishes its critical relation to official culture by revealing, again and again, in each fan's desperate twist and shout, that "we are social beings by the voice and through the voice" (14).

Mother Elvis

Mother Elvis looks down at her baby—the one who survived—and makes a special wish. This one will never leave her side—no matter what they say. He will stay in her bed, and she will dote on his eyes, his mouth, his shoulders, and his little pelvis. They will share glances, touches, feelings, sheets, scarves—and when she sings to him, he will burp and coo in kind.

Daddy's a shirker. He can barely keep a job, let alone a home. But Mama is large—she "worships" the boy, her first and last son. They love dress-up, a good laugh, tender petting, hair combing. They have their own secret language—he calls her "Satnin," and they giggle about "footies" and "sooties." And gifts—don't forget the gifts! At first, just little things, like scarves, pies, bicycles, guitars, but then, later on, gold records, pink Cadillacs, and giant colonial mansions.[39] In time, though, the doting mother has to compete for attention. As the boy grows into a star, she haunts his dressing room, tracks his tour schedule, and keeps a scrapbook of photos and clippings. The little star, for his part, insists that Mama is still his "number-one girl," but he has turned their bedroom play into the stuff of real stardom. The baby talk, the gifts, the petting, the chaste kisses and tender glances—all this becomes the basis of a new public ritual; Elvis himself becomes Mother Elvis, a big old sweaty stage mama, using all he learned in his childhood bed to woo an entire nation of children who all just want to be loved tenderly.

As we've seen, Elvis's revolt begins with the drives, and it works, thrillingly, to destabilize an obsessively conditioned corpus. He was a bumbling amateur, but his movements generated a physical ecstasy that defied most social conditioning. In this, his fame immediately sent reporters groping for an appropriate language; the King was called an "atomic explosion," a "gyrating rotary troubadour," "the Marlon Brando of the mountain music set," but none of these names seemed to fit.[40] When all was said and done, the best description turned out to be the simplest—Elvis was an "innocent," and, with this, most observers returned to his childlike simplicity and purity. As Marion Keisker said, "My total image of Elvis was as a child. It was not in him to lie or say anything malicious. He has all the intricacy of the very young" (Guralnick 65). Natalie Wood, an early Hollywood pal, dismissed romantic gossip by telling the press, "He's really great and the most totally real boy I've ever met. He's a real pixie and has a wonderful little-boy quality" (Pierce 121). Elvis himself countered charges of deviant sexuality with claims of innocence. "I can't help it," he claimed in an interview, "I just have to jump around when I sing. But it ain't vulgar. It's just the way I feel. I don't feel sexy when I'm singin'. If that was true, I'd be in some kinda institution as some kinda sex maniac."[41] In fact, as the press began to link his shows to rampant fears of juvenile delinquency, he more and more referred reporters to his relationship with his mother and the decency of his home life: "I can't figure out what I'm doing wrong. I know my mother approves of what I'm doing" (*Long Lonely* 98).

There's much to be gained by taking these statements at face value. Elvis's "innocence" lies not just in his physicality or his remarkable dumbness.

Etymologically, the word refers to indivision, a failure to part or be parted (*l. nocens*)—a refusal to leave, perhaps, the mother's bed. Elvis as innocent is Elvis unformed, unframed, resistant to socialization and cultural inscription; having never heard his father's divisive command, the boy-King remained free to become a law or state unto himself—open, expansive, Whitmanian.[42] In other words, this innocence, insofar as it entails an open play of intersubjective drives, also carries us over to the other side of the performance space—to the body of the fan. No doubt, Elvis and his adolescent fans felt each other intuitively. The star had an uncanny sense of how his gestures affected dynamic shifts of energy and emotion in his audience. His body was a finely tuned medium, shaking and shuffling by small degrees until it found the right pose for the moment. A slight shudder across his shoulders sent shrieks throughout the arena. A foot shimmy toward the left brought—row by row—a wave of fans to their knees. His left eyebrow could drop a fan to the floor at the back of the stadium. Of course, when pressed to describe his impact, Elvis was—again—completely thickheaded: "They were screaming and liked it, so I kept it up" (*Long Lonely* 126). But he was no doubt aware of his power: "If I do something good, they let me know it. If I don't, they let me know that, too. It's a give-and-take proposition in that they give me back the inspiration. I work absolutely to them. . . . They bring it out of me" (Guralnick 174). In this, we return to that creative mimicry essential to all vital musical cultures, especially the dispersed currents of repetition and exchange that occur, as we've seen, through mimetic forms such as records and radio. But whereas public history is limited when it comes to blues and country fans, the bodily exchanges of early rock and roll tell us everything and nothing at once.

By nearly all accounts, Elvis's fans genuinely experienced nameless states of bodily ecstasy—moments of powerlessness, gestural compulsion, doubled consciousness, unbearable pain, exhaustion. At first, the sheer newness, the sheer bigness of the stage show tended to short-circuit all consciousness. Elvis's presence alone—amplified from the front of the stage—created an affective surge that overwhelmed fans, obliterating thought, choice, and even ego, leaving many dumbfounded and numb. "On a deep level," one fan describes, "I was totally 'there,' but on a conscious level, I was not there. It is a rare occurrence." Another explains, "There I sat with feelings of being so ecstatic to the point where I was trembling so much that my knees were knocking together. We all sat coming apart at the seams."[43] In the lingo of the time, this intense experience was called "flipping," which, according to one fan, entails "love, hate, anger, hero worship, anxiety and a few other [extreme emotions]" (*Elvis Album* 74). The opening of the stage show brought about an affective overload that was both pleasurable and painful, welcome and feared. Many fans responded with confused violence—striking themselves, tearing out their hair, begging, "More, Elvis!" and then, "Please stop, Elvis!" In photos, their gestures suggest less desire than a wild mix of affections. They hold out their arms, hug themselves, scream, hide their eyes, and grip their heads as if they might explode.[44]

After this initial surge, though, many fans found themselves caught in an affective vice, moving and shouting without obvious reason or purpose. If the stage show first caused participants to lose their inhibitions, this release prepared them for a more complete submission to their idol's movements. As one fan remarked, "It's impossible to sit still while Elvis is on stage."[45] Another explained, "When he executed his powerful moves, it was incredibly thrilling. How could I resist?" And another, "I was so completely entranced by him that he was all that filled my mind and my consciousness" (*Elvis Now* 144, 58). Many fans confused their own actions with those around them, unsure of who did what to whom. Some emerged from the show with strange bruises and cuts, and others found themselves accused of violence. Some recall moments of self-estrangement and self-witnessing, such as, "I heard someone screaming and then realized it was me" (Guralnick 209, 303). If adults feared that Elvis spoke a "secret libidinal language" to his teenage fans, they had ample evidence in the mimic behavior of his audiences.[46] As a report from Spokane described, "White-sweatered arms swept in imitative circles and once, when he gave his famous thumb-twirling gesture, the stadium was a waving field of twirling thumbs" (*Elvis Album* 97). Another press report, from Tacoma, describes how Elvis's struts and gyrations allowed him to "blend his personality into theirs"; sound and image worked together to create a "trance" that was broken only with his exit and the frenzied rush to catch him (*Lost Lonely* 170).

But if the King was a gestural magnet, his fans soon learned to claim this power as their own. They inevitably started to mimic each other, not just copying, but embellishing and then contradicting the King's high command. Take, for example, the play of voices in the arena. As many claimed, the King's voice was capable of setting off an ecstasy of emotion. It was experienced as a medium or conduit, transferring the energy of his body into their own. As one bluntly recalled, "When Elvis sang, Patti would moan and groan and I'd do the twist."[47] Another writes, "Presley's moves were body-shouts, and the way our ears heard his voice our bodies heard his body."[48] Here, again, we find the vocal drive at work, a voice that does not merely name, but manages physiological states of attraction and repulsion. As we've seen, this voice is inherently doubled, insofar as it both establishes and denies its presence though the presence of another. Fans, in turn, found power in the space left open by the King's circular drives. They screamed as much out of anger as of love; their voices served to establish their own feelings of fear, rage, command, power, and praise. Often, in fact, their voices drowned out Elvis's own, calling into question his authority and reclaiming the entire concert experience as their own. According to a report from Buffalo, "For three solid minutes, like the high-pitched whines of a squadron of jet planes, they screamed. Elvis held up his hand for silence. He muttered something that was lost in the frenzy. Then he twitched his well-publicized pelvis, and the screams [grew] louder than ever" (*Long Lonely* 139). Voice here serves—on both ends of the concert exchange—as gesture as well as drive, circling, enveloping, capturing the other, giving pleasure, presence, and strength. One fan remembers screaming so loud that "Elvis heard me and stopped in front of me. He just stood there a second and smiled at me. I was just beside myself and came very close to having to send my clothes out to the laundry." She adds, "I guess you can say that because of Elvis, I became an independent woman" (*Elvis Now* 19–20).

This experience is way too varied and dynamic to be labeled "desire" or defined through the static language of gendered absence and presence. As these tales from the concert frontlines suggest, the stage show worked to blast through the categories of self and other, as well as any desire that might flow between them. Gestures and feelings rushed anonymously through the hot, sweaty arena, dissolving bodies in relation to each other and generating sensations that exceeded both need and want. Here, all the drives—vocal, visual, oral, genital—arc in and around the open body of each fan, between selves, between the pieces of selves, carving out new configurations of pleasure and attraction, new forms of matter and mattering. The materiality of the performance space is shot through with free-floating currents of feeling, all the shifts and swerves of fanatical attention, creating an event that was at once overdetermined and underdetermined. Again, the extremity of the situation contradicts much of what we now take for granted regarding fan culture. While the process of identification provides a certain stability to the dynamics of fandom, it accounts for very little when it comes to the physical intensity and affectionate currents that actually play across a crowd. The concert exchange suggests a mode of mediation and sociality that is neither simply erotic nor imaginary; if anything, it operates according to a charged physiology, everywhere linking up public forms and personal affects in ways that *matter* without necessarily being *meaningful*. As Erika Doss explains, "'Seeing' Elvis was never simply a matter of looking at him. . . . Elvis demanded reaction and response, the physical and emotional participation of an audience that was urged to become more than a body of listeners or viewers, but 'an audience of performers'" (9).

In a way, then, the early critics had it right: the Elvis spectacle takes us back to earlier stages of life, entailing psychological regression and the release of otherwise conditioned reflexes.[49] But they didn't go far enough, beyond adolescence, beyond the ego, to the earliest moments of life in which self and other, body and image, need and pleasure commingle in psychedelic array. This is not the terrain of Freud—or even Oedipus and the ego—but of Melanie Klein, for whom psychoanalysis begins in the nursery, with the charged exchange between infant and mother.[50] The infant's drives, Klein claims, exceed the logic of need without falling into the rigid structures of desire. Rather, they circulate in more or less erratic ways around the parts of the mother's body—breasts, hands, eyes, mouth—making demands that are at once practical and sensual. She writes, "The first gratification which the child derives from the external world is the satisfaction experienced in being fed. Analysis has shown that only one part of this satisfaction results from the alleviation of hunger and that another part, no less important, results from the pleasure which the baby experiences when his mouth is stimulated by sucking at his mother's breast" (290–91). For Klein, maternal contact is a source of intense stimulation and pleasure, but in excess to any desire-based notion of selfhood. The exchange, which consists entirely of body parts and libidinal flows, does not recognize the distinction between self and other. The infant's relations are intense, but "indifferent" to any particular body, to any restrictive order of meaning, and so imply, much like the Elvis show, more or less open configurations of power and pleasure. One body is bound up with the charismatic power of another but takes all it can get from it, uses everything it finds according to its own pleasure. As in fan culture more generally, any object will do, but each must do in its own precise way, must matter for its own sake, in its very mattering. Everything—and Klein means *everything*—serves only partially, provisionally, as a means of managing pleasure in an exchange that is at once gestural, sensual, and affective: "[B]abies of the first few months connect their feces and urine with phantasies in which these materials are regarded as presents. Not only are they presents, and as such are indications of love towards their mother or nurse, but they are also regarded as being able to affect a restoration.

On the other hand, when the destructive feelings are dominant the baby will in his phantasy defecate and urinate in anger and hatred, and use his excrements as hostile agents" (294).

Drawing upon Klein's work, Teresa Brennan argues that all affect is social in origin and physical in effect.[51] It emerges in the encounter between bodies, and it is felt primarily in the nerves, muscles, and glands. "We are not self-contained in our energies," Brennan writes, for, when it comes to affect, "There is no secure distinction between the 'individual' and the 'environment'" or even "between the biological and the social" (6–7). Brennan, in fact, explores affective transmission beyond the confines of the nursery as it persists through adult life and finds new expression in group experiences such as rock concerts. Yes, empathy and identification are important forms of social cohesion, she says, but seeing, smelling, and touch create alliances that are both deeper and potentially more dynamic. Group imitation is initiated and sustained by a physical process of contagion, a physiological linkage across bodies that can cause them to seethe and surge in unexpected ways (49, 57). The concert experience reignites the affective experiences of the infant, working through "energies" and "valences" rather than signs and meanings in order to dissolve habitual relations and effect new modes of relation and becoming (65–66). In this, Brennan distinguishes between language and the effects of sound in concert experiences. In moments of contagion, she argues, signs become sound once more, exposed—as everything else within the sensory horizon—as grainy objects of attraction and investment. Imaginary relations are upended by auditory experiences that are at once internal and external, urgent but indescribable, and thus as they threaten social stability (68–69). At such moments, perhaps, we hear, in contrast to the father's austere command, something like the vocal pleasure of the mother. As Barthes writes, the "grain" of the voice is the "mother tongue" mocking the "phallic stature" of the father's command (182). For Brennan, too, the sonic currents that spread across the group inevitably mock and challenge the law: "sights and sounds are physical matters in themselves, carriers of social matters, social in origin but physical in their effects" (71).

Indeed, at its most fun, Elvis's so-called innocence took form as sheer infantilism. The obsessive orality, the insatiable eating, his love of teddy bears and dodgem cars—the biography points everywhere toward an arrested development, a perverse yet singularly compelling performance of infantile pleasure. As the King sang "Baby, Let's Play House" or "(I Wanna Be Your) Teddy Bear," he addressed the listener as playmate, as cooing other, and his voice exhibited all the inane joy of baby babble (hiccups, burps, coos, and whispers).[52] But the King's cutesiness always contained a real explosive demand. Most performances combined tenderness with desperation and thus revived the aggressive syncopation of the infant's relation to the mother. In "I Don't Care if the Sun Don't Shine," for example, Elvis reveals, in the midst of so much child's play, all the greedy neediness of one of Klein's monster infants, one whose drive is oral and insatiable: "Well, that's when we're gonna kiss and kiss and kiss and kiss, and we're gonna kiss some more," he sings, "Who cares how many times we kiss, / 'Cause at a time like this, who keeps score?"[53] Again, Elvis transferred his intense—and intensely inarticulate—bond with his mother to the stage. Songs like this ask us to listen again to cock-rock and hear within it the very movement—the subterranean course or tour—of the infant body, or at least its sloppier drives.[54] With his thrusts and caresses, his baby talk, his pet names, and his scarves and kisses, Mother Elvis established an intimacy that was by turns tender and tough, both open and intense, but thus more radical than any simple display of phallic power. He used his body to effect a mode of social engagement that was both culturally and psychologically regressive, but also undeniably pleasurable and even, at times, ecstatic and genuinely transgressive.

In turn, fans were restored to their own affective bodies, feeling their way toward pleasure and so making new demands on an otherwise dismissive or hostile society. In fact, for many fans, the stage show revived not just the heated emotions, but also the myopic perspectives and narcissistic pleasures of infancy. One fan reported intense fear and then ecstatic relief in the presence of the King's body: "The closer I'm getting, the more paranoid you get, coming to life, getting bigger and bigger as you get closer and closer. . . . and [he] just looks like he's going to crash into your face, coming down so fast, and he gave me a blue scarf" (*Elvis Now* 62). Another recalled a sense of illicit proximity and then a kinky sublimity:

> But I couldn't sit through this show like a good little girl. . . . When I got to the second row I didn't think I would make it any closer. . . . Right after that somebody in front of me raised their arms and I ducked under. There I was, I had made it! I was actually standing right at Elvis's feet. The stage was about 6 ft. high and looked like a mountain. He had gotten to the final words of the song and the place was in pandemonium. But he just stood there like one of the Greek gods looking down over his people, his eyes seeming to touch on each face at his feet. (*Elvis Now* 2)

These accounts suggest not just the work of the drives, but Klein's specifically infantile dynamic of demand and pleasure, one marked by a complex economy of partial objects, open emotions, and an odd gift-giving exchange:

> I was in the front row and Elvis was singing many songs and giving me more kisses and scarves than I had ever received. I said to my girlfriend that I wasn't feeling well and just after I said that, Elvis came over to my table again and gave me another kiss and scarf. As he walked away, I repeated to my girlfriend that I was feeling faint and that I was going to put my head on the stage. So I watched his shoes and tried to get rid of this feeling. . . . I was then taken to first aid where they took very good care of me. Someone came to the door and asked how I was and that Elvis was concerned. (*Elvis Now* 6)

Here, the classic fetish object—the King's own shoes—proves no match for the intense (and intensely maternal) feelings at play in this moment. What would otherwise be a simple experience of desire is riddled by the more or less fortuitous circulation of bodies and things, a series of connections, linkages, and mutual recognitions characterized by various states of satisfaction and well-being—"feeling," "care," "concern." To be true to our sources, we should add that these exchanges involved a whole range of bodily functions and flows—crying, screaming, devouring, kissing, pissing, shitting, spitting, and shredding. For the Elvis fan, this Dada-like movement between readymade bodies and things was always at once physical and affective, biological as well as aesthetic, and so, in the end, celebrated the incredible plasticity of private and public being.

This exchange also allows us to rethink the blatant consumerism that accompanies fan culture. Elvis pins, Elvis dolls, Elvis perfume, Elvis clocks, Elvis guitars, Elvis jeans (black with green stitching), Elvis trading cards, Elvis charm bracelets, Elvis flavored lipsticks ("Cruel Red"), Elvis pillows, Elvis paint-by-number sets, and, of course, Elvis press-on sideburns—the vast array and sheer number of Elvis products on the market in the 1950s place the King at the center of both the culture of abundance and its voracious marketplace.[55] For me, though, consumerism, of the bloated style practiced by the King and his followers, always entails something of the body's genuine openness. Fanaticism of this era was never simply acquisitive, for it involved, in the activity of consumption, the literal use of the body as a sensual means of judgment and exchange. As we saw with blues records, country radio, and then Duchamp's readymades, the pop commodity often plays the role of fetish, promising presence and stability, but it also allows other, more transgressive kinds of pleasure. Even as consumers, obsessively hunting down all the King's relics, fans relate to these objects as potential sources of wonder and release. They approach the King's products—from cigarette butts and nail clippings to glittering mass-produced charm bracelets—in terms of the sluttish mode of affection performed by the King himself. Each cheap thing is grasped, fondled, and ultimately consumed as a means of attaining not just some connection with the King, but also his openness, his social sloppiness. Stealing blood and urine, shredding clothes, decking out one's bedroom with hundreds of photos—if fan behavior seems to approach the realm of myth and ritual, it is only to worship a body restored to its original fluidity, to reincorporate a body defined by its disincorporation. In other words, to consume Elvis is to connect with that big primal mother who gives and takes all life, to reclaim some of that early affection, that errant drive, that defines as it destroys the non-Oedipal self.[56] Take the following hotel-room binge:

> . . . we went through all the garbage cans and Tom and I ate some of the burned bacon because we figure[d] it had to be his. . . . We grabbed it with gusto and swallowed it down. And then Cathy and I, Cathy Burness, Bonnie's daughter, went around and there was Elvis' bed, ripped the covers back and just knew there would be pubic hair. I was never so disappointed in my whole life. We jumped in the bed and covered ourselves up and said, "We're in bed with Elvis . . . It's too bad he's not here.["] So I can actually say I have been in Elvis' bed, even though he wasn't in there, I have been in his bed. But I thought—this was perfect—I mean this was the height of being an Elvis fan, if I could have had a pubic hair, in a frame somewhere, that I knew came [from] his bed. . . . We took everything we could get our hand[s] on. . . . We went into Elvis' bathroom. There was like bandaid things, you know where he put little bandaids around his fingers. . . . After that we went through all the garbage cans and there was a Tab can—took that—and there was a little note pad. . . . Some doodles . . . ripped that off. I know we were really stupid cause we didn't take any sheets or anything—but the year before at Stoffers we pried the number off the door with a can opener. (*Elvis Now* 135)

As this description suggests, the "height of being an Elvis fan" is not the acquisition of some commercial fetish, but a playful romp across a charged landscape filled with hundreds of kinky totems. Every Elvis fan is essentially a Duchampian—fanaticism blossoms in a dirty, dustbin exchange that is always at once proximate and detached, sensual and sensible, convulsing the body, heaving it, joyously, from one affective state to the next. Is it any wonder that fans also wanted to bestow gifts upon the Mother

King, the kinky master of their own undoing? By alternately collecting and returning Elvis's junk, the fan both devours and restores a non-phallic god, realizes and restores that god's non-presence in ever more ridiculous forms. Ultimately, in the hotel room of Elvis culture, these exchanges are by turns transgressive and reparative, smutty and celebratory. As they allude back to the bedside pleasures of the mother's body, they generate a radical charge, one akin to *jouissance* in that, for all its deathly pleasure, it forces us to develop a more supple and perhaps more tender approach to both the fan and fan culture.

The Third Elvis

In 1957, Evelyn Fraser, age fourteen, from Long Beach, California, sent *Movie Teen Illustrated* a nineteen-point list of reasons of why she is "so ape" over Elvis. With typical adoration of the King's manliness and "yum-yum electricity," Evelyn provides detailed descriptions of her idol's voice, face, expressions, and gestures. Writing from the comfort of her four-postered, pillow-stuffed bed, she explains how her idol's movements play upon her adolescent sensibilities, shaking and twisting her own fragile frame. And yet, for all its physicality, Evelyn's account continually slips away from any desire; the teenage fan seems to locate her keenest pleasure in a certain visual detachment, as it allows a much more subtle play of affective responses:

> Elvis is so handsome the sight of his picture gives me goose bumps. No one has those blue eyes with the merry-lovin' twinkle behind them. And I wish I had a slow-moving film of that smile. I'd like to watch the crinkles start at the corners of his mouth, the way his full, lower lip opens downward and spreads, showing his wonderful even, sparkling white teeth. I could spend the rest of my days just watching this slow-motion picture of his smile.

Evelyn's language clearly emphasizes the mediation of the image. But as her attention wanders across the surfaces of her photo collection, she is also responsive to the various feelings that arise within her body. Each photo is matched by a nearly nameless but precise affection that manifests itself in shakes, chills, goose bumps, and other resonant states. Evelyn exclaims, "Even his muscles have glamour and personality!" and, with outbursts like these, the whole encounter seems both meaty and moral, gritty and idealized. No doubt, the fan's detachment grants her a certain freedom to fantasize, to indulge in sexual fantasy without consequence, but

"I sleep under an acre of Elvis pictures"

IMAGE 7 Evelyn Fraser in *Movie Teen Illustrated*, 1961.

her response is full of consequences, pleasures and pains and ultimately judgments that attest to the seriousness of her fanaticism. The fan—who claims to "sleep under an acre of Elvis pictures"—constantly conflates Elvis's powerful poses and moods with her own and thus finds something like a personal ethos (see image 7). The boundary between gaze and icon dissolves entirely, fusing fan and star in a single affective bond, one loaded with real value and strength: "I've never met Elvis, it is true, but you can't say I don't know him. Elvis is IT with me." But Evelyn doesn't stop here, because her great big teenage heart expands beyond Elvis to include a whole legion of fans, all bound by affective ties that she can feel, weigh, and ultimately defend with confidence: "I'm sure I speak the sentiments of the thousands—hundreds of thousands—of girls who feel the same way."[57]

As an Americanist, I feel inclined here to borrow from Whitman: Evelyn Fraser—*you are large! you contain multitudes!* As a modernist, though, I'm drawn to Gustave Flaubert's more elusive pronouncement: *Evelyn Fraser—c'est moi!* Either way, I must confess, I can flip through Elvis photos for hours, ogling each one, letting my eye and then my heart fill up with something like restless wonder. Each image inspires the same response, which is really no response at all, just a nearly giddy amazement that seems to emerge from the very act of looking itself, the movement of my own corporeal eye across the surface of the photo. My most critical stance (if you can call it such) takes shape as a simple, dumbstruck urgency: *Hey, you gotta see this. Do you see it? Look again—do you see it?!* Surely, here, with the image, when all of the immediacy of Elvis's song and dance becomes static, stagnant, contained by technology, I should be able to see nothing but the most obvious structures of meaning. Again, though, even in this glossy glamorized form, the star avoids easy inscription and attains something like an apotheosis of affective being. Of course, my experience is much more removed than that of the fan in 1956, but it is only more riveting insofar as it seems to defy the very detachment of my position. Simply put, looking at images of Elvis, I feel at work—in my own eye—the ceaseless renewal of a culture that otherwise seems to have been given over to visual detachment, mass reproduction, and disenchantment.

Take any photograph of Elvis. We can easily establish its referents. We can name where and when it was taken, and we can reconstruct all the historical forces—social, economic, technological—that came together to capture it. At the same time, we can read its symbolic coordinates; we can translate hair, skin, suit, and shoes, as well as posture and gesture, into a clear set of cultural meanings—a syntax, say, of class, gender, and race. And yet, at the same time, my eye is inevitably drawn to a number of seemingly irrelevant and perhaps irreverent details—the peculiar position of the feet, the odd twist of the hip, the uneven dynamism of the hands. It is not just that these features "express" adolescent pleasure or the rebellious intensity of the moment. Rather, they seem caught in the very act of posturing, in their own mediation, and thus expose the body as it is shaped and reshaped from one moment to the next. In fact, the photographed body, in its very estrangement, actually restores us to something like the body's original vitality; the image at once pushes us toward and away from the living corpus, from its own presentation, and thus recaptures something of the convulsive experience of the body as such, as it coheres and dissolves from one moment to the next. As mentioned, Elvis ventured his most outrageous gestures as he moved away from his audience, backward, receding from view. His movements were marked by aggression and retreat, and thus they commanded as they accommodated the fan's investment. In photographs, this double movement is augmented by the technology itself. The indifferent surface of the photo is open to anything that occurs within its frame, and yet it keeps the spectacle at bay, giving us presence and absence both, engagement and detachment. Again, it is not just that the photograph allows us to see what would otherwise go unnoticed in the rush of real time; rather, it amplifies the very mediation of the body, gives us a gestural body in action, at once surging and fading from one form to the next, commanding and free.

In a word, these images give us access to an *articulate* body, one that is both *flexible* and *significant*. It is a body that has been freed to gesture not according to some predetermined system of meaning, but according to its own pleasurable limit, and it allows us to experience our own bodies in kind. In one famous photo, for example, each inch of the King's arm offers a new sensation. The urgent thrust of the shoulder modulates into the defiant strength of the forearm and, then, most startlingly of all, turns into a graceful fist and dangling forefinger. Like some Dadaist montage in the flesh, the initially aggressive assemblage morphs, at the point of contact with the fan, into a gesture of genuine tenderness (see image 8). At other times, the King's body takes a more abstract turn. In another photo, Elvis reaches out, limply, lightly, with his right arm, while his left jerks inward, breaking the symmetry. His head hangs to his side, offsetting the straight line of his padded shoulders but extending the line of his opposite arm. His face—as we see in the crisp relations of mouth, nose, brow—comes off as a marvel of Euclidean geometry, Cubist portraiture, and Beale Street flash (see image 9). Tracking the curves of this form occasions a disjointed but thrilling play of feelings. We are not merely reacting to its intensity or its strangeness. Rather, our responses depend on the fact that the body on display is both posed and present, empty and full. Our pleasure exists in the movement of a specifically ocular drive, in the eye's circuit around the captured object. Take, for example, the famous photo of Elvis stretched out against his bed (see image 10). Here, too, we find a free juxtaposition of otherwise opposed gestures and emotions—torso proffered as sexy lure, fists raised in weary defiance, eyes turned upward in a mixture of love, curiosity, and resignation. The key feature, though, remains Elvis's chest, which spreads openly across the frame, available for a range of meanings and investments. It is at once exposed and weak—present, hunky, available, and yet silent, empty, blank; we can, and might, find everything and nothing written on this chest, but mostly we take pleasure in ranging across its surface, circling, fondling, caressing its mute features.

Again, we can "read" these images in other ways; semiotics and psychoanalysis are not incompatible with the pleasures of bedroom gazing. Yet, as thousands and thousands of fan letters assert, Elvis was first and foremost

IMAGE 8 Elvis Presley in concert, 1956. Courtesy of Photo Trends / Screen Gems.

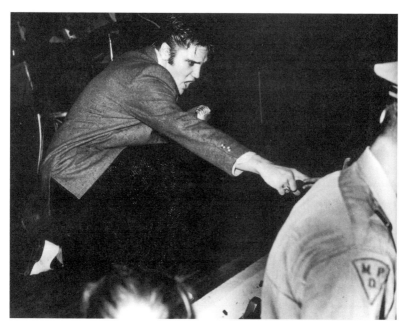

IMAGE 9 Elvis Presley in concert, 1956. Courtesy of Photo Trends / Screen Gems.

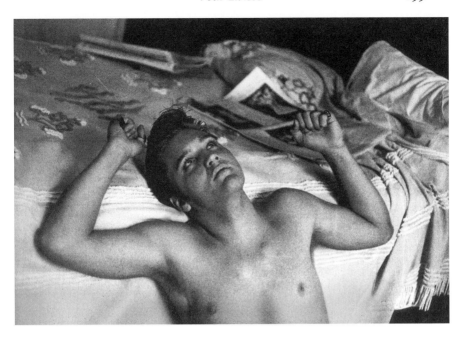

IMAGE 10 Elvis reclining against a bed. Courtesy of Michael Ochs Archives / Getty Images.

an affective/gestural phenomenon, and by rethinking his specifically visual allure in these terms, we can more carefully define the persistence of midcentury fan culture through its own technological manipulation. Elvis, we know, built his career on the cultivation and continual revision of his image. From his earliest days at Humes High, he was known for his outlandish outfits and tonsorial flair. Later, with fame, he altered his nose, smoothed his skin, and dyed his hair black; he came to favor black mascara and royal blue eye shadow, and his onstage hair regime consisted of three different kinds of oil (so only his bangs flopped when he danced).[58] He worked continually on his posture and gestures, developing a wide but idiosyncratic repertoire of steps and shrugs. "I've made a study of Marlon Brando. I've made a study of poor Jimmy Dean. I've made a study of myself," he told reporters, "and I know why girls, at least the young 'uns, go for us" (Guralnick 323–24). Further, the King loved costumes and show people—the showier, the better: clowns and daredevils and Liberace. He himself contained multitudes, taking his most outrageous moves from Beale Street musicians, gospel performers, female starlets, circus people, and burlesque dancers. As Guralnick notes, "he soaked up influences like litmus paper; he was open to new people and new ideas and new experiences in a way that defied social stereotype" (195).

But Elvis's fame rested not simply on what he mimicked, but on the very fact of mimicry. The King was so closely identified with his own mediation that he seemed to burst through to its other side. Take, for example, photo-journalist Alfred Wertheimer's account of his 1956 Elvis assignment. Wertheimer, a veteran photographer, was startled to find that he had complete access to Elvis's body—onstage, backstage, offstage, in his hotel room, on trains, at meals, in the pool, even in bathrooms. "I had never covered a subject who fell asleep in front of my camera," Wertheimer explains, "but I had my assignment." It was, in fact, in Elvis's bathroom where Wertheimer realized that all of the rules had changed. Once, the photographer stumbled on Elvis before the bathroom mirror, working through his morning routine: "I tried to find a discreet way to take his picture when I decided upon the direct approach. I asked if I could come in and take some pictures. He said, 'Sure, why not?' With one white towel around his hips and another slung over his shoulder, Elvis elevated wet combing into an art, examining each angle with a scrutiny of a portrait artist. He was a perfect subject for a photographer, unafraid and uncaring, oblivious to the invasion of my camera" (11). Flipping through Wertheimer's photos from those few tumultuous months—Elvis combing his hair, Elvis dozing on the couch, Elvis playing his own records—one becomes intimate with a figure who is at once a natural and a natural-born performer, one who is always posing because posing is innate to his very being. Elvis appears aware of his framing, but his ease of posture and attitude suggest that framing has become so casual to him that he experienced it as a state of innocence. For Wertheimer, though, the King's attitude reflected the modernity of the media that made him famous. Both star and camera, in their innocence, their visual indifference, had surpassed traditional forms of identity. Both had given up conventional notions of depth and expression for the more abstract pleasures of the public pose. Elvis the star was decisively inhuman and amoral—like the camera itself—but this estrangement always implied a more radical freedom.

I'm here reminded of Giorgio Agamben's claim that "By the end of the nineteenth century, the Western bourgeoisie had definitely lost its gestures."[59] For Agamben, early twentieth-century art, particularly the extreme histrionics of stage and screen, suggests a growing anxiety about communication. The flailing bodies of modern art and early cinema exemplify the death throes of public culture, a last-ditch effort of the bourgeoisie to record, scientifically, the expressive language of gesture as it slipped through their fingers. For Agamben, though, gesture—once stripped bare of its public usefulness—reveals itself as neither organic expression nor aesthetic wholeness; rather, it is exposed in the modern era as the exhibition of mediality, the process of making a means (here, the body as means) visible as such. As Agamben writes, "If dance is gesture, it is so, rather, because it is nothing more than the endurance and the exhibition of the media character of corporal movements. *The gesture is the exhibition of mediality: it is the process of making a means visible as such.* It allows the emergence of the being-in-a-medium of human beings and thus it opens the ethical dimension for them" ("Notes" 57). Perhaps all our modern dances—the twist, the lindy, the hop, etc.—function as a jumbled collection of more or less reified gestures calling for response. These dances—isolated, frantic, mute—arise out of communicative failure, but they also expose communicability in its purest form. As gestures, they expose the body (and its drives) as "a forceful presence in language," one that is "not exhausted with the end of communication, but persists as pure means, as pure mediality."[60] At the very least, Elvis himself, as a *gestural star*, worked through the medial dimensions of voice and body, and, as we've seen, his fans responded in kind. Here, at the end of modernity proper and with the full commodification of the public sphere, the body becomes the display of a medium, humming somewhere between reality and virtuality, everyday life and abstract art. Each gesture—as a gestural *refrain*, perhaps—appears both commanding and available, a suspension or crystallization of sensual form, waiting for another body, for an entire culture, to try out its shape and test its value. And the significance of this exchange rests precisely on its *modality* rather than its *marginality*, on its formal plasticity as it is at once conditioned and freed by consumer technology.

Here, as we saw in Phillips's studio, technology—specifically, *consumer* technology—facilitates this process. As Roland Barthes argued in a series of essays throughout the 1960s, at the moment when Elvis himself was making the shift from sonic to visual celebrity, the photographic image is a "message without a code."[61] It "reduces" as it "reproduces" reality, and so its reception is somewhat loosened from everyday relations and meanings. In fact, the photograph's contents are all—like Elvis's chest—too full and too slight, meaty and meager—alluring, but empty and inert. For Barthes, as for Evelyn Fraser and a host of other teenage gawkers, this doubleness is precisely what grants pleasure. The photo inspires a woozy sort of attentiveness, a pleasurable careening of the eye. As with any "readymade," we are drawn by its immediacy, its apparent shamelessness, and yet—lacking any

serious purpose or responsibility—we skate freely along its glossy surface. Once literal and symbolic readings are exhausted, Barthes writes, "I
am still held by the image. I read, I receive (and probably even first and
foremost) a third meaning—evident, erratic, obstinate. I do not know
what its signified is, at least I am unable to give it a name, but I can see
clearly the traits, the signifying accidents of which this—consequently
incomplete—sign is composed" (53). Here, Barthes shifts our attention
away from the vocal to the ocular drive. He describes the "third meaning" as both active and errant, a provocative but evasive "supplement" to
any direct meaning. In fact, the "third meaning" is an "obtuse meaning,"
one that is "dumb," "blunted, rounded in form"; it is experienced as a
"slip" in meaning, as a perpetual and pleasurable swerving away from any
socially sanctioned definition (54–55). As in his account of the "grain"
of the voice, Barthes here celebrates a sensual play that cuts against
formal meaning. He writes, "the obtuse meaning is outside (articulated)
language while nevertheless within interlocution. This accent . . . is not
directed towards meaning . . . does not even indicate an *elsewhere* of
meaning. . . . it outplays meaning—subverts not the content but the
whole practice of meaning" (62).

Again, we move from *meaning* to *mattering*, from established codes
and hierarchies to a more sensual mode of reflection and judgment. Born
out of consumer technology, the "third meaning," like the Third Elvis,
demands a very specific kind of "reading," an affective understanding of
form and fit, one that is charged with energy but loose in structure. Such
meaning attracts attention, demands a response, but its analysis derives
from the body's own pleasure, from the body's own ability to know just
what feels good—or not. Like the drive itself, the "third meaning" implies
not a content, but a course, a relation, an active positioning or affective
orientation; value is established and maintained through the readymade
encounter, by way of valences and intensities, shifts and swerves of attention, tics and thrusts and spastic dances that may in themselves become
new forms of investment. For me, then, the "third meaning" works best
as a theory of *popular* reading, one that explains how fans are moved in
relation to their cheap objects of affection. Barthes, like Duchamp, reads
just like fourteen-year-old Evelyn Fraser—their responses are linked by
an inarticulate but compelling logic of gesture and affection; the glossy
surface of the image allows them to pursue their own affective mediation
from one state to another, pursuing values that are decisively physical,
social, and, ultimately, transgressive. "I accept," Barthes writes, "for the

obtuse meaning the word's pejorative connotation. . . . it belongs to the family of pun, buffoonery, useless expenditure. Indifferent to moral or aesthetic categories (the trivial, the futile, the false, the pastiche), it is on the side of the carnival" (55). But, still, even as he acknowledges the ridiculousness of his affection, Barthes—like Evelyn—never shies from the language of value and judgment, for it is precisely at his most frivolous, his most superficial, that the theorist asserts something like an evaluation: "I believe," he writes, that the photo "carries a certain *emotion*. It is an emotion which simply *designates* what one loves, what one wants to defend: an emotion-value, an evaluation" (59). Clothing, hairstyles, music, dances, fast food, and fast cars—the mediated objects of pop culture are always at once empty and filling, but, as Barthes shows, in our daily encounters with these faddish inventions, we establish our greatest investments. Looking at images of Elvis, the third meaning, like all pop meaning, moves—without friction—across the face of an otherwise complacent, mediated world, casually subverting and slowly dissolving even its most stubborn values and judgments.

Ultimately, as scholars and fans, we respond to Elvis's affective body, even as it overlaps with his symbolic body, as it informs a politics of the *modal* rather than the *marginal*. His revolt took shape through gestures and their sensual resonances; at once passionate and posed, direct and detached, his body disclosed itself as a mediated body and so became something like a compelling ethical proposition, a public proposition. In this, I find myself just as much impressed by Elvis's cheap pink scarf as by any of his "authentic" rockabilly sides or his million-dollar hits. Just like that, with no explanations, no excuses, a shy boy from East Tupelo shows up to shop class wearing a pink scarf. No biographer has been able to track the causes behind this impulsive and seemingly empty declaration. No psychologist has discovered the original trauma that may have tied up this flimsy, casual knot. No cultural theorist has translated the hard chains of historical causality into the frivolous language of this insubstantial charm. The significance of the scarf—as with any readymade—lies in its unaccountability, its flamboyant uselessness, its tautological unnecessity. Elvis's scarf is—like his song, like any commodity—an emphatic gesture, a momentary pose, a tossed-off stylization of the self, easily adopted, easily discarded. In this, it does not cancel or challenge history in any direct way; rather, it operates within its own gambit, its own empty circuit of affective intensity and stylish thrust, in ways that only indirectly impact the chronicle of events and meanings. Elvis the pop star discovered the immediacy of mediation, the compelling carelessness of the commodity form, and thereby set off an accidental, incidental revolt, at once oblivious and obtuse, powerful in its very shallowness. With every useless stylish thrust, the King recreated both his body and the body politic. And through records, radio, television, and film, his revolution extended across time and space, sanctioning legions of unruly kids to try it all out on their own gangly, outcast frames.

CHAPTER FIVE

(   )

The Empty Studio

I've never been to Lubbock County, but I'm sure it must be beautiful—nothing but blue skies, open fields, and long, long roads. I imagine an immense space carved up in abstract strokes, broad swaths of color and clean, stark lines—a quiet geometry of work and rest, pain and hope. At least that's what I hear when I listen to the songs recorded in the tidy little studio designed by Norman Petty, about an hour-and-a-half drive from Lubbock proper. When Petty bought the building in the mid-1950s, it was still being used as a country store, but the enterprising producer quickly gutted the place, removed all its country clutter, and rededicated it to the production of pure sound. Working closely with his wife, Vi, he turned the front hall into a reception area, sealed off the main living area as a studio, carved a control booth out of its side, and then installed beds in the back room for musicians. He saw to the selection of proper wall materials, floor coverings, and board arrangements, a disk cutter, a Western Union clock, and, of course, recording equipment. Beer, cigarettes, and horseplay were off-limits. No clocks, no windows, no breezes. Recording sessions began and ended with quiet prayer. Thus the country store became a sonic sanctuary, both laboratory and temple. A smooth, egglike dwelling, it protected a space within space, a time within time, so that sound could reach its own undiminished limit, tracing out bright minimal patterns in the empty air. Buddy Holly's "Everyday." Buddy Knox's "Party Doll." Roy Orbison's "Ooby Dooby." Lubbock's just *got* be beautiful.[1]

Soon, in fact, Petty tiled over the unused attic space across the yard with scraps from the Holley Family Tile Business, transforming it into an echo—or, technically, a reverb—chamber. An even stranger space, this one: an empty room, hermetically sealed, containing nothing but a speaker and a microphone. The sounds made in the studio proper were wired to this other spot, where they bounced off the walls before returning to the control room to be grafted onto the original track. Petty would turn the chamber on and off from his console in the main house, but, really, the loop from one space to the other sealed off the song and sent it reeling into space: in its purest form, in the empty attic, the song had no listener, no context, no history; it was free to spin and hum in the dusty air according to its own pattern.

During the summer of 1957, however, while Petty was laying down tracks with Buddy Holly and his band, he detected a strange noise in the mix. He threw down his clipboard and stormed into the recording room. Something had found a way into the echo chamber—a darn cricket, probably. The boys put down their instruments and trudged across the yard to search for the intruder. When they entered the attic, though, they couldn't hear a thing. They looked around, shrugged it off, and returned to the studio. Again, though, when Petty turned on the booth, the cricket joined in. The boys sighed, unplugged, trudged across the yard again, and up the stairs—but, still, no cricket. They laughed it off, grabbed a few Cokes, and returned to the studio. The group continued with the session—cricket be damned—and then Petty played back some of the tapes. On one track, he noticed, the cricket let out four little chirrups at the end of the song—right on the beat. Cool stuff.[2] Something had breached the studio's thick walls and, disrupting the purity of the track, actually made it better.

In a way, the cricket affirms the entire Clovis operation. He appears in the attic like some kind of sonic aesthete, a jitterbug modernist indulging in his own strange sound. In fact, the boys in the band had already named themselves the Crickets (after flipping through an encyclopedia), and they no doubt felt a certain bond with the creature, digging his alien style as a reflection of their own—mechanical, rhythmic, groovy. Also, the group probably knew that the cricket (or at least the male of the species) only made music to attract a mate. The little insect in the attic was looking for someone to love, giving voice to all the itchy frustration that marked his lonely life in the barns and fields. His song echoed the boys' own unheeded mating cries, reassuring them, *yeah, chicks will dig it, man.* But the cricket's creak was heard everywhere in the region—in fields, basements, attics, garages. Paradoxically, its lonely air, hidden in the attic rafters, conjured

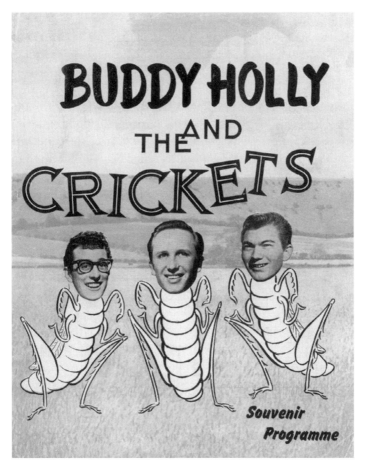

IMAGE 11 Buddy Holly and the Crickets Souvenir Programme, 1958.

up the entire lost landscape outside the studio. Similarly, the band's music, even at its quirkiest, carried with it the shape and textures of the region in which it was produced, and promotional materials consistently linked the novelty of its sound with the stark features of a decisively Texas landscape (see image 11). In all this, we're no longer dealing with pure sounds. The whole modern world seems to be rushing back into the empty studio. In fact, if the parable of the cricket suggests anything, it's that history occurs precisely when you try to deny it, and then seems to stop again when you go looking for it. The studio is never completely sealed, and the music it makes—no matter how abstract—always contains something of the very world it sought to transcend.

We might even say that the history of the modern studio "echoes" the historical dynamic of modernity at large. In the early days of the music industry, recording procedures were largely ad hoc and site-specific. Some big-city scout or aspiring folk collector would arrive on the local scene, set up his clunky machinery on the spot—in the field or the barn or the local assembly hall—and then position willing performers as close as possible to the large sound horn of the recorder. Ralph Peer conducted the famous Bristol sessions in a hat factory, covering the windows with thick quilted blankets; Alan Lomax recorded Muddy Waters in his favorite chair on the front porch of his Stovall shack. Over time, though, with advances in wiring, microphone technology, and recording devices, companies begin to construct self-contained studios in which they could more easily capture the sounds of the country. By the 1930s, in fact, most companies were running their own private studios in major cities, forcing musicians to uproot themselves and learn to play their music in foreign settings. As Paul Théberge explains, each studio was designed to function as a "non-space"—a more or less generic site removed from local traditions and identities.[3] The production of clean sound entailed not just better equipment, but a total lack of context. These spaces were designed to be "dry" or dead," and even "silent": like Petty's studio, they were emptied out and carefully sealed, stripped down to only the most essential materials and tools. At this stage, the role of the engineer began to rival that of the musician, particularly as the former was responsible for separating music from the actual activity of music making. By the time we get to Sam Phillips and Norman Petty, the engineer served to manage the studio's staggering array of equipment in its more or less inexpressive, inhuman relation to musical production. Indeed, both engineer and equipment were moved out of the studio proper into a control booth, a further abstraction, where, behind thick plates of glass, sound was handled as a flexible material rather than a form of human expression.

But engineers and producers of this era soon found themselves facing other demands. For some, the sounds that came out of the studios in the early days seemed too "dry," too "dead." Accustomed to the natural acoustics of, say, a neighbor's barn or the high school gymnasium, many listeners found the records produced in the 1930s and 1940s lacking in feel and depth. Everywhere, the demand for novelty competed with the demand for a more traditional, more "authentic" musical experience. So a further room was needed, beyond the control booth, one that could supplement the pure tones of the studio with something like reality. Hence the "echo chamber," designed to bring dead sounds back to life. As engineer Tom Lubin explains,

> [Reverb] gives the impression of power, adds drama, size and depth. It changes the edges of the sound and identifies the boundary of the image. It provides depth to the sonic picture, and constant contrast and comparison of the direct sound to the surroundings in which the music is played. . . . Reverb is an organic phenomenon that provides a locality of the general sonic scene.[4]

Oddly, the reverb chamber generated warmth by remaining completely empty. It was essentially barren—only four walls, a speaker, and a mic—and far removed from human traffic. It was tightly sealed not just to keep out extraneous noise, but so that the sound on the inside could bounce around freely and create the multiple vibrations that occurred in a "wet" or "live" space. In fact, Petty's echo chamber was nothing special. Studios around the country were using a whole array of ingenious techniques to perfect the art of reverb. Columbia Records in New York bounced sound up six flights of stairs and then sent it back to the studio. Stax Records used the bathroom of their movie-theater studio, exploiting the natural surfaces of porcelain to create a sense of soul. Bigger operations constructed multiple chambers to suit their various needs. In 1956, Capital Records in Los Angeles had six reverb chambers in its basement, each with a slightly different shape and volume to create different effects. Again, though, all of these empty rooms were designed to create a "natural" effect, to restore a sense of human space and experience.[5] Acoustic realism involved a second-order abstraction, a greater estrangement, as if only by pushing sound further beyond anything like human exchange could it attain a human function again. This is the echo effect of late modernity: in the studio as non-space, history is both lost and made, again and again, in its own estrangement and constant supplementation.

As I'll show here, then, if the recording studio figures as ground zero for the pop revolution to come, then the geeky, stuttering Buddy Holly was the first citizen (or perhaps patient zero) of the new pop order. As is well known, Holly built his reputation on sound as much as image, and he is famous the world over for crafting seemingly perfect pop songs. Still, today, stars like Paul McCartney and Keith Richards praise Holly for being the first performer to write, sing, and record his own music. For Richards, Holly led a "totally self-contained band" and created "self-contained" songs, each a "beautiful piece of precision."[6] Yet something of

Holly's unique personality and environment—something of its specific contradictions and conflicts—can be heard through and within his music's very abstraction. As suggested by his famous pair of glasses, Holly had a reputation for being neat, sober, and polite, charmingly chaste and awkward. But his biography everywhere shows that he was a red-blooded teen, prone to intense crushes, new fads, and wild drives on the Texas highways. When he found music, these two aspects of his personality—the abstract and the adolescent—found a common ground and quickly established his national fame. In fact, nearly all of Buddy's songs resound—cleanly, purely—with the same tortured love for the gal that got away, the appropriately named Echo McGuire. With each incarnation, he refined the formula, turning adolescent suffering into runic song, creating a new sonic vocabulary of purely aural intensities and relations. But if at Petty's studio, as at Sun Studio, expression gave way to the pleasures of mediation, this abstract turn did little to dampen the historical immediacy of song. As I'd like to show here, when we listen to Holly's pop hits, we still feel a certain loss, pain, anger, resentment, promise, but we feel all this in and through their very formalism, and thus as they relate to an entire lost world of commercial media and cheap consumer crap.

For me, the best pop songs produced in the 1950s, like Holly's, walked a fine line in relation to the marketplace. These songs pushed commercial alienation—of the singer, the voice, of song and musical tradition—to the point of complete emptiness, but only to affirm some new, more subtle form of presence and meaning. Their very abstraction—cold, repetitive, detached—became a site of significant engagement, a flashpoint for both personal and public feeling in an otherwise hostile marketplace. In other words, pop modernism continues the work of its vernacular precursors insofar as it uses sonic form to manage new and often bewildering sensations brought on by modernity. At the same time, though, pop modernism represents a significant break from those traditions by explicitly theorizing its own formalism in relation to the formalism of the marketplace. In fact, pop's commitment to pure sound bears within it traces of earlier traditions and styles. While some may argue that pop cheapens these traditions, slicking them up for easy mass consumption, I see these production values as a way of preserving and maintaining the original promises contained within them. Just as Petty carved an abstract space out of a traditional environment, Holly's music reworks the regional material of the past and turns it into clean, repetitive form, at once denying and preserving all the otherwise lost promises of blues, country, folk, and rock and roll. Here, then, above all else, I'd like to suggest that the pop music of the late modern period, in its administration, generates a new experience of space and time within and beyond its own frame and thus suggests another mode of history altogether—history less as linear progression, or even a postmodern series of empty citations, but as an affective echo or reverberation, a pulsating structure of regional loss and return, drawing in all the lost and lonely teens with its vague but alluring signal.

With this emphasis on the modern studio and sonic abstraction, my discussion recalls Peter Doyle's excellent book *Echo and Reverb: Fabricating Space in Popular Music Recording, 1900–1960*. Doyle similarly tracks the ways in which new studio technology revolutionized musical experience. The development of the studio, he argues, entailed a massive deterritorialization of vernacular culture, a process that culminated in a proliferation of nongeographical spaces and times, the eternal "now" of pop music as a disruption and implicit critique of everyday life. Most importantly, Doyle claims that even though sonic experience in the twentieth century moves toward virtuality—suggesting "movement in space but without any special reference to specific real-world spaces or places"—it nonetheless reflects and impacts everyday life (6). In fact, it is precisely the gap between studio-made pop music and everyday life that allows for an avant-garde intervention at the level of mass culture; the studio musician's effort to transcend the shortcomings—acoustic or otherwise—of local space signals the possibility of reinventing space altogether. As Doyle writes, "The notion here that sound qualities alone might be used to construct analogies to vision, with the potential to move between the real and the fantastic indicates an early awareness of radio's (and by implication, sound recording's) deterritorializing potentials" (33).

But Doyle, like so many critics of his generation, ends up re-territorializing this sonic potential within an all-too-familiar politics of identity and expression. For one, while Doyle celebrates the sonic transcendence of material space, his own analysis remains largely spatial. He approaches the studio mix as a visual mise-en-scène, defined by the coordinates of near and far, figure and pattern, center and margins. In turn, he interprets this scene metaphorically, so that the musical field always refers, no matter how abstract, to a political field of rebellion and authority, as if the place of each sound in the mix reflects a certain political stance (29–31). For Doyle, then, the studio recording, no matter how abstract, still serves to express human identities and positions. The new techniques at Sun, for example, suggest "a rebellious or deterritorialized presence. The answer echo, dragging just a little beyond the beat, hints strongly at a disruptive presence; there's a troublemaker on the threshold" (186). As Doyle acknowledges, these techniques create room for other kinds of listening experiences and other kinds of listeners (233). But his formulation is largely allegorical; by making sound spaces analogous to political spaces, Doyle dampens the unique properties of sound and music and (like Marcus) locks it all into an ideological paradigm (17–18). In the following discussion, you'll find, I'm not just interested in echo and reverb effects, but in the entire abstract space of the studio, as it releases musical modalities that overlap with, but are not determined by, human expressions and psychologies. I hope to show that you need to push this music way beyond the human world before it can capture the feelings of the late-modern listener and thus return to history in any dynamic way. For me, the very emptiness of pop, like the emptiness of the studio, contains and protects—in itself—all the fullness of an alternative, if undetermined, modernity.

Indeed, this chapter as a whole dwells in negatives—lacks, gaps, and silences—as they preserve, in this late stage of the capitalist era, new possibilities of experience and exchange. In this, it is dedicated not to any specific pop star or avant-garde artist, but to the silent teen, the mute fan, who, with shut mouth and open ears, signals both radical refusal and impossible revolution. In his defiant quietude, the silent kid maintains a desperate grip on the pristine purity of an unspoken life; he rejects all the generational junk served up by Ma and Pa, all the regional pap of the past, and instead holds out for the unheard song of his own utopian future. Sure, this silence is always already structured, always already a cliché, and yet it still maintains something real, some explosive demand, within and beyond any established structures. In "The Aesthetics of Silence," Susan Sontag defines the silence of the pop era as "inescapably, a form of speech . . . and an element in a dialogue."[7] She acknowledges that silence is never just silence: it can suggest resistance, refusal, deference, power; it can signal concentration, intensity, or even calm. But, overall, the silence practiced by her contemporaries in Pop Art suggests a commitment to some yet unnamed, otherworldly truth or beauty. "Silence," she writes, has become "a metaphor for a cleansed non-interfering vision. . . . the wish for a perceptual clean slate" (16–18). Similarly, the silent teen, like some human echo chamber, forever balancing narcissism and need, waiting for a sound, a voice, a world that makes sense, shoulders the entire noisy world of rock and pop, sitting alone. Think the mute generations of headphoned boys and girls, hooked on private grooves underneath the covers, in the closets, on the buses. Think the countless hidden tracks, the silent tracks, the unheard masterpieces, the lost "black" albums that shadow official music history. Think of all that unheard promise down at the bottom of the record store bin, at the yard sale, the flea market. Think the silent corpses that lay strewn across pop history—Holly in the snowy field, Elvis on the toilet, Hendrix in his bed, Joplin in the hotel room, Cobain in the greenhouse—all naked and hidden, released and ashamed, still wishing, waiting, hoping.

We have seen this destitution before—the personal trauma of the bluesman, the regional trauma of the country singer, the giddy trauma of the rock-and-roll king. Here, though, in what is undoubtedly the most absurd chapter of this book, I plan to pursue musical form at its coldest, its cheapest, its emptiest, and so, beyond its traumatic formation, as the basis of a genuinely open history. Thus the following discussion is divided into three echoing parts, tracking the ways in which pop music at once *rejects*, *recalls*, and then *returns* to something like history. The first draws on John Cage's early experience in an anechoic chamber to show how Buddy Holly's own work in the studio *rejected* the musical past and revolutionized regional songmaking as an abstract art. The second uses Jacques Derrida's theory of "expression" as a psychological echo chamber to show how Holly's voice exposes its own mediation and thereby *recalls* something like the mortal world against which it is defined. The third recasts the entire discussion in terms of the commercial echo chambers of Pop Art; it shows how Holly, like Andy Warhol, adapted the cheap commercial forms of the era to *restore* something like their original claims and historical urgency. As Lawrence Grossberg asserts, rock and roll emerged in the 1950s as a response to "experiences of alienation, powerlessness, and boredom." He describes the movement as a noisy revolt led by a generation of children that were "lonely and isolated from each other and the adult world as well."[8] Pop, of course, was never nearly so loud, so messy, so rebellious, but neither was it ever simply quiet, or quietist. I want to show here how these seemingly empty songs—in their very emptiness, their own essential silence—at once reject and restore something like modern history. I want to show how Holly's three-minute masterpieces, forged in the non-space of the studio, chirping brightly in the pop air, signal both renewal and reorientation from within the very wreckage of late modernity.

Well . . . All Right 1—The End of Tradition

In 1951, John Cage entered an anechoic chamber at Harvard University and quickly realized that he had it all wrong. Suddenly, it seemed, music needed to be freed not just from tradition, but from the composer himself and his whole habitual world. An anechoic chamber is, as the name implies, a room without any echo—without any shortwave reverb, to be precise. It is, in a way, a sonic tomb, designed to strip sound bare of its worldly resonance and positional capacity (many people report a loss of balance or an inability to move in an anechoic chamber). But Cage, expecting to hear silence in the chamber, heard himself, or, more importantly, his actual body—the operation of his nervous system and the circulation of blood. The sounds of his soma came back to him strange, yet clear; released from habit and habitual space, they revealed their inherent properties for the first time—tone, timbre, duration, rhythm. In this, the experience led him to rethink composition in Duchampian terms, as a transparent or minimal frame in and through which readymade sound—by chance and indifference—reveals its own limits and relations:

> For in this new music nothing takes place but sounds: those that are notated and those that are not. Those that are not notated appear in the written music as silence, opening the doors of the music to the sounds that happen to be in the environment. This openness exists in the fields of modern sculpture and architecture. The glass houses of Mies van der Rohe reflect their environment, presenting to the eye images of clouds, trees, or grass, according to the situation.

And so, in time, Cage's compositions became all open doors and windows, structures meant to be "heard through," transparent and transgressive.[9] Take, of course, Cage's most famous piece, *4'33"*, often referred to as the "Silent Prayer." The score—such as it is—instructs performers to do nothing more than start and stop at a set time; in fact, the only notation provided is a simple directive to be quiet—"Tacet." In this, the conventional space of performance is replaced by a new, open non-space; the three bare movements of the piece serve to reframe and so release the listener's attention into the ambient space of pure sound. What begins, in Cage's terms, as "a single idea," a "seductive" gesture, fades out into "imperceptibility," dissolving need and desire and thus making way for new sensual experience.[10] Again, though, if the piece moves beyond ego and beyond habit, it does not renounce structure in its entirety. Cage pursues freedom not *from*, but *through* form, and the minimalist score, like the minimalist studio, functions like the barest frame of all, a way to focus and enhance rather than fix sonic experience.

But Cage's understanding of silence changed over time, revealing a much deeper set of values. At first, silence seemed merely the opposite of sound, as one half of a *meaningful* syntax with sound, and thus as part of a largely binary system. Soon, though, the composer began to formulate a more intensive relation between the two phenomena, with each one persisting through the other. After the experience in the anechoic chamber, and the realization that "there's no such a thing as silence," Cage began to perceive silence as the precondition of sound itself, the very space in which sound emerges ("45'" 126):

> Where none of these [rhetorical] goals is present, silence becomes something else—not silence at all, but sounds, the ambient sounds. The nature of these is unpredictable and changing. These sounds (which are called silence only because they do not form part of a musical intention) may be depended upon to exist. The world teems with them, and is, in fact, at no point free of them.[11]

But even here, already, Cage was moving toward a third conception of silence, one with greater moral implications. Silence reveals itself as a principle of non-intentionality and thus exceeds the realm of sound in order to embrace the natural world at large. In other words, in Cage's later formulation, silence functions not simply as an empty space in which noises happen, but as a space of sonic potential, of potential as such, a "groundless ground," out of which dynamic figures emerge and recede (i.e., actualize) according to their own limits, establishing presence and significance in relation to each other[12]:

> For it is the space and emptiness that is finally urgently necessary at this point in history (not the sounds that happen in it—or their relationships) (not the stones—thinking of a Japanese stone garden—or their relationships but the emptiness of the sand which needs the stones anywhere in the space in order to be empty). When I said recently in Darmstadt that one could write music by observing the imperfections in the paper upon which one was writing, a student who did not understand because he was full of musical ideas asked, "Would one piece of paper be better than another: one for instance that had more imperfections?" He was attached to sounds and because of his attachment could not let sounds be just sounds. He needed to attach himself to the emptiness, the silence. Then things—sounds, that is—would come into being of themselves.[13]

For Cage, at his most Buddhist, silence becomes a "nothing" from which any "something" might emerge; it sustains an open field of possibility and thus a more intense experience of presence and interpenetration. It is an intentional structure of non-intentionality, an in-difference that restores the possibility of true difference, an end to expression that signals the beginning of genuine becoming.[14]

Now, Buddy Holly was no Buddhist, and the Crickets no avant-garde coterie, but the music they made together entailed a similar extinction of personality and also pushed sonic form to extreme experimental ends. On the one hand, we might say, Cage insisted on silence as the precondition of total noise, as the acceptance of sonic experience as such. On the other, Holly anxiously insisted on silence as the exclusion of all otherness; the Clovis studio was a closed space in which pure sound might resonate, in itself and for itself. Cage sought the selfless experience of an echoless field, open on all sides to the world at large (an "acoustic window," perhaps), while Holly seemed to insist on nothing but his own echo, blocking out the outside world entirely (an "acoustic mirror," as Kaja Silverman might claim).[15] Together, though, both artists saw sound and silence as constitutive and used this relation to push music beyond traditional bounds. In fact, their difference is only one of location—for they were listening through the same glass from opposite sides, working with the same minimal structures to free sound from expression and expressive forms of identity. Ultimately, for Holly, too, song ceased to exist as the expression of personal meaning and became a new domain of sonic experience, one with its own qualities and values, utterly abstract and yet also, in the end, more completely worldly.

In this, in this final push toward silence and abstraction, I hope to show that Holly's music represents the moment when popular music became "pop music," when the ad hoc and mostly local musical traditions in America became a formal aesthetic, free to explore its own sonic values in its own space and time. As Dave Laing notes, Holly's musical choices were essentially anti-lyrical, referring not "to the emotional mode or significance of the words," but "to the musical development of the record as a rock 'n' roll performance." "Instead of trying to interpret the lyric," he writes, "the singer uses it as a jumping-off point for his own stylistic inclinations. He uses it as an opportunity to play rock 'n' roll music, instead of regarding his role as one of portraying an emotion contained in the lyric."[16] In what follows, I will use Cage's own terminology—structure, form, material, and method—to organize Holly's sonic experiments and clarify their equally avant-garde thrust. But I also hope to show that Holly's experimentalism was more closely linked to the world that Cage sought to reach in more artificial ways. Simply put, Holly's music was humiliated from the start—by the crushing blows of teen love, the empty life of the Texas plains, and the falseness of the modern marketplace. These mundane restraints, which were already framed by the blues and country traditions from which Holly borrowed, inspired his music's unique formalism as well as its everyday urgency; working by night in the studio, apparently isolated from the noise of the world, Holly refined his own melancholy and frustration into abstract form, and so, each morning, another sonic masterpiece was hanging in the pop firmament, shining back brightly on the world it sought to transcend.

Of course, nearly all the songs Holly performed as a teenager were traditional bluegrass pickers and honky-tonk laments. Under the moniker "Buddy and Bob," he and high school chum Bob Montgomery played local joints like the Hi-D-Ho Drive-In and the Womble Oldsmobile Dealership. They sang local favorites in close tenor harmony, accompanied by familiar breakdowns on banjo and mandolin. Titles suggest a preponderance of broken hearts and vernacular clichés—"Flower of My Heart," "Door to My Heart," "I Gambled My Heart," and "Soft Place in My Heart."[17] Each song was more or less a quotation (sometimes literally), an expression of some feeling that some other hapless guy had already expressed:

> Tonight I'm so blue, thinking of you.
> I've got those "gotta get you near me blues."
> So hurry here to me. Darling, can't you see?
> I've got those "gotta get you near me blues."[18]

In this, perhaps, the music of "Buddy and Bob" represents a slow decadence of true country and blues—all is secondhand feeling and secondhand form. At the same time, though, their fluency with regional styles—as styles—effected something rich and strange. As can be heard on their early recordings of 1955, the boys appear to be isolating the sonic quirks of their models. Each mix becomes cleaner, leaner, more mechanical, while the sounds within it appear brighter and sharper, their musical values drawn out starkly in relation to the piece as whole. "Soft Place in My Heart," for example, thins out the dense textures of its country precursors, highlighting the relations between a few simple musical parts. The opening series of double stops becomes a model for the close harmony singing of the verses and returns throughout the song as an emphatic musical statement. Similarly, at the end of each line, two high-pitched guitar notes—"de-DING"—provide a kind of sonic exclamation point, diverting attention from the lovesick singer to the sound he's making with his guitar.

Similarly, "Don't Come Back Knockin'" takes a simple blues progression and empties out both the changes and the emotions.[19] The chords serve only as formal markers for a series of bright melodic shifts. They provide space for voice and guitar as they leap whimsically up and down the scale, each amplified note approaching the same emphatic state, becoming nothing more—and nothing less—than its own sweet sounding. Similarly, the lyrics of the song move away from the messy drama of everyday life toward the kind of pop idealism that became one of Holly's trademarks. In the third verse, the singer steps away from the scene of his own disappointment to comment on "true love—a treasure to hold," offering the listener a more generic frame in which to hang personal loss. Thus the mired world of the blues, the sick longing of country—all is pushed to the point of purity, and, in a leap of faith, something like abstract sound comes to stand in for the messiness of love itself.

So let's begin with musical "structure," which Cage defines mechanically—if not industrially—as "divisibility into successive parts from phrases to long sections."[20] As is well known, the composer rejected the traditional dynamics of harmonic structure for a series of temporal durations, more or less empty blocks of time in which sound may come into its own. But we have already seen a similar tendency at work in the popular-music industry, particularly as it came to appropriate traditional forms like country and blues. Given the limited space of the record and the rigidly programmed radio spot, artists were forced to think of their songs in standardized blocks of time and self-contained formal units. At the same time, if they had any hopes for commercial success, they needed to develop catchy hooks and riffs, signature sounds that—beyond any expressive purpose—could cut through the crowded airwaves. By the time Holly and the Crickets began recording, the impact of these demands had become part of the tradition, part of its very aesthetic, and thus an opportunity for real creative play. Indeed, having learned the blues and country on records and radio, Holly never seemed to approach song as simply expressive or even experiential, but as a set of abstract patterns, formal limits—repeatedly imposed—against which he could pursue more or less open configurations of voice and guitar.

Take, for example, the spare arrangement of his first single, "Blue Days, Black Nights."[21] In a way, this is just another brokenhearted lament, a light country moaner with a few bluesy inflections. But while the song could have easily been played for country sympathy (à la Jimmie Rodgers or Hank Williams), every aspect of the performance—from its quick opening bass run to its shimmering guitar accompaniment and Holly's own light delivery—signals the thrill of soundmaking itself. Lyrically, blue and black serve as colorful swatches in a more or less abstract field (Rothko's color-field paintings come to mind), while the music itself is full of thrilling yet utterly meaningless transitions between its bright tones and figures:

> Blue days, black nights.
> Blue tears keep on fallin' for you dear.
> Now you're gone.

One first hears the basic spaciousness of the mix, as if the emptiness of loss has become a space for sonic play. The song's minimal structure provides plenty of room for each instrument, and the silence that surrounds each part gives it a neat, sharp clarity. The three-chord progression is simple, clean, and repetitive—factory-made and wrapped in cellophane. One chord follows another with assembly-line precision round and round the neck of the guitar, each a simple space, available for the free play of voice and guitar within it. The voice leaps lightly up the scale in short two- and three-note doodles, filling in each measure before hurrying along to the next. The two-string guitar solo follows the same line, first with a series of whimsical slides and then, the second time around, breaking everything up again, skipping from one figure to another. As we follow these more or less open leads, we realize how far we've come from the thick textures and infinite rambling of the blues or the intricate fingerpicking patterns of country. If loss comes across in the end, it does so less in Holly's cheeky performance than in the song's stark abstraction and nearly bashful haste. Given the pervasive silence and emptiness that surrounds each line, the song seems to hover over a great void, working its compelling "something" within and through an overwhelming "nothing." But, in this, emptiness everywhere turns into its opposite, the joy of sound itself, neither fetish nor fantasy—the quirky tumult of a bright sonic field, buzzing, rumbling, according to its own formal logic.

At the same time, Holly pursued the possibilities of three-dimensional "structure," approaching each song as something like a miniature diorama of synchronous sound. On recordings such as "Words of Love" and "Listen to Me," he and Petty layered first percussion, then guitars, and finally vo-cals.[22] On the final mix, the gaps between parts work to distinguish sounds from each another, creating a less organic, but certainly more striking, listening experience. While each instrument follows its own quirky lead, the ensemble together creates a mesmerizing arabesque of continuous

sound, grabbing the ear over and over again with its unexpected corre-
spondences and divergences. "Everyday," for example, neatly extends its
lyrical themes to the song's actual form:

> Everyday seems a little longer.
> Every way love's a little stronger.
> Come what may.[23]

The lyrics cleverly outline something like a Zeno's paradox of romance—
distance increases the desire for closeness, while closeness is merely an
anxious form of distance. But this frustrating logic of presence and proximity truly comes to life in the song's own mix, which is a miniature marvel
of contrasting timbres and rhythms. Famously, the song is accompanied
by a celesta (played by Vi Petty) and knee-slapping (provided by Jerry Allison). On its own, Holly's vocal track seems sincere, beckoning the listener
with its simple message of love and hope. Its melody fits the hesitancy of
the lyrics well, rising and falling with the singer's own confidence. The
refrain "Love like yours will surely come my way," for example, coasts
confidently at first, stumbles on the fifth word, and then dips into uncertainty at the end. Holly's performance, though, attains much greater
weight and complexity when layered within the accompaniment. The
gentle echo of the celesta, for example, first seems to support Holly's delivery but soon proves a distraction. Over time, its quirky sustain begins
to suggest desperation, and the slight trill it adds at the end of each line
mocks the singer's hopefulness. The knee-slapping, on the other hand,
suggests all the panting rush of the horny teenage heart. At times, the two
hands themselves seem out of sync with each other, and this clumsy effect
casts a shadow over the song's pristine wish. But, again, the formalism of
the song frees it from its own demands; its spatial structure generates a
thrilling temporal experience. Above all else, "Everyday" recalls the rise
and fall of a roller-coaster ride at a kiddie fair. Its mechanical cheapness
is also its quirky grace, and the song's final phrase is its most stunning.
"A-hey, a-hey-hey"—this is pop nonsense, to be sure, but it consolidates
all the giddy wistfulness of Holly's late modernism.

Thus we come to "form," which, for Cage, refers to the "continuity" of
a piece, the movement of each instrument from one section to the next.
Here, spatial abstraction is inextricably bound to the temporal dynamism
of sound, its unique and momentous course in time and thus its shifting
relations of intensity and interpenetration. Importantly, Cage defined
"form" as a "freedom" element. Whereas "structure" establishes the basic
rules of the piece through mechanical units, "form only wants the freedom

to be"; the truly gifted composer, Cage explains, integrates both of these principles, mobilizing one through the other, "bringing about, ideally, a freely moving continuity within a strict division of parts" ("Forerunners" 62; "Composition" 18). Similarly, Holly quickly broke through the stark structuralism of his earlier songs to create a more fluid continuity of parts across each piece. Each track found him further dissolving the differences between verse and chorus, rhythm guitar and lead guitar, backing vocal and lead vocal, working with shorter chordal fragments and shifts, and reshuffling standard progressions. Lyrically, too, he began to use simpler, shorter refrains and internal rhyming, so that the vocal line could flow smoothly across the surface of the song, working subtle shifts in tone and phrasing. In all this, song became less a stark series of empty spaces in which to hang sounds, but a multilayered transit or *modality* in which a series of fluid sounds could develop according to their own limits and in relation to each other.

Such effects are brilliantly deployed on "Peggy Sue."[24] Jerry Allison's paradiddles rumble behind the piece like a summer storm, while the rhythm guitar—a barrage of manic downstrokes—gives the song its force, carrying us along like a gale wind. With the vocal, Holly gives full rein to all his characteristic burps and growls; the constant repetition of the girl's name blurs the distinction of verse and chorus, allowing us to focus on the swerving power of his voice. "It's So Easy" puts similar effects to more giddy ends.[25] Here, each part of the mix, rather than following its own continuous track, flows with and from all the others. Lead vocal is followed by a backing vocal that is then carried off by Tommy Allsup's one-string solo and so on and so on. In Laing's terms, the record "gives the impression of being one, long flowing unit, instead of . . . a series of structurally regular sections" (81). Again, lyrics match up perfectly with form, referring as much to the musical riskiness of the piece as to the recklessness of young love:

> People tell me love's for fools,
> So here I go breakin' all the rules.
> It seems so easy (*seems so easy, seems so easy*).
> Oh-oh-oh, so doggone easy (*doggone easy, doggone easy*).

So easily, too, the song shifts in sound and rhythm, following its own giddy whims from one lead to the next. Everywhere in Holly's music, a certain clichéd casualness—"It's So Easy," "Well . . . All Right," "It Doesn't Matter Anymore," etc.—signals the liberation of the ego and its music-making possibilities. In fact, the very emptiness of cliché—both lyrical cliché and musical cliché—signals the death of personal expression and opens the way for genuine experimentation—"breakin' all the rules." But this song's openness mostly derives, as suggested above, from the formal emptiness of the studio. Its smoothly interlocking parts could never have come together so brilliantly in a bar or gymnasium; in fact, each of its separately recorded parts carries with it a different kind of reverb and thus a different spatial effect, and so the "continuity" of the whole exists only in its sheer "discontinuity"—its estrangement from anything like habitual space and time. At this point, we might think that silence is no longer part of the song, for it is hardly to be heard in this thick multi-instrumental mix. And yet, the entire off-kilter assemblage everywhere affirms the smooth, featureless space in which it was made, and its thrilling movement would not have been possible apart from the blank technology used to record it.

Cage's third term, "material," includes "sound and silence" and everything in between ("Forerunners" 62). He refers here to the coldly predetermined range of tones and non-tones available for a given composition. As he explains in his "Lecture on Nothing," this range is only ever truly opened through some other restriction, the banning of the self and its expressive urges:

> The other day a pupil said, after trying to compose a melody using only three tones, "I felt limited." Had she concerned herself with the three tones—the materials—she would not have felt limited, and since materials are without feeling, there would not have been any limitation. It was all in her mind, whereas it be-longed [sic] in the materials. It became something by not being nothing; it would have been nothing by being something. (115)

Holly's access to materials was restricted by his own empty pockets and the minimal talents of his bandmates. For the most part, his recorded output consisted of the same four instruments, the same three chords, one or two strings for soloing, and, of course, his voice. But his commitment to this minimalist "gamut," as Cage might have called it, allowed him to achieve the most varied effects. First and foremost, Holly was a tone freak. Famously, he traded in his Les Paul Gold Top for a solid-body Stratocaster, a guitar known then for its extra pickup and sleek, futuristic design. As Philip Norman explains, Holly spent hours and hours exploring the instrument's range, venturing up and down the neck, messing around with attack and timbre, experimenting with volume and its three electric pickups (73). In the studio, Holly and his band lavished the same attention on each instrument. The boys tinkered constantly with levels and mixes, pushing—as we saw at Sun—each tool beyond its expected uses, opening up tones and textures in ways that were impossible on the stage or at home. Over time, their sounds lost their conventionally expressive qualities to become part of a purely sonic mix, communicating with each other in their own pop idiom. Drums emerged as a significant object of attention, no longer simply providing rhythmic support for the ensemble. The guitar shed its bluesy wail, offering instead sharp single-note attacks and chunky chordal rhythms. And, most dramatically of all, Holly's voice shook itself free of the country-ballad tradition; with its huffs and growls and coos, it became a promiscuous sound-making machine, often, like his guitar, claiming nothing but its own giddy virtuosity.

Take, for example, "That'll Be the Day," the group's first unexpected hit.[26] When the boys debuted the song on *American Bandstand*, Dick Clark was at a compete loss for words. The otherwise unflappable host stammered for a moment and then simply declared the song "highly unusual."[27] As Norman explains, the song's reception was stymied by its sonic strangeness. Not only had few pop songs at that time featured such a heavy electric guitar, but Holly's voice "sounded unlike that of a potential teenage idol, being totally lacking in sexual suggestiveness." In fact, the overall sound of the tune—from tone to rhythm to structure—could only be defined by its complete lack of definition: "not quite dance tune, not quite love song, not quite fast, not quite slow, not funny yet not quite serious" (128–29). But perhaps the most striking aspect of the song was that all of the instruments sounded like instruments. The carelessness of the title (a refrain here borrowed from John Wayne) freed the performance from any explicit message and gave it over entirely to its sonic "materials." It certainly begins abruptly, with its famous set of descending triplets and then a full-blown chorus. All starts at once, as if someone had just flicked the power on, unleashing a thick current of voice–drum–guitar. And then nothing seems to determine the movement from one part to the next; the song tears along, sounds and voices emerging out of the mix according to their own capacity and threshold. Each instrument is both loud and dumb, proclaiming itself and communicating nothing, drawing all attention to its own sound rather than the singer's dilemma. Holly and the Crickets express nothing here and yet give it their all, gracefully relinquish their own needs to the inherent qualities of the "material"—the fat bass guitar, the sharp snare drum, the jangly guitars—all of which find a much more thrilling sound on their own.

Finally, "method"—"the means of controlling the continuity from note to note" ("Forerunners" 62). This category includes Cage's most experimental efforts to free composition from his own intentions—tossing coins, poking holes in a written score, reading the *I Ching*. Holly's method, though, seems closer to what Cage cryptically suggested at the end of "Lecture on Nothing": "All I know about method is that when I am not working I sometimes think I know something, but when I am working, it is quite clear that I know nothing" (126). In a similar way, Holly's method was extramusical and inexpressive, deriving from his actual transit to and from the studio. His friends recall him often exiting the studio suddenly, driving down the highway in his red Caddy, sometimes all the way to Abilene or Albuquerque, and then returning back at night with a new tune. In turn, his songs bear all the features of that specific transit—its speed, its duration, its straight lines, and sharp turns. At the beginning of his guitar solos, for example, Holly often shouts, "Go! Go! Go!" as if pushing the pedal down to the floor. All here is velocity and valence, pure movement in sonic space, not bound to any specific route or destination. As David Thomas asserts, the automobile is the most significant site for musical experience in the modern age. In fact, the non-space of the automobile distinctly resembles the non-space of the studio—think of the glass windows, the levered consoles, the seemingly frictionless shifts in sound and speed. The listener-driver, like the studio engineer, navigates a "whacked landscape from within this resonating soundscape frame-container," one in which "all the scales are fracturing . . . and the gyroscope of the sixth sense of body awareness is flipping around, getting pleasantly enervated or irrepressibly enthused."[28] In a similar way, we can describe Holly's "method" as initially automotive—composition as a kind of sonic cruising within a minimally structured landscape, testing durations, experimenting with shifts in rhythm and melody, pushing the entire body-sound continuum toward sound alone, toward the inherent dynamism of the sonic field and its integral values.

For Holly, though, each long drive necessarily ended back at the studio, where he would get his bearings, hang with friends, record his songs, and send them out into the world. In this, the studio becomes a space of ritual restriction again, a place where Holly willingly gave his song over to a series of nearly arbitrary but utterly essential constraints. First there was the constraint of his band—a bunch of local buddies with clear but limited talents and tastes (country, rockabilly, etc.). Then there were the constraints of the space itself: the quirky mix of instruments assembled for Petty's pop trio, the specific layout of rooms and hallways (Allison recorded drums for "Peggy Sue" out in the reception area), and the producer's own tight schedule and rules (no smoking, prayer circles, etc.).[29]

Finally, Holly had to confront the constraints of himself—his looks, his voice, his vision, his own shyness and diffidence—each of which, he knew, seriously restricted his range.[30] Yet all of these constraints were met in the spirit of adventure, and Holly and the boys exploited them fully. In this back-and-forth from car to studio, from studio to song and back again, music-making became something like an open question, a thrilling proposition, at once underdetermined and overdetermined by environment. Of course, in this, we're discussing "spaces" more than "methods," "motions" as much as "techniques," but the slippage says a lot about pop music and the uneven ways in which it relates to the modern world. Holly's songs seem to spin in their own quirky orbits within a purely sonic space, offering nothing more than their own empty shifts and swerves, but they always somehow—in their very formalism—point us back to real space and time. Indeed, as I've already suggested, there's always "something" in the mix that is not so easily given over to "nothing": there's always something there in or around its own sound, in its very voicing, some barely discernible hint or trace of its human orientation and intention. If we want to hear this cricket, though, we need to be very quiet indeed.

Well . . . All Right 2—The End of Expression

In *Speech and Phenomena*, written in 1967, Jacques Derrida compares the human mind to an empty echo chamber, one in which voice, bouncing from ear to ear, becomes a pleasing source of "self-presence" and "auto-affection."[31] When the self speaks to itself, Derrida argues, its voice appears both proximate and distinct. Its very sound doubles the self within the self, and so, both present and meaningful, real and sublime, it gives a certain life—like some holy breath—to an otherwise meaningless form:

> When I speak, it belongs to the phenomenological essence of this operation that *I hear myself at the same time* that I speak. The signifier animated by my breath and by the meaning-intention . . . is in absolute proximity to me. The living act, the life-giving act . . . which animates the body of the signifier and transforms it into a meaningful expression, the soul of language, seems not to separate itself from itself, from its own self-presence. (77)

Importantly, though, for Derrida, internal speech, as "expression," always entails a certain slippage. Paradoxically, the inner voice—as an "acoustic mirror"—also appears as an external voice, its power arriving from somewhere else within the self. At best, inside and outside overlap in pleasing ways; the mind is drawn out of and into itself in one self-affirmative, but ultimately "empty" and "unproductive," echo (33). But this structure threatens the very consistency of expression. The expressive voice is inherently anxious, fragile, always at work denying its own doubleness, its dependence on speech and, ultimately, the outside world. In fact, according to Derrida, this voice must remain deaf, dumb, and blind to its own work. Living speech—the actual sounds and words of communication—would only muddy its reflection, exposing its derivative nature: "My words are alive because they seem not to leave me: not to fall outside me, outside my breath, at a visible distance; not to cease to belong to me, to be at my disposition" (76). Similarly, other bodies, other people would only disrupt its narcissistic purity: "Visibility and spatiality," Derrida writes, "could only destroy the self-presence of will and spiritual animation which opens up discourse. *They are literally the death of that self-presence*" (35).

For Derrida, then, the pleasing "immediacy" and "presence" of the expressive voice depends, paradoxically, on a set of mediating forms and the very denial of those forms, on the very *silencing* of language in its social aspect. But this is precisely where it gets interesting, for insofar as expression relies on language, no matter how rarefied, it cannot deny the latter's "indicative" function. For Derrida, indication is the gestural dimension embedded in all language, its tendency to point toward something else, some other term or form in the mix. Voice, even as internal voice, remains an inherently external or exteriorizing phenomenon, faced—forever—outward. It inevitably brings the entire physical world back into play—"the living present"—even if only as a dark potential, as "non-presence" (37). In other words, indication—as mere pointing, as a minimal frame of reference—does not simply represent, but calls forth all that expression would rather ignore, and it does so by relinquishing that egotistical unity that is blindly asserted in expression. It anxiously extends toward the world and sustains something like the self only within an unstructured and radically uncertain field of intensities: "If communication or intimation is essentially indicative, this is because we have no primordial intuition of the presence of the other's lived experience" (40). There is risk here, to be sure. Derrida, like Cage, pushes the expressive ego toward silence, darkness, the unknown, but only as these categories signal a new life altogether. As Derrida explains, the distinction between "expression" and "indication" is nothing less than this relation to difference and change—to mortal time itself. Expression is "*present to the self* in the life of a present that has not yet gone forth from itself into the world*," while "indication, which thus far includes practically the whole surface of language, is the process of death at work in signs. As soon as the other appears, indicative language—another name for the relation with death—can no longer be effaced" (40).

Thus the silence of *expression* signals a refusal to speak, a refusal to expose oneself to the openness of language and other people. The silence of *indication*—its dark, risky work—entails an openness to speech, to the unknowability of others, and the uncertainty of the self in relation to others—the uncertainty of time and history itself. But for Derrida, as for Cage, the coiled inwardness of the voice always *inevitably* unravels the self back into the world. In fact, it opens up space and time as the space and time of performance, where re-presentation becomes an act of social engagement. "Hearing oneself speak," Derrida writes, "is not the inward-ness of an inside that is closed in upon itself; it is the irreducible openness in the inside; it is the eye and the world within speech. *Phenomenological reduction is a scene, a theater stage*" (86). Derrida's turn to performance here is startling, given his structuralist bent. Nonetheless, it suggests the voice's ultimate exposure to the world, or, rather, not just its exposure, but its spectacle, its dramatic movement within a field of intensities. Toward the end of his study, in fact, Derrida defines "indication" as a mode of "orientation," one that is "essentially occasional," conditioned by relations of speaker and situation. "Indication," he claims, "enters speech whenever a reference to the subject's situation is not reducible, wherever this subject's situation is designated by a personal pronoun, or a 'subjective' adverb such as *here, there, above, below, now, yesterday, tomorrow, before, after*, etc." (94). These phrases—which oddly resemble the generic phrases of pop—clearly display their indicative functions; for the "I" who speaks in this way, Derrida notes, meaning is immediately "carried off into indica-tion" and becomes "real intended speech for someone else" (94). Suddenly, speech exposes itself, exposes the speaker, in mortal space and time, and thus sets the stage for a dramatic performance, for the work of orientation in relation to an audience.

The lead vocal of any pop mix serves as an important point of "expres-sive" identification, at once establishing intimacy and presenting itself as a source of authority. In songs about love and loss, specifically, this voice becomes a powerful surrogate, a sonic imago or fetish, filling up the lis-tener's ear, and thus his empty head, with its own narcissistic pleasure. As Sean Cubitt explains, the needy listener readily internalizes this voice, taking the singer's "expression" (in all its tricky "difference") as his own; "The amplified voice," he writes, "commands an awareness of difference and of identity, of another greater than oneself yet like oneself, both admirable and available: all the conditions of identification are present."[32] But we have just seen—via Derrida—how the presumed presence and authority of this voice emerges out of a certain doubleness and rests upon established patterns of speech, and, so, as much as it entails a momentary satisfaction, it also always frustrates its own coherence and complicates the listening experience. Cubitt adds, concerning the lack of closure in classic rock-and-roll songs such as Chuck Berry's "Maybelline," "The subject's presence in the song is in fact an absence, a lack. Its activity in listening is pursuing this felt lack with all the energy of its desires along the stream of signifiers in search of an impossible completion" (221). For me, the most thrilling pop songs—like "Maybelline"—allow us to recognize this impossibility as a formal matter as much as a psychological one. In Holly's pop, specifically, the voice, even at its most expressive, reveals its constructedness and thus upends its narcissistic function, unraveling self-presence in a more or less open field of indication. Certainly, this voice sings of love and loss, and in this it serves as a wonderful point of identification for the adolescent ear, but lurking within its emphatic structure is a powerful case for the "not I," a risky disavowal of subjective coherence and thus an opening out toward the world.

Barbara Bradby and Brian Torode, for example, argue that Holly's best songs dramatize the psychological process of learning to speak and becoming a subject. They hear "Peggy Sue" as an Oedipal drama in miniature, one in which a geeky teenager tries to claim his expressive voice and thus something like paternal authority. The offbeat stammering and falsetto whining of the first few verses, they argue, slowly gives way to a more consistent pattern of enunciation, and finally, after the amplified guitar solo, emerges as a confident display of control—deep, steady, and on the beat.[33] This interpretation is compelling in its own Freudian terms, but it fails to follow through on its own logic regarding the instability of voice. To me, the song's power and allure rest on Holly's embrace of his voice's own radical inconsistency; while, lyrically, the song repeats all the clichés of loss and love, the lead vocal everywhere slips away from this tired narrative of the male ego, reveling instead in its very groundlessness:

> Pretty pretty pretty pretty Peggy Sue—
> Oh-uh-oh Peggy, my Peggy Sue
> Oh well, I love you, gal,
> And I need you, Peggy Sue.

This vocal line is remarkably unconcerned with the fact that it continually misses its mark. Holly's voice trips giddily away from "Peggy Sue" as both a name and an intended object of desire, stammering and stuttering all the way through the song, falling unevenly before or after each beat, pitching itself above or below each note. The singer finds a certain thrilling pleasure in his own vocal syncopation as it cuts within and against the song as a whole, losing and finding the structure of expression, and thus the self, in more and more circuitous ways. Most importantly, the voice is playing with its orientations. Not only is there no consistency to its changes, there is also no clear development of its identity. Rather, it shifts instantly and arbitrarily between different attitudes and stances—by turns tough, tender, cutesy, and quirky—and all of these modes seem to be variations of the pop voices in circulation at the time. Beyond the frame of the song, this voice is ceaselessly at work positioning itself in relation to an indeterminate field of intentions. Nothing is signified here but the performance of pop itself, and, with its simple gamut of pop phrases and sounds, the voice deploys different modes of address and display—some personal, some tentative, some detached, some aggressive, etc. Identity is established provisionally, tentatively, over and over again, in its multiple "orientations," and its power and pleasure is always subject to the presence and position of others—the elusive Peggy, his backing buddies, and, of course, the listener.

Similarly, let's take Holly's famous hiccup technique, which emerges from an obscure southern tradition of eefing (a kind of hillbilly beatboxing) and looks ahead to DJ scratching. At first, Holly's hiccup seems to erupt from within the melodic line like some unruly somatic force, an irrepressible presence in a more or less canned pop performance. We may take pleasure in its quirky immediacy, as a physical disruption of linguistic and melodic structure—sheer expression. But Holly's hiccup actually consists of two parts—a catch and a thrust, a silence and its echo. He cuts off the sound at the back of the throat, blocking the flow of sound so that it pops out again with greater intensity—hic-a! A sharp break or silence is immediately followed by a loud burp, an extra "supplemental" syllable. In songs such as "I'm Gonna Love You Too" and "Mailman, Bring Me No Blues," Holly runs with the effect, so that his words sound more or less like arbitrary cuts in an otherwise homogenous sonic matter.[34] He seems to be toying with the very structure of speech as a system of differentiation, emptying out his own voice again and again, so that he can assert it more forcefully. Presence thus becomes the effect of multiple arbitrary differences—the hiccup appears as no primary expression, but as part of a larger structure of emptiness. And, yet, in this alone, it still bears—like the DJ's own scratching—traces of something else, something irrepressibly human. This hiccup—in its very emptiness, its momentary silence—*indicates* or *marks* the space and time of linguistic production itself, the work of orientation that occurs within and beyond all expression, and thus the place in which the listener may lose and find him- or herself all over again.

Here, then, we can consider three essential vocal strategies in Holly's music, as each in turn releases the expressive power of the voice within an expansive field of sonic indication and intensity. First, backup vocals. Typically, in Holly's songs, these voices establish a kind of basic but meaningless field of vocal sound against which the main voice emerges. They lend neither authority nor consensus, but an empty, airy substance—mere wind—against which the singer cuts and shapes his own voice.[35] In "I'm Looking for Someone to Love," for example, the boys first lay down a bright sonic palette, forcefully humming the chord changes and then, with the chorus, providing a rough, mumbling version of the lyrics.[36] Holly's voice emerges shakily against this background, drawing an unstable presence from and against its simple but meaningless drone:

> Playin' the field
> All day long
> Since I found out I was wrong

Here, the desire for distinction, for difference, leads only to another fall, a leveling of the playing field, but this irony is rooted in the arc of the voice itself. For one, the originality of the voice is undermined by its own use of cliché, which it everywhere applies and then applies again. At the same time, its momentary coherence is dissolved in the echo of the backing band, and so the singer becomes just another randy cat, part of a larger, indistinct colony of howling boys on the market. In this, though, Holly seems to open himself up to a much wider space of indication. He's just "lookin' for someone to love," using his voice to navigate an undetermined scene. Indeed, above all else, the singer seems to have made peace with his own lack of distinction, turning, as we saw with Elvis, his own inconsequence into a condition of openness. As he reminds us with each chorus, he's just "playin' the field" (both the field of romance and the field of sound), open to all the possibilities of someone or something else down the line.

"Oh Boy" pursues this dynamic toward more ridiculously giddy ends.[37] It is yet another song in Holly's repertoire that pushes a clichéd, everyday phrase—"Oh Boy," "That'll Be the Day," "It's So Easy"—toward something like an original exchange. The exclamatory title seems to refer here not only to the naive pleasures of the adolescent body, but also to the joyful emptiness of its own sounding. At first, the boys sing only of themselves, narcissistically echoing "Oh, Boy" with "Oh, Boy" in delicious harmony—sheer narcissistic "auto-affection." Then, as if falling joyfully into indifference, each "boy" dissolving into all the others, they let out a giant roar of meaningless sound, mouths open wide, full of nothing but air, against which the lead singer begins to trace his unique presence:

> All of my love, all of my kissin'.
> You don't know what you've been a-missin'.
> Oh, boy, when you're with me,
> Oh, boy, the world can see that you were meant for me.

Here, Holly's all gutsy vows and threats. Yet each assertion is tinged with a goofy smirk. His claims pop emptily in the air, while the boys shout out "dum de de dum dum" over and over again. Then, during the break, all signs fall by the wayside, and the boys' voices blend into one, washing over any established difference with another solid block of sound. Here, they lead us to the brink of sonic emptiness as the pleasurable extinction of difference, as the wide-open potential of voice as such, a space to cut and mark with all the pleasure of our own emptiness.

   Holly, though, also tracks his own voice against itself and in this, paradoxically, more clearly exposes its strange and risky relation to the listener. Along with Les Paul, Holly was one of the first pop artists to explore the possibilities of vocal overdubbing, but his experiments in self-echoing everywhere suggest a deep anxiety about the mediating qualities of the voice. In songs such as "Words of Love" and "Listen to Me," for example, the most intimate vocal sounds are layered on top of one other, but rather than shoring each other up, they appear oddly detached from anything like a "true" self. The supplemental logic of the echo, like the supplemental logic of the echo chamber, draws us in with a certain "realism" or "presence" but here ultimately pushes us away with its uncanny abstraction. In "Words of Love," for example, two double-tracked and doubly echoed voices whisper into the listener's ear. The effect is unsettling, as the singer's seeming directness flickers in and out of focus, slipping from one voice to the other and ultimately back into the mix and its woozy samba beat. Rather than establishing presence or sensual fullness, the echo de-centers and dissolves the immediacy of the singing voice, taking the listener's own desire for presence along with it:

> Words of love you whisper soft and true.
> Darling, I love you . . . hm-mm-mm-mm.

Let me hear you say the words I want to hear.
Darling, when you're near . . . hm-mm-mm-mm.

This vocal slippage is only exacerbated by the self-conscious lyrics, which suggest an infinite deferral of love and presence. While multitracking denies the internal coherence of the singer, the language of the song itself suggests the incompletion of linguistic expression, its need for constant supplementation via the presence of some other. In other words, these words—as "words of love"—appear only as copies, clichés, of themselves. The sincerity of "expression" disappears in the redoubling of its surface, in the desperate supplementation of more "words." In this, though, the song remains a testament to the need and place for some other voice. Apparently, all these "words of love" come from somewhere else and prove meaningful, effective, only in their repetition by another. One lover borrows them from another and yet demands that another repeat them in turn. In fact, the most compelling "words of love" here are not words at all, but the gentle humming that ends each line. Stripped of its representational function, the hummed sound leads with its indicative aspect, pointing openly, emptily, beyond the ego toward some genuine, if vague, comfort of another.

Finally, though, Holly's voice is tracked within and against its own silence. Not only does it resound in the frictionless space of the cut, in its own gap or breach, but it is also always already fading in time, expiring in its very aspiration. On all sides, it comes up against its immanent death, as if shrouded, shadowed by the very emptiness it sought to fill. In a way, this tendency to fade always grants power to the otherwise empty act of speech. In order to become truly significant, voice must be transubstantiated into spirit, breathy, transient, hushed. As Mladen Dolar notes, following Derrida, "The body distracts the spirit, it is a cumbersome impediment, so it has to be reduced to the spectrality of mere voice, and entrusted to its disembodied body" (62). Holly's words of love are always whispered "soft and true." He coos and sighs his way toward a certain enigmatic presence, his spirit rising as his voice fades, establishing himself in the fullness of his own soulful silence. But this fading is also the precondition for some other kind of presence, and perhaps some genuine exchange. It announces the singer's own inevitable non-presence as the appearance of some tender other. It indicates the space and time, within and beyond the space and time of the song, within and beyond expression itself, in which some other may appear. Take, for example, "Not Fade Away."[38] Here, with a jerky Bo Diddley beat behind him, Holly belts out a bunch of tough-guy threats,

but one by one they all fade to black. At the end of each line, as if in opposition to the song's own title phrase, the voice falls into a gap, complete
silence, taking us along with it:

> I'm a-gonna tell you how it's gonna be.
> You're gonna give your love to me.
> I wanna love you night and day.
> You know my love a-not fade away.

Buddy has never sung so forcefully, but in this insistence on presence
and persistence, the voice ultimately declares its emptiness. As a lover, he
knows, his presence exists only in the reciprocation of the other, in the
way that some other might in turn give shape to his existence. Similarly, as
a singer, he depends on the reciprocation of the listener, who must, with
his or her sustained concentration, shoulder the song as it falls—again
and again—into silence. The last few lines intensify this logic, with Holly's
voice dipping lower than ever, barely audible above the mix, and thus calling on us to make good on its original logic. In fact, these lines invite us
to invert their explicit meaning. A "love that's love" is a bland tautology,
empty in its own insistent echo, but a love that fades is one that endures.
A love that fades is a love that recognizes its need for some other. A love
that fades is a mortal love and it embraces the entire mortal world.

There is always a moment in listening to pop music when silence becomes unbearably present. We don't hear it when we're *just listening*, when
we allow the bright sound of pop to play out behind us, and we lose track
of its presence. At such moments, we merely inhabit the music as perfect
silence, hearing nothing, accepting all; it surrounds us, fills the ear, fills the
wounds, and—as a form of expression, narcissistic and echoey—seems to
heal or at least cover over an otherwise painful difference. However, with
a slight shift in attention, a more forceful or attentive ear, we hear a more
radical silence, a continual vanishing of voice, and thus a continual loss.
In an instant, the voice dissolves, becomes thin and weak, and the very
source of comfort becomes an overwhelming sadness, the sound fading
so quickly that it obliterates all listening, leaving in its wake only a dull
ache. This silence—this nothingness—is not the absence or obverse of
sound; it is not opposed to voice, but stitched into it, carried along with
it, rising and fading in one and the same noisiness. As Sontag argues, if
language "points to its own transcendence in silence," then silence "points
to its own transcendence—to a speech beyond silence," a world in which
one's own voice makes sense (18). In pop music, too, such silence signals
not just song's emptiness and falseness, but also some more radical sense

of idealism. Holly's wisdom resides not in his wistful platitudes, but in the actual delivery of the vocal line, in its eventual fade, it broken openness to the listener, to the world.

To take one more example, "Well . . . All Right" has often been cited as Holly's most political song, a precursor to the socially conscious music that would flower in the 1960s.[39] But if we ascribe political value to what, on the surface, seems to be only another banal love song, it perhaps exists in the hushed repetition of the title phrase and its marked pauses:

> Well . . . all right,
> Well . . . all right,
> Our lifetime love will be all right.

Once more, Holly establishes a certain affective presence through an otherwise empty pop expression. "Well . . . All Right" follows in the vein of "That'll Be the Day," "It's So Easy," and "Oh Boy," revitalizing a stale cliché, giving it a new directness and urgency for the listener. The phrase is first sung in a low and uncertain register, and the slight gap marked by the ellipses suggests hesitation, a lack of confidence. Yet, with each repetition, the phrase—with its quickly ascending melody—begins to attain a certain force; it slowly fills itself with its own emptiness, embracing each obstacle it encounters, and thus begins to assert itself, lovingly and then forcefully, as a formidable presence in its own right. In this, the brief space of silence between "Well" and "all right" becomes a space of anticipation, one that accepts all, abides all. In other words, this voice, or, rather, its silence, represents nothing—it speaks for neither left nor right, center nor margins. In fact, it doesn't speak at all, and thereby opens itself not only to the voice of another, but to the uncertainty of time itself. It uses its own negation to contradict the insistent negativity of the crowd. Its silence seeps up through the cracks of everyday speech, dissolving distinctions between love and hate, dream and reality, foolishness and wisdom. It even refuses to distinguish itself from those who want to distinguish themselves from it, and so it transcends the mundane logic of expression, becoming the groundless ground of some more essential exchange, anticipating, for all those "foolish kids," the time and place of genuine presence. Yeah, kids, it's all right . . . it'll all be all right.

Well . . . All Right 3—The End of Song

We can now perhaps consider how Holly's music—for all its airy abstraction—returns to something like actual history. For this, though, we need to recognize that, with its stark formalism, bright emotional coloring, and expressive clichés, it anticipates not so much the campus riots or civil-rights protests of the 1960s, but the emergent Pop Art movement of the same era. In fact, while Holly was using the studio to abstract the formal patterns of an increasingly commercialized musical tradition, Pop Artists across the country were already beginning to push the mass-mediated world beyond its own surfaces toward something like genuine presence. Andy Warhol, for example, used a photo-silkscreen process to explore the emotional effects of media technology; his obsessively copied images of dead stars and violent car crashes dramatized, in their own blank way, all the desensitization and addictive violence of a thickly mediated public sphere. Roy Lichtenstein, for his part, enlarged images from the world of advertising and comic books to question the commodification of public feeling; with his giant Benday dot reproductions of crying women and exploding rockets, he put on display both the mechanical construction of everyday emotion and the explosive powers that lurk within it. Wayne Thiebaud used the bright, creamy textures of oil paint to mimic the surfaces of the consumer marketplace; his frosted paintings of cupcakes, ice cream cones, and carnival prizes played with the frustrated appetite of the consumer, forcing the viewer to question the inherent worth and appeal of the commodity form. Altogether, though, by miming the surfaces and textures of modern commerce, Pop Artists showed how the consumer marketplace concealed and preserved more subtle modes of human engagement. Their work adopted the two-dimensional forms of the modern world to expose and then claim their communicative potential and persistent emotional weight. In other words, Pop Art—like pop music—becomes realistic and historical precisely in its abstraction, insofar as that abstraction corresponds to a whole world of plastic products and mass media. Most importantly, this art preserves and protects human invest-ment within that very abstraction, within its own glamorous structures and surfaces. As Lawrence Alloway explains, "Pop Art is neither abstract nor realistic, though it has contacts in both directions. . . . The human markers are there, but implied and not insistent."[40]

Holly's music and the Pop Art movement are most clearly linked by a remarkable melancholy. Much of the Pop Art of this era is marked not just by silence and emptiness, but by a vague sadness, one that, despite its apparent superficial or clichéd expression, gives it a real critical edge. Take, for example, Warhol's obsessive silkscreen reproductions of Marilyn Monroe (see image 12). As Thomas Crow explains, these seemingly cheap and meaningless reproductions are deeply memorial.[41] They reinvest the

consumer logic of desire, in its ceaseless repetition and constant deferral, with a real sense of value and loss. "The screened image," he writes,
"reproduced whole, has the character of an involuntary trace: it is memorial in the sense of resembling memory, which is sometimes vividly
present, sometimes elusive, and always open to embellishment as well as
loss" (133). Warhol's repetitions dramatize the consumer's own efforts to
restore presence through the very forms that continue to chase it away. In
this, though, they also generate something like "the real," or, at least, an
"orientation" toward it. In Warhol's reproductions of Monroe, the dead star
fades and returns in the very repetition of her image; she becomes "most
real and best remembered in the flickering passage of film exposures, no
one of which is ever wholly present to perception. . . . she is most present
where her image is least permanent" (134). This sad art, forever fading,
forever deferred, like Holly's own voice, both repeats and reframes the
experience of consumer life, anticipating some future moment of genuine
return or reparation. Faced with the deep loss brought about by consumer
culture, it embraces form itself—blank, repetitive form—as the minimal
precondition for some more genuine sense of presence and difference.
Thus, looking at these images, Hal Foster depicts Warhol not as a "blank
subject," but as a "shocked subject," one who, in his sadness and fear,
"takes on the nature of what shocks him as a mimetic defense against this
shock."[42] As Foster suggests, Warhol's sadness persists in and through each
repetition, becoming, in itself, a sign of humanness and engagement: "If
you can't beat it, Warhol suggests, join it. More, if you enter it totally, you
might expose it; that is, you might reveal its automatism, even its autism,
through your own excessive example" (41).

Again, no way but through. The sad emptiness of the machine age is
embraced in order to attain some purchase on it, if only in an ideal, utopian form. Pop music, however, enacts this tension with the voice itself.
It constructs an echo chamber via sonic forms only to crack open again
along the otherwise unbearable mediations of time and space, disturbing
the commercial song of the self with the noise of everyday life. Indeed,
while Holly also limits himself to the market's forms—all the clichés of
commercial blues and country—his music everywhere reverberates with
human connections and exchanges. His song follows the very shape of
consumer desire; in its own bright blankness, it conjures up something
like deep yearning and genuine loss and thereby offers itself as both the
apotheosis of commercial form and its own immanent critique. Again,
though, this dynamic is defined mostly through negation; it exists everywhere at the fading borders of Holly's song and in its ultimate silence.

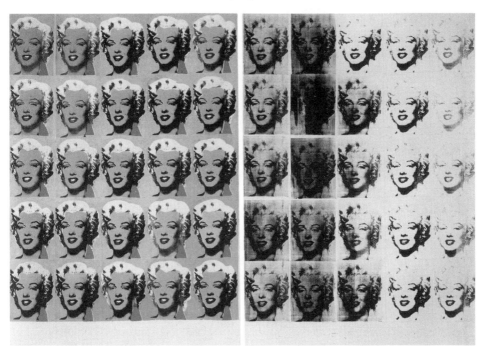

IMAGE 12 *Marilyn Diptych*, Andy Warhol, 1962. (ARS)

On one level, Holly's music simply fails to deliver the goods. His tragic relation to commercial life traces out, inversely, all the human pleasure and camaraderie routinely denied by the market. On another level entirely, though, the structure of his music simply unravels itself. Each song is a marvel of egotistical expression, a desperate cry for distinction and differentiation, but each then also proves a form of indication, pointing toward a now common condition and affirming the larger hostility and alienation of the world in which it was created. Indeed, the very medium of Holly's expression—its clichéd lyrics, mechanical repetitions, and sonic abstraction—connects it, its own isolation, to a common world of common uses and manipulations. Like Jeff Koons's metallic balloon "Rabbit," the bright surfaces of his song everywhere reflect the bright surfaces of the culture and history that surround it, conjuring up everything we would rather leave behind. Ultimately, the singer loses and finds himself in a cheap, prefabricated line and thus points, however awkwardly, toward *all* that can be won and lost in a world given over to comic strips, drive-in movies, and *American Bandstand*.

Of course, it's a fine line between this critique and acquiescence, and, for some, pop music never really *pops*. As mentioned above, music produced for the commercial market tends to trap the listener within a cruel echo chamber of "expression." Its slick surfaces and easy emotions double over and ultimately mask the real pain of being modern, conjuring false obstacles and weak resolutions in order to distract us from the pains of everyday life. Lyrically, these songs proffer empty promises of puppy love, class rings, and backseat snuggles and thereby translate historical despair into a merely personal struggle for love and recognition. Musically, their sound—with its jarring hooks, manic solos, and easy melodic resolution—recasts the violence of the marketplace in charming miniature, locking all its pain within a carefully coordinated play of rebellion and restoration.[43] But what if we take this pain seriously? What if the very sadness of pop, no matter how cheap, proves the precondition of its transcendence? What if these adolescent dramas of hope and loss reveal—on radios and records and television shows across the country—a much more urgent condition? No doubt, Holly's music, with its soft play of tragic emotions, simple harmonies, and glossy textures, confronts us as a textbook pop commodity. The lyrical tension of humility and hope, backed everywhere by bright tones and catchy hooks, seems to mimic as well as glamorize the tragic deferral and compulsive repetition of the age. In this, though, each song does not so much name, but repeat, in its own movement and strange sonic ontology, the very structure of commercial desire, and thus each also marks a troubling dissonance—or, perhaps, a remarkable opening—within the life of the listener. As we saw with the blues in chapter one, a second-order trauma works to dissolve the first. Each song transmutes the emotional trauma of modernity into something pure, perfect, and commercially viable, but only to unravel the entire structure, expose its deficiencies, reveal its demand, giving it all over to the listener, the world, and history at large.

Again, in Holly's music, this dynamic most often takes a subdued, wistful form. In "An Empty Cup," for example, the singer's romantic plight is directly linked to the forms and structures of commerce.[44] As he describes his lonely night at a local drive-in, waiting for his gal, his voice becomes a tiny marvel of hope and hopelessness, at once inspired and denied by all the commodities on the horizon. Each line swells and fades like some cheap wish, a mighty painful could-have-been, but this dynamic maintains, again and again, a sense of fulfillment, if not in its own sonic motion, than elsewhere, on the other side, just beyond this lame movie, this empty cup, this lonely song. The last verse, a small pop haiku, entirely reverses the song's loser fatalism: focusing on the now empty cup of Coke, it neatly summarizes the market's damning logic but, with the return of the backup voices, dissolves it back, along with the singer's loneliness, into a collective state of hope and despair:

> Just like this Coke (*just like this Coke*)
> My love is gone (*my love is gone*).
> I've hit the bottom.
> Now I'm all alone (*all alone*).

A similar dynamic is put to more obscure and thus more radical ends in Holly's threefold pop mantra "Crying, Waiting, Hoping."[45] This uptempo rocker, with its swooping slides and clanging cymbals, resounds somewhere among its three titular emotions. The first and last terms imply each other, as, for Holly, the experience of loss always entails—negatively—the persistence of some ideal. The middle term, though—"waiting"—is the condition of their mutual possibility, at once consistent and open. Thus the pop crush—in all its adolescent pathos—takes on a tragic glory and becomes a statement of both real loss and steady commitment:

> Crying . . . my tears keep a-fallin' all night long
> Waiting . . . it feels so useless, I know it's wrong
> To keep a-crying, waiting, hoping . . . you'll come back
> Maybe someday soon things will change and you'll be mine

The singer's yearning here exceeds any clear need or demand. Yet by refining and intensifying his longing through its abstraction, he allows us to hear what may yet be possible on its other side. His predicament is defined by refusal on all ends, but the remaining configuration—precisely in its repetition and elliptical sadness—maintains, as in Warhol's work, the possibility of "someday soon."

Elsewhere, the pop music of this era reveals a much more aggressive demand, yet still working by its own negativity and formal negation to suggest alternatives. Eddie Cochran's "Something Else," for example, angrily outlines the perpetual deferral of the teen marketplace.[46] The title phrase, which is really only an advertising slogan, lures both singer and listener, linking girl to car to gas to job to song in an apparently endless loop of working and spending. Each verse is followed by a thudding beat that suggests all the anxious repetition and empty urgency of consumer life in the pop age. The whole piece is nothing less than thrilling, nervous, and angsty but, in the end, simply exhausting. Not surprisingly, Cochran later sang of a "Nervous Breakdown."[47] In this song, his delivery, all clenched teeth and nervous stutter, exposes all the barely contained rage and spite of the marketplace as a whole:

> See my hands how they shiver.
> See my knees how they quiver.
> My whole body's in a jitter.
> I'm a-havin' a nervous breakdown.

And let's not forget the era's overwhelming number of songs about teen death and suicide. As R. Serge Denisoff argues, these "coffin songs" present death as an ultimate rebellion, a final, extreme negation of an unbearably conformist and oppressive social order.[48] We should add, though, that this rebellion is essentially economic, as death always proves a release from the market's false system of value. Listen to Jody Reynolds's "Endless Sleep," Ray Peterson's "Tell Laura I Love Her," or Mark Dinning's "Teen Angel." These teen tragedies almost all begin with a desire for some empty commodity—a ring, a car, a high school jacket—and end with death as both an ironic release from the humiliations of consumer culture and a preservation of its original claims.

Female pop artists used this same angry dialectic to comment on the gendering of the market. Wanda Jackson, for example, consistently turned the tables on her own sources, gritting her teeth as she busted open the false promises of commercial blues and country. For example, in "I Gotta Know" (penned by Thelma Blackman), she depicts the classic rockabilly cat as a con man, all show and no delivery.[49] Beautifully, she exposes the dance-floor economy of romantic desire as an expression of the economy at large:

> Well, I thought that you was a wantin' romance,
> But all you ever do is dance, dance, dance . . .
> One thing I gotta know, I gotta know, I gotta know,
> *If our love's the real thing where's my weddin' ring?*

Jackson performs each verse of this song in a supercharged rockabilly style until the last line (italicized above), at which point, with a fiddle breakdown, she slows down the mix for a bit of country soul. By switching in this way from rock to country—presumably to "the real thing"—Jackson upends both traditions at once, exposing each as a form of manipulation and finding a new powerful space for herself in the emptiness between them. Drawing upon similar reversals, girl groups of the later 1950s and early 1960s—the Ronettes, the Shirelles, the Shangri-Las, etc.—re-inflected the entire language of commercial desire and dissatisfaction. By layering vocals and refrains within a single wall of reverberant sound (thanks to Phil Spector), their slow-burn pop became at once the market's greatest expression and its own sad self-critique. Their songs about rings, kisses, candy, and motorcycles beckoned the listener with promises of love lost and lost again, re-making the entire market of romance and desire into a place of exquisite sadness. Andy Warhol's own favorite song was the Jaynetts' "Sally Go 'Round the Roses," a gorgeous girl-group jam that consists of multiple overlapping voices that never quite explain the title girl's great sadness.[50] Backed by a hypnotic samba beat, the voices by turns hint, reveal, counsel, console, and mock, until they occupy the entire dilemma with their own sad swing:

> Sit and cry with the door closed
> Sit and cry so no one knows
> Sally, baby, cry, let your hair hang down
> Sally, baby, cry, let your hair hang down
> Saddest thing in the whole wide world

It's a masterpiece, as cold as plastic and yet full of its own obscure languor, just like Warhol's best work. Its multiple voices break up the mystery of the narrative into a strangely amorphous and open-ended space of melancholic pleasure. Sally's loss becomes a formal emptiness around which a new aesthetic experience begins to cohere, a ceaseless proliferation of desire and affect, sadness whipped up round and round by a go-go beat, sentimental and senseless at once, the saddest, giddiest thing in the whole wide world.

All of these artists pattern the empty air of the marketplace with abstract constellations of hope and despair. Through sound alone, they push the very alienation of the age to its breaking point and thus indicate, with their own inhuman voices, something like human emotion once more. Sure, every one of these artists believes in personal "expression," in the singularity of his or her own hurt against the massive violence and conformity of the marketplace. But even as each tries to drown out the pain of the world with an individual echo, their songs reflect the conditions of society at large—indeed, the very *effort* to drown out that pain attests to the power and impact of that society. Moreover, each of these songs embraces—one clichéd line after another—an entire world of false forms. With every further abstraction, something like reality, as mediated reality, finds itself confronted and renewed. No way but through—the pop artist, in his or her desire for immediacy and presence, winds up testifying to the opposite, sheer mediation and self-difference. Expression maintains the possibility of self-fulfillment yet, in its very abstraction, its own empty formalism, gives voice to the manipulation of all. This logic should sound familiar enough—it is the echo effect of modernity itself, the noise of the modern world as it loses and finds itself in its own formal mediation. Pop music, even at its emptiest, its most abstract, remains a historical proposition, a human proposition, and it is through its own airy sound that it attains its most demanding effect.[51]

* * *

In a way, all pop music is sad. Every pop song is a sad song, suffering in its own time and space. We need to listen to this quiet pain, closely, to realize something of its deep promise. We need to hear the silent song within the song, and thus the silent world beyond this one, the one waiting to be created. Because, really, you can't go back—song, no matter how nostalgic, always inevitably points us toward something like the present—our orientation in everyday space and time. Pop music more so, for it tries to push the pain and promise of its moment beyond itself, toward some impossible future, and yet inevitably breaks open upon the real, or something like it. Holly himself went down in a snowy field. The wreckage sat in silence all night long, three musicians lying facedown in the field, their bodies frozen and twisted. But, more than a monument to lost talent or tragic youth, the downed flight points—in its very stillness—toward all the great and reckless hopefulness of pop modernism at large (see image 13). The sound of this crash echoes throughout history like a cheap pop song, at once silly and tragic, mechanical and human. In fact, here, we come to the most radical sound of all: the one never heard at the Winter Dance Party. Holly, Ritchie Valens, J. P. Richardson—all those silent kids, all those silenced fans—we can still hear them singing about nothing to no one. Some pop songs remind us of this emptiness with their loudness; some remind us with their softness. And some remind us with their silence, with their own refusal to be heard. But all of them gesture toward this promise as well as the deeper quiet beyond it, the silence of a world that no longer needs any music.

So, picking through the wreckage of Buddy's career, I found a short but unbearably heartbreaking version of Fats Domino's "Valley of Tears."[52] Another lost track, nearly silent—another sad track, almost too sad to hear—but it chugs along at its own pace and ultimately turns its loss into something bright, shiny, and hopeful. There's a valley of tears in Syria, another one in India, and even one in Texas (Valle de las Lágrimas, where you can still hear the cries of kidnapped mothers and children). But the

IMAGE 13 Buddy Holly plane wreck, February 3, 1959. Courtesy of Michael Ochs Archives / Getty Images.

valley depicted in this song does not exist in any region I know of—not in Mississippi, not in Virginia, or Oklahoma, or Tennessee, or Lubbock. It does not exist anywhere in this country, or even this world—for it is always elsewhere, a utopia, a non-space, off in the distance, shimmering in its own impossible contradiction. It's a place for those without any place, and it accepts all those who won't be accepted anywhere else. It provides comfort through its own interminable sadness, and relief through the shared pain of all the lost and lonely folks who are not there:

I want you to take me where I belong . . .
Where hearts have been broken with a kiss and a song.
Spend the rest of my days, dear, without any cares.
Everyone understands me in the valley of tears.

The paradoxes of the valley extend through to its performance. The singer's loneliness is an indication of his social condition and calls out to all his lost friends and lovers. In his performance, he sings *of* his loneliness and *through* his loneliness, mapping all over again the entire lost world, providing a new orientation for anyone who cares to listen. In fact, this is a cover song. It has been sung by Fats and Buddy and Slim Whitman and Brenda Lee, Faron Young, Ray Stevens, Van Broussard, and a whole bunch of other unknown, unnamed artists. Some real community persists in its empty sounding, in its airy passage from one mouth to another, one region to another. In this, the "Valley of Tears" becomes simply the place of pop itself, where misunderstanding precedes understanding, and carelessness is performed with great care, where all vows are broken and words always fade away. Here, in this valley, love is sustained in its loss, over and over again, and the self is born in its death, through the crushing presence of some other form, some other voice, some other self. Ultimately, all pop leads to this valley. And most of us would spend the rest of our days there, if its sweet airs didn't make us want to live again.

Notes

INTRODUCTION *From a Basement on Long Island to a Mansion on the Hill*

1. Robert Palmer, *Deep Blues: A Musical and Cultural History, from the Mississippi Delta to Chicago's South Side to the World* (New York: Penguin, 1982); Guthrie P. Ramsay, *Race Music: Black Cultures* (Berkeley: University of California Press, 2003); Adam Gussow, *Seems Like Murder Here: Southern Violence and the Blues Tradition* (Chicago: University of Chicago Press, 2002); Bill C. Malone, *Country Music, U.S.A.*, 2nd ed. (Austin: University of Texas Press, 2002); Richard A. Peterson, *Creating Country Music: Fabricating Authenticity* (Chicago: University of Chicago Press, 1997); Nick Tosches, *Country: The Twisted Roots of Rock 'n' Roll* (Cambridge, Mass.: Da Capo Press, 1996); Greil Marcus, "American Folk," *Granta* 76 (Winter 2001): 301–15, and "Dock Boggs in Thomas Jefferson's Virginia," *representations* 58 (Spring 1997): 1–23.

2. Elijah Wald, *Escaping the Delta: Robert Johnson and the Invention of the Blues* (New York: HarperCollins, 2004), xiv.

3. Carl Wilson, *Let's Talk about Love: A Journey to the End of Taste* (New York: Continuum, 2007), 15.

4. Josh Kun, *Audiotopia: Music, Race, and America* (Berkeley: University of California Press, 2005).

5. Robert Musil, "On Stupidity," in *Precision and Soul: Essays and Addresses*, trans. Burton Pike and David Luft (Chicago: University of Chicago Press, 1990), 268–86.

6. Miriam Hansen, "The Mass Production of the Senses: Classical Cinema as Vernacular Modernism," *Modernism/Modernity* 6:2 (1999): 59–77.

7. Andreas Huyssen, *After the Great Divide: Modernism, Mass Culture, Postmodernism* (Bloomington: Indiana University Press, 1986).

8. Rei Terada, *Feeling in Theory: Emotion after the "Death of the Subject"* (Cambridge, Mass.: Harvard University Press, 2003); Sianne Ngai, *Ugly Feelings* (Cambridge, Mass.: Harvard University Press, 2005).

9. Justus Nieland, *Feeling Modern: The Eccentricities of Public Life* (Urbana: University of Illinois Press, 2008).

10. See Michael Levenson, *Modernism and the Fate of Individuality: Character and Novelistic Form from Conrad to Woolf* (Cambridge, UK: Cambridge University Press, 1991); Tyrus Miller, *Late Modernism: Politics, Fiction, and the Arts between the World Wars* (Berkeley: University of California Press, 1999); Tim Armstrong, *Modernism, Technology, and the Body: A Cultural Study* (Cambridge, UK: Cambridge University Press, 1998).

11. This tension is most thoroughly and compellingly explored in Charles Altieri, *The Particulars of Rapture: An Aesthetics of the Affects* (Ithaca, N.Y.: Cornell University Press, 2004).

12. Ezra Pound, "A Retrospect," *Literary Essays of Ezra Pound*, ed. T. S. Eliot (New York: New Directions, 1968), 3–14 (4).

13. Such perspectives have been most famously expressed by Fredric Jameson, *Postmodernism, or, The Cultural Logic of Late Capitalism* (Durham, N.C.: Duke University Press, 1991) and Francis Fukuyama, *The End of History and the Last Man* (New York: Free Press, 2006).

14. Bernard Gendron, *Between Montmartre and the Mudd Club: Popular Music and the Avant-Garde* (Chicago: University of Chicago Press, 2002).

15. Guthrie P. Ramsay, *Race Music: Black Cultures* (Berkeley: University of California Press, 2003).

16. Eric Lott, *Love and Theft: Blackface Minstrelsy and the American Working Class* (Oxford, UK: Oxford University Press, 1995).

17. Alexander G. Weheliye, *Phonographies: Grooves in Sonic Afro-Modernity* (Durham, N.C.: Duke University Press, 2005).

18. Greil Marcus, *The Old, Weird America: The World of Bob Dylan's Basement Tapes* (New York: Picador, 1997), originally published in 1997 by Henry Holt and Company under the title *Invisible Republic: Bob Dylan's Basement Tapes*.

19. Greil Marcus, *Mystery Train: Images of America in Rock 'n' Roll Music*, 4th ed. (New York: Plume, 1997).

20. Herbert Marcuse, "The Affirmative Character of Culture," in *Negations: Essays in Critical Theory*, trans. Jeremy J. Shapiro (London: Penguin Press, 1968), 65–98.

21. Admittedly, I think Marcus's writing on the rock and punk movements of the 1960s and 1970s is better attuned to the possibilities of mass culture in the twentieth century. See, for example, *Lipstick Traces: A Secret History of the Twentieth Century* (Cambridge, Mass.: Harvard University Press, 2009) and Marcus's essays on the Beatles and the Sex Pistols in the *Rolling Stone Illustrated History of Rock & Roll* (New York: Random House, 1992).

CHAPTER ONE *Lord, It Just Won't Stop! Work and Blues in the Industrial Delta*

1. Richard Wright, *Native Son*, restored ed. (New York: Perennial Classics, 1993), 10.

2. T. S. Eliot, "The Metaphysical Poets," in *Selected Prose*, ed. Frank Kermode (New York: Farrar, Straus and Giroux, 1975), 59–67 (64), and Ezra Pound, "A Retrospect," *Literary Essays of Ezra Pound*, ed. T. S. Eliot (New York: New Directions, 1968), 3–14 (4), respectively.

3. Martin Scorsese (director) and Peter Guralnick (writer), *Feel Like Going Home* (Sony, 2004).

4. James C. Cobb, *The Most Southern Place on Earth: The Mississippi Delta and the Roots of Regional Identity* (Oxford, UK: Oxford University Press, 1992), 6–7, 98.

5. Harold D. Woodman, "Postbellum Social Change and Its Effects on Marketing the South's Cotton Crop," *Agricultural History* 56:1 (January 1982): 215–30 (220).

6. "Biggest Cotton Plantation," *Fortune* (March 1937), 125–32.

7. See Cobb, *The Most Southern Place on Earth*, 61.

8. See commentary in LeRoi Jones (Amiri Baraka), *Blues People: Negro Music in White America* (New York: William Morrow, 1963), 6–7, 12–13, 64.

9. See Slavoj Žižek "Why Are There Always Two *Fathers*?" in *Enjoy Your Symptom! Jacques Lacan in Hollywood and Out* (New York: Routledge, 2001), 149–92.

10. Alan Lomax, *The Land Where the Blues Began* (New York: New Press, 1993), ix.

11. See commentary in Paul Oliver, "Got to Work or Leave," in *Blues Fell This Morning: Meaning in the Blues* (Cambridge, UK: Cambridge University Press, 196), 12–42.

12. Qtd. in Samuel C. Adams, "Changing Negro Life in the Delta," in *Lost Delta Found: Rediscovering the Fisk University Library of Congress Coahoma County Study, 1941–1942*, ed. Robert Gordon and Bruce Nemerov (Nashville: Vanderbilt University Press, 2005), 223–90 (259).

13. Sampson Pittman, "Cotton Farmer Blues," *The Devil Is Busy* (Laurie Records, 1992), track 7.

14. Bessie Smith, "House Rent Blues," *The Complete Recordings*, vol. 2 (Columbia/Legacy, 1991), disc 1, track 6. Ida Cox, "Pink Slip Blues," *Complete Recorded Works in Chronological Order*, vol. 5 (Document Records, 1999), track 9.

15. Son House, "Country Farm Blues," *The Complete Library of Congress Sessions: 1941–2* (Travelin' Man Records, 1996), track 16.

16. See Lawrence W. Levine, *Black Culture and Black Consciousness: Afro-American Folk Thought from Slavery to Freedom* (Oxford, UK: Oxford University Press, 1977), 217, 221–23.

17. See Cobb, *The Most Southern Place on Earth*, 106ff.

18. Charley Patton, "Revenue Man Blues," *Screamin' and Hollerin' the Blues* (Revenant Records, 2001), disc 5, track 20.

19. Clara Smith, "Every Woman's Blues," *Complete Recorded Works in Chronological Order*, vol. 1 (Document Records, 1995), track 2.

20. See *commentary in* Elijah Wald, *Escaping the Delta: Robert Johnson and the Invention of the Blues* (New York: HarperCollins, 2004), 86–102.

21. See Cobb, *The Most Southern Place on Earth*, 115, 140ff, and Wald, 84ff.

22. Robert Johnson, "Hell Hound on My Trail," *The Complete Recordings* (Columbia/Legacy, 1996), disc 2, track 6.

23. Jeff Todd Titon, *Early Downhome Blues: A Musical and Cultural Analysis* (Urbana: University of Illinois Press, 1977), 15–16.

24. Robert Johnson, "Me and the Devil Blues," *Complete*, disc 2, track 12; Charley Patton, "34 Blues," *Screamin'*, disc 5, track 17.

25. Cleo Gibson, "I've Got a Ford Engine Movement in My Hips," *Ultimate Blues Collection*, vol. 3 (Mbop Global–OvcMedia, 2009), track 10.

26. See Titon, *Early Downhome Blues*, 11, and Angela Y. Davis, *Blues Legacies and Black Feminism: Gertrude "Ma" Rainey, Bessie Smith, and Billie Holiday* (New York: Vintage Books, 1999), 18ff.

27. Bessie Smith, "In the House Blues," *Complete*, vol. 4, disc 2, track 17.

28. Bessie Smith, "Sam Jones Blues," *Complete*, vol. 1, disc 1, track 19. On traveling themes in women's blues, see Davis, *Blues Legacies and Black Feminism*, 66–90.

29. On African American sociability, see John Dollard, *Caste and Class in a Southern Town* (New Haven, Conn.: Yale University Press, 1937). For commentary on sociality and the architecture of the juke joint, see Jennifer Nardone, "Roomful of Blues: Juke Joints and the Cultural Landscape of the Mississippi Delta," *Perspectives in Vernacular Architecture* 9 (2003): 166–75.

30. See Daphne Duval Harrison, *Black Pearls: Blues Queens of the 1920s* (Brunswick, N.J.: Rutgers University Press, 1988), 35–36.

31. See images in ibid., 83–84.

32. Clara Smith, "Mama's Gone, Goodbye," *Complete*, vol. 2, track 14.

33. See Harrison, *Black Pearls*, 6–10.

34. Clara Smith, "Kansas City Man Blues," *Complete*, vol. 1, track 13. Bertha Chippie Hill, "Pratt City Blues," *Complete Recorded Works: 1925–9* (Document Records, 1995), track 10.

35. Bertha Idaho, "Down on Pennsylvania Avenue," *Female Blues Singers*, vol. 10 (Document Records, 1997), track 8.

36. See Jones (Baraka), *Blues People* 61–2; Lomax, *The Land Where the Blues Began,* 232–23; Cobb, *The Most Southern Place on Earth*, 282; and Levine, *Black Culture and Black Consciousness,* 335ff.

37. For these and other details, see John Fahey, *Charley Patton* (London: Studio Vista, 1970); David Evans, "Charley Patton and the Conscience of the Delta," in *The Voice of the Delta: Charley Patton and the Mississippi Blues Tradition*, ed. Robert Sacre (Liège, France: Presses Universitaires de Liège, 1987), 111–214; Robert Palmer, *Deep Blues: A Musical and Cultural History from the Mississippi Delta to Chicago's South Side to the World* (New York: Penguin Books, 1981), 48–89.

38. See *The Chicago Defender* (national edition, January 11, 1930), 7.

39. Charley Patton, "Mean Black Moan," *Screamin'*, disc 2, track 13.

40. Charley Patton, "High Water Everywhere, Parts 1 and 2," *Screamin'*, disc 2, tracks 1–2.

41. Charley Patton, "Screamin' and Hollerin' the Blues," *Screamin'*, disc 1, track 6.

42. Charley Patton, "Green River Blues," *Screamin'*, disc 2, track 14.

43. On the difference between feeling and form ("embodied" and "designative" meanings) in music, see Leonard B. Meyer, *Emotion and Meaning in Music* (Chicago: University of Chicago Press, 1956). For an excellent account of work done on musical "code usage," see Patrik N. Juslin, "Communicating Emotion in Music Performance," in *Music and Emotion: Theory and Research*, ed. Patrik N. Juslin and John A. Sloboda (Oxford: Oxford University Press, 2001), 309–37. For an account of music as an "affective lexicon," see Nicholas Cook and Nicola Dibben, "Musicological Approaches to Emotion," in *Music and Emotion*, 45–70.

44. Brian Massumi, "The Autonomy of Affect," *Cultural Critique* 31 (1995): 83–109 (88). For emotion as a "dimensional structure," see J. A. Russell, "A Circumplex Model of Affect," *Journal of Personality and Social Psychology* 39 (1980): 1161–78, and Daniel N. Stern, *The Interpersonal World of the Infant: A View from Psychoanalysis and Developmental Psychology* (New York: Basic Books, 1985). Many have adapted such concepts specifically for music study; see John A. Sloboda and Patrik N. Juslin, "Psychological Perspectives on Music and Emotion," in *Music and Emotion*, 71–104; Ivan Nykliček, Julian F. Thayer, and Lorenz J. P. van Doornen, "Cardiorespiratory Differentiations of Musically-Induced Emotions," *Journal of Psychophysiology* 11 (1997): 304–21; Mitch Waterman, "Emotional Responses to Music: Implicit and Explicit Effects in Listeners and Performers," *Psychology of Music* 24 (1996): 53–67.

45. Simon Frith, *Performing Rites: On the Value of Popular Music* (Cambridge, Mass,: Harvard University Press, 1996), 138.

46. "Prayer of Death, Parts 1 and 2," *Screamin'*, disc 1, tracks 4–5.

47. Roland Barthes, "The Grain of the Voice," in *Image-Music-Text*, ed. and trans. Stephen Heath (New York: Hill and Wang, 1977), 179–89. See chapter four.

48. David Evans, *Big Road Blues: Tradition and Creativity in the Folk Blues* (Berkeley: University of California Press, 1982), 56, 153, 31.

49. Charley Patton, "Down the Dirt Road Blues," *Screamin'*, disc 1, track 3.

50. Charley Patton, "Bird Nest Bound," *Screamin'*, disc 4, track 2.

51. *Bukka White and Son House: Masters of the Country Blues* (Yazoo, 2000), track 2.

52. Adam Gussow, *Seems Like Murder Here: Southern Violence and the Blues Tradition* (Chicago: University of Chicago Press, 2002).

53. For these terms, see Sigmund Freud, *Beyond the Pleasure Principle* (1920), std. ed., trans. James Strachey (New York: W. W. Norton, 1961), and Sigmund Freud, "Remembering, Repeating and Working-Through (Further Recommendations on the Technique of Psycho-analysis II)" (1914), in *The Standard Edition of the Complete Works of Sigmund Freud*, vol. 12, trans. James Strachey (London: Hogarth Press, 1958), 147–56.

54. Skip James, "22–20 Blues," *Complete Early Recordings* (Yazoo, 1994), track 11.

55. Robert Johnson, "32–20 Blues," *Complete*, disc 1, track 14.

56. Johnny Lee Hooker, "Boom Boom," *The Ultimate Collection, 1948–90* (Rhino, 1991), disc 2, track 1.

57. See Davis, "I Used to Be Your Sweet Mama," in *Blues Legacies*, 3–41; Hazel V. Carby, "It Jus Be's Dat Way Sometime: The Sexual Politics of Women's Blues," in *The Jazz Cadence of American Culture*, ed. Robert G. O'Meally (New York: Columbia University Press, 1998), 471–83.

58. Memphis Minnie, "Bumble Bee," *Queen of the Country Blues, 1929–37* (JSP Records, 2003), disc 1, track 3. Ma Rainey, "Sweet Rough Man," *Complete Recorded Works: 1928 Sessions* (Document Records, 1994), track 15.

59. Bessie Smith, "Hard Driving Papa," *Complete*, vol. 3, disc 1, track 12, and "Empty Bed Blues, Part 2," *Complete*, vol. 4, disc 1, track 5.

60. Qtd. in Davis, "I Used to Be Your Sweet Mama," 30.

61. Ralph Ellison, "Richard Wright's Blues," in *Shadow and Act* (New York: Signet Books, 1966), 90.

62. W. C. Handy, *Father of the Blues: An Autobiography* (New York: Macmillan, 1944), 143.

63. Theodor Adorno, "On the Fetish-Character in Music and the Regression of Listening," in *Essays on Music*, ed. Richard Leppert (Berkeley: University of California Press, 2002), 288–317. For a more recent critique, see Evan Eisenberg, *The Recording Angel: Explorations in Phonography* (New York: McGraw-Hill, 1987).

64. Robert Johnson, "Phonograph Blues," *Complete,* disc 1, track 12.

65. For gender, consumerism, and the modern marketplace, see Rita Felski, *The Gender of Modernity* (Cambridge: Harvard University Press, 1995), 61–90.

66. Theodor Adorno, "The Curves of the Needle," in *Essays on Music*, 271–76.

67. See William Howland Kenney, *Recorded Music in American Life: The Phonograph and Popular Memory, 1890–1945* (Oxford, UK: Oxford University Press, 1999), 24ff.; Andre Millard, *America on Record: A History of Recorded Sound* (Cambridge, UK: Cambridge University Press, 1995), 24–64.

68. Zora Neale Hurston, "Characteristics of Negro Expression," in *The Sanctified Church* (Berkeley: Turtle Island Foundation, 1983), 49–68.

69. Sigmund Freud, *Totem and Taboo: Some Points of Agreement between the Mental Lives of Savages and Neurotics*, std. ed., trans. James Strachey (New York: W. W. Norton, 1950).

70. Muddy Waters, "Louisiana Blues," *His Best: 1947 to 1955* (Geffen, 1997), track 6.

71. Ma Rainey, "Lucky Rock Blues," *Complete*, vol. 1, track 17, and "Louisiana Hoodoo Blues," *Complete*, vol. 2, track 14.

72. Here, my argument draws on Michael Taussig's astounding observations in *Mimesis and Alterity: A Particular History of the Senses* (New York: Routledge, 1993). 44ff.

73. Joel Dinerstein, *Swinging the Machine: Modernity, Technology, and African American Culture between the World Wars* (Amherst: University of Massachusetts Press, 2003), 78.

74. Robert Johnson, "Terraplane Blues," *Complete*, disc 1, track 11. Ma Rainey, "Black Cat Hoot Owl Blues," *Complete: 1928 Sessions*, track 1.

75. John Work, untitled manuscript, in *Lost Delta Found*, 53–126 (86–87).

76. See Levine, *Black Culture and Black Consciousness*, 227ff.

77. WPA Manuscripts, Florida File, Archive of Folk Song. Qtd. in Levine, *Black Culture and Black Consciousness*, 231.

78. Again, see Taussig, *Mimesis and Alterity*, 19ff, which, in turn, draws upon Walter Benjamin, "A Small History of Photography," in *One-Way Street and Other Writings*, trans. Edmund Jephcott and Kingsley Shorter (London: New Left Books, 1979), 240–57, and "The Work of Art in the Age of Mechanical Reproduction," in *Illuminations*, ed. Hannah Arendt, trans. Harry Zohn (New York: Schocken, 1969), 217–51.

79. Alexander G. Weheliye, *Phonographies: Grooves in Sonic Afro-Modernity* (Durham, N.C.: Duke University Press, 2005).

CHAPTER TWO *Thought I Had Your Heart Forever:*
Death, Detachment, and the Modernity of Early Country Music

1. Bob Coltman, "Look Out, Here He Comes! Fiddlin' John Carson, One of a Kind and Twice as Feisty," *Old Time Music* 9 (Summer 1973), 16–21 (20).

2. Richard A. Peterson, *Creating Country Music: Fabricating Authenticity* (Chicago: University of Chicago Press, 1997).

3. Aaron Fox, "The Jukebox of History: Narrative of Loss and Desire in the Discourse of Country Music," *Popular Music* 11:1 (1992), 53.

4. Kathleen Stewart, "Nostalgia—A Polemic," in *Cultural Anthropology* 3:3 (August 1988): 227–41.

5. Qtd. in Wayne W. Daniel, *Pickin' on Peachtree: A History of Country Music in Atlanta, Georgia* (Urbana: University of Illinois Press, 1990), 24.

6. Gene Wiggins, *Fiddlin' Georgia Crazy: Fiddlin' John Carson, His Real World, and the World of His Songs* (Urbana: University of Illinois Press, 1987), 5, 49.

7. Patrick Huber, *Linthead Stomp: The Creation of Country Music in the Piedmont South* (Chapel Hill: University of North Carolina Press, 2008), 70–71.

8. All details in Wiggins, *Fiddlin' Georgia Crazy*, 74–76.

9. Bill C. Malone, *Country Music, U.S.A.*, 2nd ed. (Austin: University of Texas Press, 2002), 27–28, 9–10.

10. See commentary in Wiggins, *Fiddlin' Georgia Crazy*, 250, 169ff, 234.

11. Wiggins, *Fiddlin' Georgia Crazy*, 246–47, 206, 32–33, 194, and Daniel, *Pickin' on Peachtree*, 90. All tracks on Fiddlin' John Carson, *Complete Recorded Works in Chronological Order* (Document, 1997).

12. Carson, *Complete*, vol. 1, track 1.

13. See commentary in Bill C. Malone, *Don't Get above Your Raisin'* (Urbana: University of Illinois Press, 2002), 56.

14. Pamela Fox, *Natural Acts: Gender, Race, and Rusticity in Country Music* (Ann Arbor: University of Michigan Press, 2009).

15. Malone, *Raisin'*, ix; Curtis W. Ellison, *Country Music Culture: From Hard Times to Heaven* (Jackson: University Press of Mississippi, 1995), xvi; Dorothy Horstman, *Sing Your Heart Out, Country Boy* (Nashville: Country Music Foundation, 1996), 240–41.

16. For an analysis of this discourse and its ideological overtones, see Barbara Ching, "Country Music," in *A Companion to the Literature and Culture of the American South*, ed. Richard Gray and Owen Robinson (Malden, Mass.: Blackwell, 2004), 203–20; David Brackett, "When You're Looking at Hank (You're Looking at Country)," *Interpreting Popular Music* (Berkeley: University of California Press, 2000), 75–107; Diane Pecknold, "The Selling Sound of Country Music: Class, Culture, and Early Radio Marketing Strategy of the Country Music Association," in *Country Music Annual 2002*, ed. Charles K. Wolfe and James Akenson (Lexington: University of Kentucky Press, 2002), 54–81.

17. Charles K. Wolfe, *A Good-Natured Riot: The Birth of the Grand Ole Opry* (Nashville: Country Music Foundation Press and Vanderbilt University Press, 1999), 179–89.

18. Recording available at Country Music Hall of Fame, Recorded Sound Collection.

19. Wolfe, *Riot*, 211ff.

20. Delmore Brothers, "The Frozen Girl," *Classic Cuts, 1933–41* (JSP Records, 2004), disc A, track 10.

21. *Rural Radio* 1:9 (October 1938): 10–11.

22. George D. Hay, *A Story of the Grand Ole Opry* (George D. Hay, 1945), 8, 9, 26–27.

23. The Vagabonds, *Collection of Mountain Ballads, Old-Time Songs, and Hymns* (Nashville: Old Cabin Company, 1932), 6.

24. Benedict Anderson, *Imagined Communities: Reflections on the Origins and Spread of Nationalism* (London: Verso, 1983).

25. Qtd. in Mark Zwonitzer, with Charles Hirshberg, *Will You Miss Me When I'm Gone? The Carter Family and Their Legacy in American Music* (New York: Simon and Schuster, 2002), 7, 8–10.

26. Regarding the evolution of traditional modes and singing style, see Norm Cohen, *Folk Music: A Regional Exploration* (Westport, Conn.: Greenwood Press, 2005), 77–80.

27. See Bob Coltman, "An Appreciation of A. P. Carter," in *The Carter Family: Old Time Music Booklet 1*, ed. John Atkins (London: Old Time Music, 1973), 24–33 (26).

28. See John Robert Moore, "Omission and the Central Action in English Ballads," *Modern Philology* 11:3 (Jan 1914): 391–406, and Phillips Barry, *Folk Music in America* (New York: Works Progress Administration, Federal Theatre Project, National Service Bureau, 1939). For later commentary, Tristram P. Coffin, "'Mary Hamilton' and the Anglo-American Ballad as an Art Form," *The Journal of American Folklore* 70:277 (July–September 1957), 208–14; Peggy A. Bulger, "'Don't

Forget This Song': Recorded Balladry of the A. P. Carter Family," *Mid-America Folklore* 10: 2–3 (Fall–Winter 1982): 1–16; Susan Key, "Sound and Sentimentality: Nostalgia in the Songs of Stephen Foster," *American Music* (Summer 1995): 145–66.

29. On the Carters' revision of Child's ballads, see Bulger, "'Don't Forget This Song,'" 4–6. On the prominence of these themes in the larger southern musical tradition, see Norm Cohen, "The Songs," in *The Carter Family on Border Radio, JEMF101* (Los Angeles: John Edward Memorial Foundation, 1972), 23.

30. See related commentary in Katie Doman, "Something Old, Something New: The Carter Family's Bristol Sessions Recordings," in *The Bristol Sessions: Writings about the Big Bang of Country Music*, ed. Charles K. Wolfe and Ted Olson (Jefferson, N.C.: McFarland, 2005), 66–86 (84).

31. T. S. Eliot, "Tradition and the Individual Talent," in *Selected Prose of T. S. Eliot*, ed. Frank Kermode (New York: Farrar, Straus and Giroux, 1975), 37–44 (40).

32. On Appalachian singing styles and traditions, see Peggy Langrell, "Appalachian Folk Music: From Foothills to Footlights," *Music Educators Journal* 72:7 (March 1986): 37–39.

33. See comments by Janette Carter in Bulger, "'Don't Forget This Song,'" 4.

34. Zwonitzer, *Will You Miss Me When I'm Gone?*, 59 and 28–29.

35. Zwonitzer, ibid, 120. The Carter Family, "My Clinch Mountain Home," *The Carter Family: 1927–34* (JSP Records, 2001), disc A, track 20. By A. P. Carter. Copyright 1929 by Peer International Corporation. Copyright Renewed. Used by Permission. All Rights Reserved.

36. "Lulu Walls," *The Carter Family*, disc A, track 24.

37. The Carter Family, "Single Girl, Married Girl," *The Bristol Sessions: Historic Recordings from Bristol, Tennessee* (Country Music Foundation, 1991), disc 2, track 8.

38. The Carter Family, "The Wandering Boy," *Bristol Sessions*, disc 2, track 3.

39. Shane Vogel, "Lena Horne's Impersona," *Camera Obscura* 23:1 (2008): 10–45.

40. Zwonitzer, *Will You Miss Me When I'm Gone?*, 35, 100.

41. The Carter Family, "Bury Me under the Weeping Willow" and "Will You Miss Me When I'm Gone," *The Carter Family*, disc A, tracks 1 and 13, respectively.

42. The Carter Family, "Can the Circle Be Unbroken," *Smithsonian Collection of Classic Country Music*, vol. 1 (Smithsonian Folkways Recordings, 1991), track 9.

43. Sigmund Freud, "Mourning and Melancholia" (1917), in *Collected Papers*, vol. 4, ed. Ernest Jones (London: Hogarth Press, 1948), 152–70.

44. Tammy Clewell, "Mourning Melancholia: Freud's Psychoanalysis of Loss," *Journal of the American Psychoanalytic Association* 52:1 (2004): 43–67 (48–49).

45. Michele Hilmes, *Radio Voices: American Broadcasting, 1922–1952* (Minneapolis: University of Minnesota Press, 1997).

46. Aaron Jaffe, "Inventing the Radiocosmopolitan: Vernacular Modernism at a Standstill," in *Broadcasting Modernism*, ed. Michael Coyle, Debra Rae Cohen, and Jane Lewty (Miami: University of Florida Press, 2009), 11–30 (27). For further

commentary, see Daniel Tiffany, "Phantom Transmissions: The Radio Broadcasts of Ezra Pound," *SubStance* 19:1:61 (1990): 53–75; Timothy C. Campbell, *Wireless Writing in the Age of Marconi* (Minneapolis: University of Minnesota Press, 2006).

47. Jeffrey Sconce, *Haunted Media: Electronic Presence from Telegraphy to Television* (Durham, N.C.: Duke University Press, 2000), 94.

48. For rural listeners' early responses, see Derek Valliant, "'Your Voice Came in Last Night . . . But I Thought It Sounded a Little Scared': Rural Radio Listening and 'Talking Back' during the Progressive Era in Wisconsin, 1920–1932," in *Radio Reader: Essays in the Cultural History of Radio*, ed. Michele Hilmes and Jason Loviglio (New York: Routledge, 2002), 63–88.

49. William McKinley Randle Jr., *History of Radio Broadcasting and Its Social and Economic Effect on the Entertainment Industry, 1920–1930 (Vols. I–III)* (William McKinley Randle Jr., 1967), 472.

50. Malone, *Raisin'*, 55–56, and Ray Barfield, *Listening to Radio, 1920–1950* (Westport, Conn.: Praeger, 1996), 39ff.

51. Carmen Malone, "The Sweetest Hour," *Rural Radio* 1:4 (May 1938): 20.

52. Qtd. in William F. Danaher and Vincent J. Roscigno, "Cultural Production, Media, and Meaning: Hillbilly Music and the Southern Textile Mills," *Poetics* 32 (2004), 51–71 (67).

53. Foreword, *Stand By!* (February 16, 1935), 2.

54. Bob Coltman, "Across the Chasm: How the Depression Changed Country Music," *Old Time Music* 23 (Winter 1976–77), 6–12 (6, 9).

55. See, for example, the WHO Barn Dance Frolic Souvenir Program (Des Moines; n.d.) and *Rural Radio* 1:4 (May 1938), 20, and 1:1 (February 1938), 13.

56. *Rural Radio* 1:4 (May 1938): 1–2.

57. "Rural Radio Roundup," *Rural Radio* 1:4 (May 1938): 10, 13 ; "Family Gossip," *Rural Radio* 1:4 (May 1938): 18.

58. See commentary in Barfield, *Listening to Radio*, 45ff, and letters reprinted in Charles Wolfe, "The Triumph of the Hills: Country Radio, 1920–50," in *Country: The Music and the Musicians*, ed. Paul Kingsbury, Alan Axelrod, and Susan Costello for the Country Music Foundation (New York: Abbeville Press, 1994), 70–77.

59. McCusker, "'Dear Radio Friend,'" 181, and Malone, *Raisin'*, 66.

60. See ads for "Rural Radio Saturday Night Barn Dance Club" in *Rural Radio* 1:2 (March 1938): 19.

61. John Lair, *Renfro Valley, Then and Now* (John Lair, 1957), 31.

62. *Renfro Valley Keepsake* (Renfro Valley Enterprises, 1940), 3.

63. Charles K. Wolfe, *Kentucky Country: Folk and Country Music of Kentucky* (Lexington: University Press of Kentucky, 1982), 78.

64. John Lair, WLS interview, Berea College, John Lair Papers, Series VI, Box 31 (1930).

65. Testimony of John Lair before the Federal Communications Commission (Clear Channel Hearing), John Lair Collection, Southern Appalachian Archives,

Hutchins Library, Berea College, Series II, Box 12, WHAS 1941–[1959], (April 29, 1946), 4–5.

66. Jürgen Habermas, *The Structural Transformation of the Public Sphere: An Inquiry into a Category of Bourgeois Society*, trans. Thomas Burger (Cambridge, Mass.: MIT Press, 1991).

67. Michael Warner, "The Mass Public and the Mass Subject," in *The Phantom Public Sphere*, ed. Bruce Robbins (Minneapolis: University of Minnesota Press, 1993), 234–56.

CHAPTER THREE *A Rambling Funny Streak:
Woody Guthrie, Revolutionary Folk Song,
and the Migrant Art of the Refrain*

1. Woody Guthrie, *Bound for Glory* (New York: Plume, 1983), 260.

2. Woody Guthrie, *Seeds of Man: An Experience Lived and Dreamed* (Lincoln: University of Nebraska Press, 1995).

3. See Diane Pecknold's excellent account of boomer soundtracks in "Holding Out Hope for the Creedence: Music and the Search for the Real Thing in *The Big Lebowski*," in *The Year's Work in Lebowski Studies*, ed. Edward P. Comentale and Aaron Jaffe (Bloomington: Indiana University Press, 2009), 276–94.

4. Simon Frith, *Performing Rites: On the Value of Popular Music* (Cambridge, Mass.: Harvard University Press, 1996), 164, 169.

5. Woody Guthrie, *Pastures of Plenty: A Self-Portrait*, ed. Dave Marsh and Harold Leventhal (New York: HarperPerennial, 1992), 115–16.

6. Michael Denning, *The Cultural Front: The Laboring of American Culture in the Twentieth Century* (New York: Verso, 1997), xvi–xvii, 29. See also Warren Susman, *Culture as History: The Transformation of American Society in the Twentieth Century* (New York: Pantheon Books, 1984), 152, 156, 160.

7. See Peter Bürger, *Theory of the Avant-Garde*, trans. Michael Shaw (Minneapolis: University of Minneapolis Press, 1984).

8. Peter La Chapelle, *Proud to Be an Okie: Cultural Politics, Country Music, and Migration to Southern California* (Berkeley: University of California Press, 2007), 56, 53.

9. See commentary in Denning, *The Cultural Front*, 265ff.

10. Karl Marx, *Economic and Philosophic Manuscripts of 1844 and The Communist Manifesto* (New York: Prometheus Books, 1988), 212.

11. See *Bound for Glory*, 250.

12. Qtd. in Ed Cray, *Ramblin' Man: The Life and Times of Woody Guthrie* (New York: W. W. Norton, 2004), 79.

13. Eric Lott, *Love and Theft: Blackface Minstrelsy and the American Working Class* (Oxford, UK: Oxford University Press, 1995), 51.

14. Janet Lyon, "Gadže Modernism," *Modernism/Modernity* 11:3 (2004): 517–38 (526).

15. See Robbie Lieberman, *"My Song Is My Weapon": People's Songs, American Communism, and the Politics of Culture, 1930–50* (Urbana: University of Illinois Press, 1995), 37–39.

16. Shelly Romalis, *Pistol Packin' Mama: Aunt Molly Jackson and the Politics of Folksong* (Urbana: University of Illinois Press, 1999), 158.

17. See ibid., 158, 169–70.

18. For documentary realism, see Denning, *The Cultural Front*, 177ff.; Susman, *Culture as History*, 160ff.; Alfred Kazin, *On Native Grounds: An Interpretation of Modern American Prose Literature* (New York: Harcourt, Brace, 1942), 490ff. For "superrealism," see James Johnson Sweeney, *Plastic Redirections in 20th Century Painting* (Chicago: University of Chicago Press, 1934), 87ff.

19. James Agee and Walker Evans, *Let Us Now Praise Famous Men: Three Tenant Families* (New York: Mariner Books, 2001), 10. See excellent commentary in T. V. Reed, "Unimagined Existence and the Fiction of the Real: Postmodernist Realism in *Let Us Now Praise Famous Men*," *Representations* 24 (Autumn 1988), 156–76.

20. Kenneth Burke, *Attitudes toward History*, vol. 2 (New York: New Republic, 1937), 73, 87–88. William Solomon similarly uses the term "grotesque" to character-ize the literary negotiation of bodies and technology in the 1930s; see *Literature, Amusement, and Technology in the Great Depression* (Cambridge, UK: Cambridge University Press, 2002), 8–10.

21. See Cray, 206, 228.

22. See Cray, 223; Ellen G. Landau, "Classic in Its Own Little Way: The Art of Woody Guthrie," in *Hard Travelin': The Life and Legacy of Woody Guthrie*, ed. Robert Santelli and Emily Davidson (Hanover: Wesleyan University Press, 1999), 83–107 (88); John Greenaway, *American Folksongs of Protest* (Philadelphia: University of Pennsylvania Press, 1953), 287–8.

23. Woody Guthrie, "My People," in *Born to Win*, ed. Robert Shelton (New York: Macmillan, 1965), 215–17. © Copyright Woody Guthrie Publications, Inc. All rights reserved. Used by permission.

24. See Cray, *Ramblin' Man*, 260, 287.

25. Woody Guthrie, "Ludlow Massacre," *Asch Recordings*, vol. 1–4 (Smithsonian Folkways Recordings, 1999), disc 3, track 20.

26. Woody Guthrie, "The Sinking of the Rueben James," *Asch*, disc 1, track 25.

27. All details in Cray, *Ramblin' Man*, 138.

28. Woody Guthrie, "Folk Music" (unpublished manuscript), Woody Guthrie Archives (Box 4, Folder 7), July 25, 1944.

29. Woody Guthrie, "Babe O' Mine," *Songs for Political Action: Folk Music, Topical Songs and the American Left, 1935–54* (Bear Family Records, 1996), disc 3, track 15.

30. Sarah Ogan Gunning, "I'm Going to Organize," *Sarah Ogan Gunning: "Girl of Constant Sorrow"* (Folk-Legacy, 1965), track 8. For background details, see Archie Green's useful liner notes to this collection.

31. C. Wright Mills, "Situated Actions and Vocabularies of Motive," in *Power,*

Politics, and People: The Collected Essays of C. Wright Mills (London: Oxford University Press, 1967), 439–41.

32. Woody Guthrie, *Ballads of Sacco & Vanzetti* (Smithsonian Folkways Recordings, 1960).

33. Details in Cray, *Ramblin' Man*, 299–30.

34. Henri Bergson, "Laughter," in *Comedy*, ed. Wylie Sypher (Baltimore: Johns Hopkins University Press, 1980), 59–190 (73–74).

35. See commentary in Cray, *Ramblin' Man*, 54, 71, 125.

36. Woody Guthrie, *Woody Sez*, ed. Marjorie Guthrie et. al. (New York: E. P. Dutton, 1975), 117.

37. Alan Lomax, Woody Guthrie, and Pete Seeger, *Hard Hitting Songs for Hard-Hit People* (New York: Oak Publications, 1967), 17.

38. Woody Guthrie, "Talking Dust Bowl Blues," *Dust Bowl Ballads* (Buddha Records, 2000), track 2.

39. Woody Guthrie, "Blowin' Down the Road (I ain't going to be treated this way)," *Dust Bowl Ballads*, track 6.

40. Woody Guthrie, "Dusty Old Dust (So Long, It's Been Good to Know You)," *Dust Bowl Ballads*, track 4. Excerpts from "So Long It's Been Good to Know Yuh" by Woody Guthrie. © Copyright Woody Guthrie Publications, Inc. / TRO-Ludlow Music, Inc. All rights reserved. Used by permission.

41. Woody Guthrie, "Pastures of Plenty," *Asch*, disc 1, track 8.

42. Woody Guthrie, "This Land Is Your Land," *Asch*, disc 1, track 14; for analysis of the song's many versions, see Mark Allen Jackson, "Is This Song Your Song Anymore? Revisioning Woody Guthrie's 'This Land Is Your Land,'" *American Music* 20:3 (Autumn 2002): 249–76.

43. Gilles Deleuze and Félix Guattari, *A Thousand Plateaus: Capitalism and Schizophrenia*, trans. Brian Massumi (Minneapolis: University of Minnesota Press, 1987), 313.

44. Woody Guthrie, "Mermaid's Avenue" (1950). Words © Copyright 2001 by Woody Guthrie Publications, Inc.

45. Michel de Certeau, *The Practice of Everyday Life* (Berkeley: University of California Press, 1988).

46. Josh Kun, *Audiotopia: Music, Race, and America* (Berkeley: University of California Press, 2005), 22.

CHAPTER FOUR *Four Elvises: On the Dada Possibilities of Midcentury Rock and Roll and Modern Fan Culture*

1. See Calvin Tomkins, *Duchamp: A Biography* (New York: Henry Holt, 1996), 179ff.

2. Albert Goldman, *Elvis* (New York: McGraw-Hill, 1981), 80ff.; Peter Guralnick, *Last Train to Memphis: The Rise of Elvis Presley* (Boston: Little, Brown, 1994), 49ff.

3. James and Annette Baxter, "The Man in the Blue Suede Shoes," rpt. in *The Elvis Reader: Texts and Sources on the King of Rock 'n' Roll*, ed. Kevin Quain (N.p.: Kevin Quain, 1992), 31–35 (33–34).

4. Nick Tosches, *Country: The Twisted Roots of Rock 'n' Roll* (Cambridge, Mass.: Da Capo Press, 1996) and Greil Marcus, *Mystery Train: Images of America in Rock 'n' Roll Music*, 4th ed. (New York: Plume, 1997).

5. See also Linda Ray Pratt, "Elvis, Or the Ironies of a Southern Identity," *Elvis Reader*, 93–103; Van K. Brock, "Images of Elvis, The South and America," *Elvis Reader*, 126–58.

6. See also Anne Mandlsohn, "The Church of Risen Elvis: Female Initiation through Sacred Souvenirs," in *Canadian Woman Studies: An Introductory Reader*, ed. Nuzhat Amin et al. (Toronto: Inanna Publications, 1999), 450–59; Peter Stromberg, "Elvis Alive?: The Ideology of American Consumerism," *Journal of Popular Culture* xxiv:3 (Winter 1990): 11–19.

7. Barbara Ehrenreich, Elizabeth Hess, and Gloria Jacobs, "Beatlemania: Girls Just Want to Have Fun," in *The Adoring Audience: Fan Culture and Popular Media*, ed. Lisa A. Lewis (London: Routledge, 1992), 84–106 (96–97). See also Stephen Hinerman, "'I'll Be Here with You': Fans, Fantasy and the Figure of Elvis," in *Adoring Audience*, 107–34; Simon Frith and Angela McRobbie, "Rock and Sexuality," in *On Record: Rock, Pop, and the Written Word*, ed. Simon Frith and Andrew Goodwin (New York: Routledge, 1990), 371–89; Sue Wise, "Sexing Elvis," in *On Record: Rock, Pop, and the Written Word*, 390–98.

8. David R. Shumway, "Watching Elvis: The Male Rock Star as Object of the Gaze" in *The Other Fifties: Interrogating Midcentury American Icons*, ed. Joel Foreman (Urbana: University of Illinois Press, 1997), 124–43 (137–38).

9. Eric Lott, *Love and Theft: Blackface Minstrelsy and the American Working Class* (Oxford, UK: Oxford University Press, 1995), 5.

10. For a comprehensive account of Elvis and racial performance, see Michael T. Bertrand, *Race, Rock, and Elvis* (Urbana: University of Illinois Press, 2000).

11. Lawrence Grossberg, *We Gotta Get Out of This Place: Popular Conservatism and Postmodern Culture* (New York: Routledge, 1992), 152–56.

12. Lawrence Grossberg, "Is There a Fan in the House?: The Affective Sensibility of Fandom," in *Adoring Audience*, 50–65 (55–57).

13. On Elvis's trash aesthetic, see Gael Sweeney, "The King of White Trash Culture: Elvis Presley and the Aesthetics of Excess," in *White Trash: Race and Class in America*, ed. Matt Wray and Annalee Newitz (New York: Routledge, 1997), 249–66 (250, 263).

14. See Tomkins, *Duchamp: A Biography*, 117, and Dawn Ades, Neil Cox, and David Hopkins, *Marcel Duchamp* (London: Thames and Hudson, 1999), 166.

15. See Katherine Kuh's interview with Duchamp in *The Artist's Voice: Talks with Seventeen Artists* (New York: Harper and Row, 1962), 81–93, and commentary in Arturo Schwarz, *The Complete Works of Marcel Duchamp*, vols. 1–2, 3rd ed. (New York: Delano Greenidge Editions, 1997), 19–20, 26.

16. For Duchamp's "indifference," see Jean-Michel Rabaté, "Duchamp's Ego," *Textual Practice* 18:2 (2004): 221–31 (223), and Margaret Iverson, "Readymade, Found Object, Photograph," *Art Journal* 63:2 (Summer 2004): 44–57 (46).

17. Qtd. in William A. Camfield, *Marcel Duchamp: Fountain* (Houston: Menil Foundation, 1989), 44, 97.

18. Jean-François Lyotard, *Duchamp's TRANS/formers: A Book*, trans. Ian McLeod (Venice, Calif.: Lapis Press, 1990), 15.

19. See Iverson, "Readymade, Found Object, Photograph," 48–50.

20. Qtd. in Colin Escott, with Martin Hawkins, *Good Rockin' Tonight: Sun Records and the Birth of Rock 'n' Roll* (New York: St. Martin's Press, 1991), 156.

21. Qtd. in Peter Doyle, *Echo and Reverb: Fabricating Space in Popular Music Recording, 1900–1960* (Middletown, Conn.: Wesleyan University Press, 2005), 167.

22. See ibid., 186ff.

23. See Steve Waksman, *Instruments of Desire: The Electric Guitar and the Shaping of Musical Experience* (Cambridge, Mass.: Harvard University Press, 1999), 60, 80.

24. See ibid., 138–40, and Robert Cantwell, *Bluegrass Breakdown: The Making of the Old Southern Sound* (New York: Da Capo Press, 1992), 155.

25. Jackie Brenston and His Delta Cats, "Rocket 88," *The Sun Records Collection* (Rhino, 1994), disc 1, track 2.

26. Elvis Presley, "That's All Right," *The Sun Sessions CD* (RCA, 1990), track 1.

27. Arthur "Big Boy" Crudup, "That's All Right," *His 22 Greatest Songs* (Wolf/ Blues Classics, 2003), track 13.

28. Details in Escott, *Good Rockin' Tonight*, 63; Guralnick, *Last Train to Memphis*, 95.

29. See Goldman, *Elvis*, 114.

30. Information about Elvis's performances can be found in Guralnick and Patricia Jobe Pierce, *The Ultimate Elvis: Elvis Presley Day by Day* (New York: Simon and Schuster, 1994).

31. Jacques Lacan, *The Four Fundamental Concepts of Psychoanalysis: The Seminar of Jacques Lacan, Book XI*, ed. Jacques-Alain Miller, trans. Alan Sheridan (New York: W. W. Norton, 1981).

32. See reports in *Long Lonely Highway: A 1950's Elvis Scrapbook*, compiled by Ger Rijff (Ann Arbor, Mich.: Pierian Press, 1987), 87–108, and Alfred Wertheimer's commentary in *Elvis '56: In the Beginning* (New York: Collier Books, 1979), 37–38.

33. Elvis Presley, "All Shook Up" and "Shake, Rattle and Roll," *The King of Rock 'n' Roll: The Complete 50's Masters* (RCA, 1992), disc 2, tracks 2 and 27.

34. Elvis Presley, "Blue Moon of Kentucky," *Sun Sessions*, track 2.

35. Roland Barthes, "The Grain of the Voice," in *Image-Music-Text*, ed. and trans. Stephen Heath (New York: Hill and Wang, 1977), 179–89 (181).

36. Richard Middleton, "All Shook Up?: Innovation and Continuity in Elvis Presley's Vocal Style," in *Elvis Reader*, 3–12 (12).

37. Elvis Presley, "Baby, Let's Play House," *Sun Sessions*, track 7.

38. Mladen Dolar, *A Voice and Nothing More* (Cambridge, Mass.: MIT Press, 2006), 47.

39. See details in Goldman, *Elvis*, 61ff. and Guralnick, *Last Train to Memphis*, 12ff.

40. See press reports reprinted in Bill DeNight, Sharon Fox, and Ger Rijff, eds., *Elvis Album* (Lincolnwood, Ill.: Publications International, 2001), 46–52.

41. Qtd. in Stanley Booth, "A Hound Dog, to the Manor Born," in *Elvis Reader*, 159–71 (165).

42. See Shumway, "Watching Elvis," 134ff.

43. Qtd. in Bob Olmetti and Sue McCasland, eds., *Elvis Now—Ours Forever* (San Jose, Calif.: S.p., 1984), 144, 16.

44. See commentary in *Long Lonely*, 124–25 and 130–34.

45. Qtd. in Erika Doss, *Elvis Culture: Fans, Faith, and Image* (Lawrence: University Press of Kansas, 1999), 9.

46. Qtd. in Jane and Michael Stern, *Elvis World* (New York: Alfred A. Knopf, 1987), 20.

47. Jeannie Deen, "A Young Girl's Fancy," in *Elvis: Images and Fancies*, ed. Jac L. Tharpe (Jackson: University of Mississippi Press, 1979), 169.

48. Michael Ventura, "Hear that Long Snake Moan," in *Shadow Dancing in the U.S.A.* (Los Angeles: Jeremy P. Tarcher, 1985), 152–53.

49. See, for example, *Elvis Album*, 78.

50. Melanie Klein, "Weaning," in *Love, Guilt and Reparation and Other Works, 1921–1945* (New York: The Free Press, 1975), 290–305.

51. Teresa Brennan, *The Transmission of Affect* (Ithaca, N.Y.: Cornell University Press, 2004).

52. Elvis Presley, "Baby, Let's Play House," *Sun Sessions*, track 7, and "(I Wanna Be Your) Teddy Bear," *50's Masters*, disc 3, track 11.

53. Elvis Presley, "I Don't Care If the Sun Don't Shine," *Sun Sessions*, track 21.

54. See Richard Middleton, "Mum's the Word: Men's Singing and Maternal Law," in *Oh Boy!: Masculinities and Popular Music*, ed. Freya Jarman-Ivens (London: Routledge, 2007), 103–24.

55. For negative accounts of Elvis's relation to consumer culture, see Mandlsohn and Stromberg.

56. See related commentary in Sweeney, "The Church of Risen Elvis," 263ff.

57. "An Elvis Fan Tells All," *Movie Teen Illustrated: Special Elvis Issue* 4:1 (August 1961), 36–37.

58. See Doss, *Elvis Culture*, 127, and Guralnick, *Last Train to Memphis*, 172.

59. Giorgio Agamben, "Notes on Gesture," in *Means without Ends: Notes on Politics*, trans. Vincenzo Binetti and Cesare Casarino (Minneapolis: University of Minnesota Press, 2000), 49–60 (49).

60. Giorgio Agamben, "Kommerell, or on Gesture," in *Potentialities: Collected Essays in Philosophy*, ed. and trans. Daniel Heller-Roazen (Stanford, Calif.: Stanford University Press, 1999), 77–85 (77).

61. See "The Photographic Image," "Rhetoric of the Image," and "The Third Meaning," in *Image-Music-Text*, 15–68.

CHAPTER FIVE ( )

1. See John Goldrosen and John Beecher, *Remembering Buddy: The Definitive Biography* (New York: Penguin Books, 1987), 45ff.; Philip Norman, *Rave On: The Biography of Buddy Holly* (New York: Simon and Schuster, 1996), 84ff.

2. Goldrosen and Beecher, *Remembering Buddy*, 52–53; Norman, *Rave On*, 122–23. Buddy Holly and the Crickets, "I'm Gonna Love You Too," *The Buddy Holly Collection* (MCA, 1993), disc 2, track 1.

3. Paul Théberge, "The Network Studio: Historical and Technological Paths to a New Ideal in Music Making," *Social Studies of Science* 34:5 (October 2004): 759–81 (763).

4. Qtd. in Peter Doyle, *Echo and Reverb: Fabricating Space in Popular Music Recording, 1900–1960* (Middletown, Conn.: Wesleyan University Press, 2005), 28.

5. Michael Rettinger, "Reverberation Chambers for Broadcasting and Recording Studios," *Journal of the Audio Engineering Society* 5:1 (January 1957): 18–22 (20).

6. See interviews in *The Real Buddy Holly Story* (White Star, 2004).

7. Susan Sontag, "The Aesthetics of Silence," in *Styles of Radical Will* (New York: Farrar, Straus and Giroux, 1969), 3–34 (11).

8. Lawrence Grossberg, *Dancing in Spite of Myself: Essays on Popular Culture* (Durham, N.C.: Duke University Press, 1997), 32–33.

9. John Cage, "Experimental Music," in *Silence: Lectures and Writings* (Middletown, Conn.: Wesleyan University Press, 1961), 7–13 (8–9); John Cage, "45' for a Speaker," in *Silence*, 146–94 (174).

10. John Cage, "A Composer's Confession," qtd. in Eric De Visscher, "'There's no such a thing as silence . . .': John Cage's Poetics of Silence," in *Writings about John Cage*, ed. Richard Kostelanetz (Ann Arbor: University of Michigan Press, 1993), 117–33 (118).

11. John Cage, "Composition as Process," in *Silence*, 18–57 (22–23).

12. My phrasing here comes from Gilles Deleuze, *Difference and Repetition*, trans. Paul Patton (New York: Columbia University Press, 1994), 28ff.

13. John Cage, "History of Experimental Music in the United States," in *Silence*, 67–75 (70).

14. See Cage's "Lecture on Nothing" and "Lecture on Something," in *Silence*, 109–46.

15. Kaja Silverman, *The Acoustic Mirror: The Female Voice in Psychoanalysis and Cinema* (Bloomington: Indiana University Press, 1988).

16. Dave Laing, *Buddy Holly* (New York: Macmillan, 1971), 86, 90.

17. All tracks on *The Complete Buddy Holly*, vols. 1–10, (Purple Chick, 2005), disc 1.

18. Buddy Holly, "Gotta Get You Near Me Blues," *Complete*, disc 1, track 10.

19. Buddy Holly, "Don't Come Back Knockin'," *Complete*, disc 1, track 23.

20. John Cage, "Forerunners of Modern Music," in *Silence*, 62–67 (62).

21. Buddy Holly, "Blue Days, Black Nights," *Collection*, disc 1, track 4.

22. Buddy Holly, "Words of Love" and "Listen to Me," *Collection*, disc 1, tracks 17 and 22.

23. Buddy Holly, "Everyday," *Collection*, disc 1, track 19.

24. Buddy Holly, "Peggy Sue," *Collection*, disc 1, track 25.

25. Buddy Holly, "It's So Easy," *Collection*, disc 2, track 15.

26. Buddy Holly, "That'll Be the Day," *Collection*, disc 1, track 15.

27. "Dick Clark Interview: October, 1958," on *The Complete Buddy Holly*, disc 9, track 20.

28. David Thomas, "Destiny in My Right Hand: 'The Wreck of Old 97' and 'Dead Man's Curve,'" in *The Rose and the Briar: Death, Love and Liberty in the American Ballad*, ed. Sean Wilentz and Greil Marcus (New York: W. W. Norton, 2005), 161–74 (173).

29. See Norman, *Rave* On, 87–104.

30. See Laing, *Buddy* Holly, 81–90.

31. Jacques Derrida, *Speech and Phenomena, and Other Essays on Husserl's Theory of Signs*, trans. David B. Allison (Evanston, Ill.: Northwestern University Press, 1973).

32. Sean Cubitt, "'Maybelline': Meaning and the Listening Subject," *Popular Music*, vol. 4: Performers and Audiences (1984), 207–24 (221).

33. Barbara Bradby and Brian Torode, "Pity Peggy Sue," *Popular Music*, vol. 4: Performers and Audiences (1984), 183–205.

34. Buddy Holly, "Mailman Bring Me No More Blues," *Complete*, disc 3, track 13.

35. For an alternative take, see Bradby's Freudian reading of "Oh Boy" and its backing vocals: "Oh, Boy! (Oh, Boy!): Mutual Desirability and Musical Structure in the Buddy Group," *Popular Music* 21:1 (2002): 63–91.

36. Buddy Holly, "I'm Looking for Someone to Love," *Collection*, disc 1, track 16.

37. Buddy Holly, "Oh, Boy!" *Collection*, disc 1, track 23.

38. Buddy Holly, "Not Fade Away," *Collection*, disc 1, track 18.

39. Buddy Holly, "Well . . . All Right," *Collection*, disc 2, track 11.

40. Lawrence Alloway, *American Pop Art* (New York: Collier Books, 1974), 7, 32.

41. Thomas Crow, "Saturday Disasters: Trace and Reference in Early Warhol," *Art in America* (May 1987), 128–36.

42. Hal Foster, "Death in Warhol," *October* 75 (Winter 1996): 36–59 (39–40).

43. See Theodor W. Adorno, "On Popular Music," in *Essays on Music*, ed. Richard Leppert (Berkeley: University of California Press, 2002), 437–69, as well as Jon Stratton, "Capitalism and Romantic Ideology in the Record Business," *Popular Music*, vol. 3: Producers and Markets (1983), 143–56, and Terry Bloomfield, "Resisting Songs: Negative Dialectics in Pop," *Popular Music* 12:1 (January 1993): 13–31.

44. Buddy Holly, "An Empty Cup," *Complete*, disc 3, track 34.

45. Buddy Holly, "Crying, Waiting, Hoping," *Collection*, disc 2, track 23.

46. Eddie Cochran, "Somethin' Else," *Somethin' Else: The Fine Lookin' Hits of Eddie Cochran* (Razor & Tie Music, 1998), track 14.

47. Eddie Cochran, "Nervous Breakdown," *Somethin' Else*, track 10.

48. R. Serge Denisoff, "'Teen Angel': Resistance, Rebellion and Death—Revisited," *The Journal of Popular Culture* 16:4 (1983): 116–22.

49. Wanda Jackson, "I Gotta Know," *Vintage Collections Series* (Capitol, 1996), track 1.

50. The Jaynetts, "Sally Go Round the Roses," *The Best of the Girl Groups* (Rhino, 1987), track 6.

51. See Theodor W. Adorno, "On Lyric Poetry and Society," *Notes to Literature*, vol. 1, ed. Rolf Tiedemann, trans. Shierry Weber Nicholsen (New York: Columbia University Press, 1991), 37–54, and Richard Leppert, "Music 'Pushed to the Edge of Existence' (Adorno, Listening, and the Question of Hope)," *Cultural Critique* 60 (Spring 2005): 92–133.

52. Buddy Holly, "Valley of Tears," *Complete*, disc 3, track 19.

Index

Page numbers in *italics* refer to illustrations.

abstraction: abstraction/commoditization of labor, 10, 32, 37–38; affective performance as, 21–22; of authentic/rooted music, 4–5; Buddy Holly and, 210, 219–20, 231; Carter Family and, 93, 103; city as space of, 44–45; clichéd phrases and, 221–22; deterritorialization and, 155; folk song and, 134, 144–45; minstrelsy as abstraction of culture, 16–17; as modernist experience of reality, 10–11; motivated forms and, 25; of musical space/time, 7–8; music performance as abstract labor, 47–48; phonograph as device for, 64–65, 69; pop music consumption and, 26–27, 235–42; progressive country music and, 75, 85, 90; studio space and production of, 170, 208–11. *See also* airiness; intention/meaning

Ades, Dawn, 169

Adorno, Theodor, 63–65, 250, 262–63

aesthetics: aesthetic awareness of sensual experience, 5–6; aesthetics of the readymade, 160–61, 166–72, *167, 172*; blues composition/creativity and, 54–55

affective form: blues as affective history, 71; Buddy Holly as exemplar of, 21–22; distancing in progressive country music, 85–87; drives as bodily manifestation of, 181–82; Elvis Presley as affective body, 201–4; emotive force in Woody Guthrie, 119; as engine of folk sentiment, 120–21, 139–41; fan experience and, 186–202; identification in rock concerts and, 189–94; the mass public sphere and, 114–15; as political discourse, 20, 85; radio technology and, 104–5; readymade affect in Sun recordings, 175–76; technology as medium for, 52–53, 195–202

African Americans: Afro-modernism and, 14–15; blackness in Elvis Presley, 162, 164–65; Fiddlin' John Carson racial views, 82–83; mimicry as mode of being, 65–66; minstrelsy as a "sonic republic," 16; music as resource for agency, 17; naming tradition of, 61, 66; post-Emancipation musical agency, 16–17, 32, 45, 51; post-plantation Delta agriculture, 35–36, 41; race records, 23, *48,* 49; symbolic magic as theme for, 67

Afro-modernism, 14–15, 69–70

Agamben, Giorgio, 200–201

Agee, James, 99, 121, 134–35

agency: affirmative culture and, 19–20; African American musical agency, 16–17, 32, 45, 51; in blues performance vs. text, 39; music as surrendered agency in *Native Son*, 29–31; personal identity/agency in blues, 7, 32; self-negation in vernacular modernism and, 12. *See also* identity; political discourse

EDWARD P. COMENTALE is an associate professor of English at Indiana University and the author of *Modernism, Cultural Production, and the British Avant Garde.*

Music in American Life

Juilliard: A History   *Andrea Olmstead*
Understanding Charles Seeger, Pioneer in American Musicology
   Edited by Bell Yung and Helen Rees
Mountains of Music: West Virginia Traditional Music from *Goldenseal*
   Edited by John Lilly
Alice Tully: An Intimate Portrait   *Albert Fuller*
A Blues Life   *Henry Townsend, as told to Bill Greensmith*
Long Steel Rail: The Railroad in American Folksong (2d ed.)   *Norm Cohen*
The Golden Age of Gospel   *Text by Horace Clarence Boyer;*
   photography by Lloyd Yearwood
Aaron Copland: The Life and Work of an Uncommon Man   *Howard Pollack*
Louis Moreau Gottschalk   *S. Frederick Starr*
Race, Rock, and Elvis   *Michael T. Bertrand*
Theremin: Ether Music and Espionage   *Albert Glinsky*
Poetry and Violence: The Ballad Tradition of Mexico's Costa Chica
   John H. McDowell
The Bill Monroe Reader   *Edited by Tom Ewing*
Music in Lubavitcher Life   *Ellen Koskoff*
Zarzuela: Spanish Operetta, American Stage   *Janet L. Sturman*
Bluegrass Odyssey: A Documentary in Pictures and Words, 1966–86
   Carl Fleischhauer and Neil V. Rosenberg
That Old-Time Rock & Roll: A Chronicle of an Era, 1954–63   *Richard Aquila*
Labor's Troubadour   *Joe Glazer*
American Opera   *Elise K. Kirk*
Don't Get above Your Raisin': Country Music and the Southern
   Working Class   *Bill C. Malone*
John Alden Carpenter: A Chicago Composer   *Howard Pollack*
Heartbeat of the People: Music and Dance of the Northern Pow-wow
   Tara Browner
My Lord, What a Morning: An Autobiography   *Marian Anderson*
Marian Anderson: A Singer's Journey   *Allan Keiler*
Charles Ives Remembered: An Oral History   *Vivian Perlis*
Henry Cowell, Bohemian   *Michael Hicks*
Rap Music and Street Consciousness   *Cheryl L. Keyes*
Louis Prima   *Garry Boulard*
Marian McPartland's Jazz World: All in Good Time   *Marian McPartland*
Robert Johnson: Lost and Found   *Barry Lee Pearson and Bill McCulloch*
Bound for America: Three British Composers   *Nicholas Temperley*
Lost Sounds: Blacks and the Birth of the Recording Industry, 1890–1919
   Tim Brooks
Burn, Baby! BURN! The Autobiography of Magnificent Montague
   Magnificent Montague with Bob Baker

Charles Ives in the Mirror: American Histories of an Iconic Composer
  David C. Paul
Southern Soul-Blues   *David Whiteis*
Sweet Air: Modernism, Regionalism, and American Popular Song
  Edward P. Comentale
Pretty Good for a Girl: Women in Bluegrass   *Murphy Henry*

The University of Illinois Press
is a founding member of the
Association of American University Presses.

Composed in 10.5/13 Adobe Minion
with Scala Sans display
by Jim Proefrock
at the University of Illinois Press
Manufactured by Thomson-Shore, Inc.

University of Illinois Press
1325 South Oak Street
Champaign, IL 61820-6903
www.press.uillinois.edu